Whole Brain® Learning in Higher Education

CHANDOS

LEARNING AND TEACHING SERIES

Series Editors: Professor Chenicheri Sid Nair and Dr Patricie Mertova
(emails: *sid.nair@uwa.edu.au* and *patricie.mertova@education.ox.ac.uk*)

This series of books is aimed at practitioners in the higher education quality arena. This includes academics, managers and leaders involved in higher education quality, as well as those involved in the design and administration of questionnaires, surveys and courses. Designed as a resource to complement the understanding of issues relating to student feedback, books in this series will respond to these issues with practical applications. If you would like a full listing of current and forthcoming titles, please visit our website, *www.chandospublishing.com*, email *wp@woodheadpublishing.com* or telephone +44 (0) 1223 399140.

New authors: we are always pleased to receive ideas for new titles; if you would like to write a book for Chandos, please contact Dr Glyn Jones on *gjones@chandospublishing.com* or telephone +44 (0) 1993 848726.

Bulk orders: some organisations buy a number of copies of our books. If you are interested in doing this, we would be pleased to discuss a discount. Please email *wp@woodheadpublishing.com* or telephone +44 (0) 1223 499140.

Chandos Learning and Teaching Series

Whole Brain® Learning in Higher Education

Evidence-based practice

Ann-Louise de Boer, Pieter H. du Toit,
M. Detken Scheepers and
Theo J. D. Bothma

CHANDOS
PUBLISHING

Oxford Cambridge New Delhi

Chandos Publishing
Hexagon House
Avenue 4
Station Lane
Witney
Oxford OX28 4BN
UK
Tel: +44(0) 1993 848726
Email: *info@chandospublishing.com*
www.chandospublishing.com
www.chandospublishingonline.com

Chandos Publishing is an imprint of Woodhead Publishing Limited

Woodhead Publishing Limited
80 High Street
Sawston
Cambridge CB22 3HJ
UK
Tel: +44(0) 1223 499140
Fax: +44(0) 1223 832819
www.woodheadpublishing.com

First published in 2013

ISBN 978–1–84334–742–2 (print)
ISBN 978–1–78063–408–1 (online)
Chandos Learning and Teaching Series ISSN: 2052–2088 (print)
and ISSN: 2052–2096 (online)

Library of Congress Control Number: 2013942534

British Library Cataloguing-in-Publication Data.
A catalogue record for this book is available from the British Library.

Typeset by RefineCatch Ltd, Bungay, Suffolk

Contents

List of figures and tables

Figures

Tables

Acknowledgements

There are many acknowledgements due when a book represents 15 years of experience and work. We as authors would like to thank the following people and entities sincerely for their unconditional support in advocating Whole Brain® Thinking as an asset to the higher education community:

- Ned Herrmann, the father of Whole Brain® Thinking, whose lifetime work on Whole Brain® Thinking inspired us to start the project at the University of Pretoria

- Dr Johan van Zyl, former Principal of the University of Pretoria, who at the time of his term of office supported our initiatives to conduct the base line study through a research grant

- Ann Herrmann-Nedhi, CEO of Herrmann International, and Mac Sutherland for carefully reviewing the manuscript, ensuring concepts and terminology are accurate

- Isabel Claassen, proofreader and editor par excellence, for taking care of our draft manuscript

- Hettie Mans, our graphic designer, for designing the cover of the book and for her professional conduct in meeting our demands regarding quality graphic design

- the heads of department who were excited by our ideas and supported our efforts, allowing their staff to experiment with Whole Brain® ideas, and to apply the principles of Whole Brain® teaching and learning in their respective departments

- the lecturers who saw the potential of Whole Brain® Thinking as an innovative option for facilitating of learning, and embarked on a scholarly journey of action research on the application of Whole Brain® Thinking in their practices

- the hundreds of students from the University of Pretoria who kept us excited about teaching and learning the Whole Brain® way

- the Department for Education Innovation and Director Prof Wendy Kilfoil for their monetary investment, innovative support and active contributions in changing the information literacy textbook to accommodate and develop Whole Brain® learners

- Susannah Wight whose copy editing speaks of the highest quality
- Ed Gibbons, the production editor overseeing the final product in what we would call a Whole Brain® editing way
- Chandos Publishing – a publication house with an inspirational group of professionals who saw the potential of the core of our book: Whole Brain® Thinking
- the University of Pretoria, that creates space for innovation and supports us and the research of the community of practice, as our scholarly focus is aligned with the vision of the University as a research-driven higher education institute.

Foreword

If you are in education you are in the business of brain development.

Dr John Medina, Brain Rules

The link between brain development and education seems obvious, yet it continues to surprise many in the learning profession. With a focus primarily on content concerns and the learning process, our main operating system for that process – the brain – is often overlooked or forgotten.

Over a hundred years of dogma have led us to believe that after a certain age our brains stop growing and evolving. Nothing could be further from the truth. The last 30 years of neurological research have demonstrated that neurogenesis – the creation of new neurons – is indeed possible, and this has led to a new understanding of the connections between the brain and learning. In fact, all of the current neurological research demonstrates that brain development continues throughout life and education has everything to do with it.

If we agree with Dr Leo Buscaglia, professor at the University of Southern California, that 'change is the end result of all true learning' (Buscaglia, n.d.), what can educators do in practical terms to engage learners' brains so they can successfully drive desired outcomes and change?

This book addresses many of the questions that immediately come to mind:

- What models exist to help understand learning styles in order to improve learning outcomes?
- How do I engage learners' brains in a way that works for them?
- What really works in learning design to drive the change we seek?

The answer is Whole Brain® learning design. This book gives the reader a complete analysis and concrete examples of how educators can effect change and better engage learners by applying Whole Brain® Thinking to meet their greatest learning challenges.

My father, Ned Herrmann, started his research in this domain over 30 years ago, seeking to apply what we knew about the brain to improve learning outcomes. This book takes his research even further by providing a comprehensive understanding of the options available and a practical set of examples that will inform any educator, trainer or researcher looking for insight into ways of improving learning outcomes.

The authors have extensive experience in the academic research that validates this methodology, as well as hands-on practice in its application, providing a richness and depth to the content that readers will greatly enjoy.

Nelson Mandela once said that 'education is the most powerful weapon which you can use to change the world' (Mandela, 2012). This work provides a critical place to start that change. And as my late father would say, 'the Whole Brain® concept, once understood, becomes irresistible'.

If you are ready to initiate a change with far-reaching impact, reading *Whole Brain® Learning in Higher Education: Evidence-based practice* is the best way forward.

Ann Herrmann
CEO: Herrmann International Global

Authors' prologue

As any teaching practice in higher education is multi-dimensional in nature, we can only touch on a small part of this educational reality in our book. Our focus is on the practical application of learning theories for adults, of which Whole Brain® Thinking constitutes the essence. All theories are to be integrated and made relevant to a specific context, which includes a specific field of specialisation. Such integration would enhance the quality of facilitating learning and the quality of learning *per se*. With a view to determining quality, we propose that lecturers as higher education practitioners research their own practice. In this way a research-driven approach to teaching practice is promoted.

As indicated above and highlighted in the title of our book, Whole Brain® Thinking is the learning theory that runs as a golden thread throughout our book. This theory is discussed in Chapter 1 and sets the scene for what is to come. However, we extensively deliberate on this important subject and link it with some of the responsibilities each lecturer has, such as facilitating learning, curriculum development and assessment. The thinking behind these deliberations is that all the aspects pertaining to teaching practice can be enhanced if based on the principles of Whole Brain® Thinking. In general, it is about developing the full potential of students. At the same time, developing the full potential of lecturers should be considered a complementary act focused on their continuing professional development.

This prologue serves as a fanfare to the entire book. Our message is that all the constructs introduced are connected to Whole Brain® Thinking. When referring to 'construct' as a verb, it is one of the aims of our book that readers or practitioners should construct their own meaning in relation to higher education practice. This becomes a reality when one reads about some aspect of teaching practice, discusses it with peers, applies the relevant principles in practice, and investigates one's own practice. Constructs will differ from one lecturer to the next as we all have a different understanding of the realities we face. In this way, lecturers as higher education practitioners contribute to and expand the current body of knowledge.

In writing this book, as a group of lecturers with divergent thinking preferences we were challenged to actually portray the notion of a Whole Brain® approach to writing. Most books mainly consist of narratives, and our book also revolves greatly around fact-based reading material. However, it also reflects the idea that thinking goes beyond this notion and thus our book includes a number of illustrations and is structured for those who prefer step-by-step reading. We propose that you share the content and your new construction of meaning with others. We invite you to solve, as you read, the riddle concealed in this paragraph, in other words to identify the different ways of reading and thinking according to the Whole Brain® Model we are about to introduce to you. Your journey with us will be multi-coloured and multi-layered, and we wish you a practice-focused, visual, productive and constructivist Whole Brain® read. All those who will engage in the unpacking of the title and content of our book surely will endeavour to contribute to painting their teaching practice onto a canvas, as we believe this is the way forward in establishing communities of practice.

Whole Brain® Thinking is well established in the business world, but less so in higher education. The case studies discussed give insight into the possibilities of enhancing the quality of higher education in general and teaching practice specifically. Instead of suggesting an external quality assurance locus of control (such as the top-down approaches adopted by most higher education institutions), we promote an intrapersonal locus of control approach to quality assurance in which the lecturer takes full responsibility. The different chapters in our book are aimed at supporting lecturers in succeeding with this task.

Whole Brain® Thinking should enhance the quality of lecturers' teaching practice. It represents a wide, soft brush, with the most delicate hair, that is evenly stroked time and again over the teaching practice canvas – a multi-layered mix of colours that is continuously added to enhance the colours on the palette to create different hues. Each separate colour is applied to the canvas with the finest of brushes, depending on the extent to which it should take prominence in the landscape of higher education practice. Thus, these fine brushes that represent the application of the principles of learning theories for adults, provide another dimension to quality assurance. Theories such as action learning and constructivist learning are blended on the palette to construct new meaning in the sense that we promote Whole Brain® co-operative learning, Whole Brain® constructivism and Whole Brain® action learning. We see action learning as a theory and a practice that promotes student learning. In addition to enhancing students' thinking preferences, lecturers take responsibility for continuously monitoring their own professional development. We are convinced that action research is the most appropriate means of doing this and ensuring quality practice. How else could one substantiate practice-based evidence? Such an action research design is more often than not complemented by a mixed-methods approach. Again, as proponents of constructivist learning, we would like to give more substance to action research by promoting the idea of Whole Brain® action research.

We invite you to acquaint yourself with the constructs discussed and to share any new constructs with your fellow lecturers. You are invited to experiment with different novel ideas in your teaching practice with a view to promoting the quality of learning and your facilitating of learning. Experimenting with Whole Brain® Thinking as a novel idea and integrating it with other learning theories in one's own field of specialisation does not pose a challenge to you alone, but to everyone who is responsible for teaching practice in the context of higher education.

About the authors

Prof Ann-Louise de Boer

Department of Information Science
University of Pretoria
South Africa
ann-louise.deboer@up.ac.za

Ann-Louise de Boer is an associate professor in the Department of Information Science and holds a PhD degree in curriculum studies. Her teaching and research focus the past 15 years has been on the application of Whole Brain® facilitating of learning, an interest that extended into designing and presenting leadership programmes for middle and senior managers for organisations. She is the author and co-author of numerous articles on the application of Whole Brain® teaching and learning and has presented numerous papers at local and international level. She is also the CEO of Herrmann International Africa representing Herrmann International on the African continent.

Dr Pieter H du Toit

Department of Humanities Education
University of Pretoria
South Africa
pieter.dutoit@up.ac.za

Pieter du Toit is a senior lecturer in the Department of Humanities Education, Faculty of Education, University of Pretoria. He is programme coordinator of the Postgraduate Certificate in Higher Education, a professional education qualification for academic staff. He has been involved in academic staff development for more than 20 years. His interests are, *inter alia*, action research, learning styles, professional development and education innovation. He held a post-doctoral fellowship from the University of Antwerp, Belgium, sponsored by the Flemish Government, during 2004 and 2005. He was a guest lecturer there and at the Iowa State University and University of Oklahoma. He was the vice-president of the South African Association for Research and Development, which recently merged with the Higher Education Learning and Teaching Associaton, and currently serves on the Executive Committee. He is a registered practitioner with the Ned Herrmann group in South Africa.

M Detken Scheepers

Department for Education Innovation
University of Pretoria
South Africa
detken.scheepers@up.ac.za

Detken Scheepers is Head of e-Learning at the Department for Education Innovation, University of Pretoria. She holds an MSc (Anatomy) and an MEd (Computer-Assisted Education) from the University of Pretoria. Prior to her adventures in education innovation, she was a lecturer in the Department of Anatomy, Faculty of Health Sciences, University of Pretoria. Her interests are, *inter alia*, professional development of e-learning practice, change management and education innovation. Ms Scheepers has published several articles and presented numerous papers at local and international conferences.

Prof Theo JD Bothma

Department of Information Science
University of Pretoria
South Africa
theo.bothma@up.ac.za

Theo Bothma is a professor and Head of the Department of Information Science at the University of Pretoria, as well as chair person of the School of Information Technology. His teaching and research focus is on information organisation and retrieval (including information literacy), web development and electronic publishing, as well as on curriculum development. He has published widely and presented numerous papers at local and international conferences. He is an advisory editor and a member of the editing board of a number of local and international journals.

Theoretical framework

Abstract: In this chapter we give an overview of what Whole Brain®
learning is, and discuss in depth the Whole Brain® Model of
Herrmann (1995) as a tool to understand the diverse thinking
preferences that individuals have. We highlight what a single
dominant HBDI® profile looks like in each of the quadrants.

Acknowledging that we have a diverse representation of
thinking preferences in our classrooms, we emphasise that learning
opportunities should be designed in such a way that they factor in
the uniqueness of the individual student – this creates a challenge to
all lecturers.

Keywords: Whole Brain® learning, facilitating of Whole Brain®
learning, thinking preferences.

1.1 Introduction

Our knowledge of the functioning brain has not only increased more
over the past 40 years than in all previous centuries together, but is also
still evolving. It has long been recognised that people vary significantly in
their styles of thinking and learning, and models have been created in an
attempt to capture these differences. The construct 'learning style' is
often used by Kolb (1984), Felder (1996) and other researchers in this
field, but in this book we use the constructs 'thinking style' and 'thinking
preference' throughout (Herrmann, 1995; 1996). These are some of the
questions raised by researchers such as Coffield et al. (2004), who study
styles of thinking and learning:

- How can student learning be facilitated if lecturers do not know how
  students learn?

- How can the teaching practice of academic staff be optimised and transformed if they do not know how students learn?
- What models of learning and facilitating of learning do lecturers use?

It is our intention to demonstrate and substantiate the value of acknowledging different thinking preferences that students and lecturers have. Furthermore, we propose a comprehensive, flexible Whole Brain® Model for learning and facilitating learning (see Figure 6.5) to be adopted by lecturers. This 'inclusive' model reflects a merging of aspects that come under scrutiny in different sections of the book. It embraces the original work by Herrmann (1995; 1996) and expands it by promoting Whole Brain® learning and a Whole Brain® Thinking approach to facilitating learning. The comprehensive Whole Brain® Model for learning and facilitating learning can provide a tool for lecturers to accommodate students' diverse thinking preferences, and to develop areas of lesser preferred modes of learning, thus contributing to the development of students' potential. According to Herrmann (1996) it is important to note that a preference for a particular thinking style becomes a motivational factor for the individual. Individuals who constantly have to operate in their least preferred modes become demotivated and their learning can be affected in a negative way because they lose interest.

Most lecturers take the traditional view that students are a homogeneous learning group, with similar interests and aptitudes for subjects. They therefore facilitate learning in a style where 'one size fits all', but the truth is that quality learning and understanding can only be accomplished if the learning group is assumed to be heterogeneous – highly dissimilar in interest and aptitude. The only safe assumption is that every learning group represents a composite of Whole Brain® Thinking (Herrmann, 1996).

1.2 Key contributors

Earlier brain research typified the left hemisphere as being logical, analytical, quantitative and rational, whereas the right hemisphere deals with conceptual, holistic, intuitive, imaginative and non-verbal aspects of thought. The split-brain research carried out by Nobel Prize winner Roger Sperry and his co-workers confirmed that different hemispheres are responsible for different learning tasks (Herrmann, 1995).

Ongoing research has reaffirmed that the two hemispheres control vastly different aspects of thought and action. Each half has its own specialisation, advantages and limitations (Gazzaniga, 1998). Research shows that the left hemisphere breaks everything down into different elements, while the right hemisphere considers the whole and searches systematically for connections, analogies and similarities.

MacLean's model, the Triune Brain Model (Herrmann, 1995), explains his research as an evolutionary model comprising a three-layered structure. Each layer represents a different evolutionary state. The deepest layer, known as the reptilian or R-layer, contains the cerebellum and brainstem and is important for survival. The next layer, the limbic system, consists of the amygdala, hippocampus and hypothalamus. It is responsible for emotions, and records memories of behaviours that produced pleasant and unpleasant experiences. The neocortex, the third layer, comprises the two hemispheres of the brain (cerebral cortex) and is involved with voluntary movement, processing sensory information, language, logical thinking, planning, imagination and consciousness. It is important to keep in mind that all three layers are interconnected and dependent on one another for survival through the *corpus callosum* (Herrmann, 1996).

1.3 Herrmann's metaphoric Whole Brain® Model

Herrmann, acknowledged in literature as the father of brain dominance technology (Morris, 2006), focused his initial research not on brain dominance, but on understanding how the creativity of the human brain is unleashed. His valuable contribution to brain research during the 1990s involves his documentation of the fact that the human brain comprises four distinct learning modes and not only two hemispheres, where each of the modes has its own ways of processing information and functioning (Herrmann, 1995). His research proved that the brain functions as a whole, and there is a validated metaphoric Thinking Styles™ Model describing specialised clusters, or quadrants, of processing in the left, right, upper and lower modes, inspired by the physiological brain's division into left and right hemispheres, embodying the left–right hemisphere brain theory of Sperry and his co-workers (based on research in the field of neuroscience during the 1980s), as well as the triune brain theory of MacLean (based on insights gained from anthropology during the 1970s). Herrmann further determined that each quadrant has very distinct clusters of cognitive functions within, called specialised modes of learning, and each quadrant has its own language, different ways to solve problems, values and ways of knowing (Herrmann, 1995). Every person embodies a coalition of these specialised processes in various proportions. Because of the nature of the brain's serial processing, when one part of the brain is activated or challenged to learn in a specific way, the other parts may be less involved. However, when solving a complex problem, more than one mode is required and thus the brain switches signals back and forth very rapidly between different specialised areas within and across the hemispheres, functioning as a whole system (Lumsdaine and Binks, 2003).

Figure 1.1 is a schematic representation of Herrmann's metaphoric Whole Brain® Model (Herrmann, 1995).

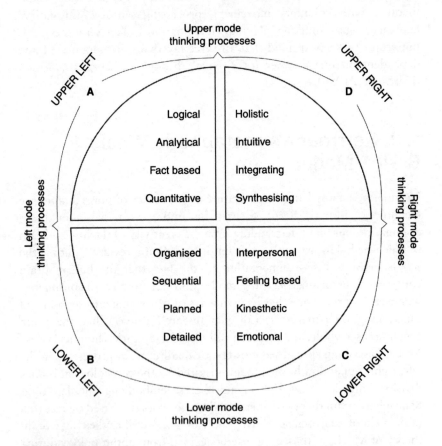

Figure 1.1   Herrmann's metaphoric Whole Brain® Model

Source: Herrmann (1995, 411; 1996, 30)

Figure 1.1 shows the upper left mode, or A-quadrant, associated with logical, analytical, fact-based and quantitative thinking. The lower left mode is associated with organised, sequential, planned and detailed thinking. The lower right mode is associated with interpersonal, feeling-based, kinaesthetic, emotional thinking, and the upper right mode is associated with holistic, intuitive, integrating and synthesising thinking.

Although the four-quadrant model is inspired by a division within the physical brain, Herrmann's Whole Brain® Model is metaphoric, as an individual's degree of preference for each of the four modes can be determined by the relative attraction or aversion to each of the mode descriptors (Herrmann, 1996) and current research affirms that the brain functions as a whole system.

Herrmann's research led to the development of a scientifically validated instrument that can quantify the degree of thinking preferences for specific modes within the Whole Brain® Model. The Herrmann Brain Dominance Instrument® (HBDI®) of 1981 is a questionnaire consisting of 120 items that quantifies mental (thinking) preferences. The results of the questionnaire are a visual plot of the thinking preferences of the individual (see Figures 1.2, 1.3, 1.4 and 1.5). Accompanied by a data summary sheet, the model gives a breakdown of what each individual selected and registers it according to the different quadrants (Tables 1.1, 1.2, 1.3 and 1.4). Finally these data are complemented by an explanation report that describes and highlights important aspects of the profile.

In order to understand the profile, it is important to explain quadrants and modes of thinking, the preference code, the adjective pair data, the profile score and the data summary.

1.3.1 Quadrants and modes of thinking

Thinking preferences are measured not only by the four quadrants (A, B, C or D), but also by four modes (upper left, lower left, upper right and lower right). The upper modes (right and left), combining quadrants A and D, are more cognitive and intellectual, preferring thinking in abstract, conceptual modes. The left modes, combining the A- and B-quadrants, prefer concise, efficient processes with realistic, disciplined and orderly approaches. The right modes, combining the C- and D-quadrants, include key mental processes such as intuitive and perceptive thinking, as well as idealistic, expressive and open approaches. The lower modes, combining the B- and C-quadrants, are grounded and emotional in nature. These modes often prefer visceral, 'gut' and concrete approaches (Herrmann International, 2009).

1.3.2 The preference code

The preference code is a categorisation of the profiles and is helpful in identifying generally similar profile configurations (see Section 1.3.4.1):

- A code 1 corresponds to a preference (a numerical value of 67–99). Visibility of a strong preference typically will be associated with a numerical value of 100 or more (Herrmann, 1996).

- A code 2 corresponds to an intermediate preference of generally being comfortable to use the thinking activities of the quadrant (a numerical value between 33 and 66).

- A code 3 indicates a low preference or even lack of interest for that specific quadrant's thinking, and for some cases even avoidance (a numerical value of 33 or below) (Herrmann, 1996; Herrmann International, 2009).

1.3.3 The adjective pair data

This data derive from the forced choice pairing section in the HBDI® Survey and reveals the thinking style distribution that is most instinctive to the individual. The adjective pair data help indicate the individual's 'backup' style of preferred thinking. There are 24 pairs, and therefore 24 points distributed between the four quadrants. The highest score (maximum 12) typically reveals the Thinking Styles™ favoured in 'pressured' or stressful situations, which may differ from the preferred style. The distribution of responses into A-, B-, C- and D-quadrants under pressure could therefore also indicate perhaps a less preferred quadrant becoming more dominant or a generally preferred one receding into the background (Herrmann International, 2009).

1.3.4 The profile score

The profile score, the total scores allocated to the four quadrants based on individuals' responses to the HBDI® survey form, constitutes the basis of the profile. This visual profile (see Figures 1.2, 1.3, 1.4 and 1.5) is a graphic display of the diagonal axes (A and C; B and D). The scores within each quadrant have been plotted based on each individual's responses to the HBDI® survey form. It is a visual representation that synthesises the responses into a global visual profile. At the top of the profile are displayed the individual's preference code, adjective pairs and profile scores for easy reference (Herrmann International, 2009).

Without going into the detail of all the possible combinations that emanate from the clusters within the quadrants and modes (Herrmann, 1995; Herrmann International, 2009), the purpose of the book is to highlight the main dominances.

1.3.4.1 Single dominant profiles

Of the more than three million profiles in Herrmann's database, only 5 per cent of the profiles are for a single dominance. The single dominance can occur across all the four quadrants, with a preference code of 1222, 2122, 2212 or 2221. The advantage of having a single dominant profile is that the individual experiences relatively little internal conflict. Perceptions and decision-making processes tend to be harmonious, predictable, coherent and comfortable. The single dominant person tends to see the world through a consistent set of lenses. The downside to single dominance is that it can be quite a challenge getting along smoothly with others since those with multi-dominant preferences have the ability to see the world from different points of view.

1.3.4.2 Double dominant profiles

A majority of people (58 per cent of profiles in Herrmann's database International, 2009) have a preference for two quadrants. Double dominance can occur between left 1122, right 2211, upper 1221 or lower 2112 with the advantage being that the two quadrants tend to reinforce each other. However, like single dominant profiles, a profile with two primaries in the same mode tends to access the other modes less frequently. Opposing double dominant profiles, left–right 1212 or 2121, experience some internal conflict between the two primary quadrants, but individuals with this profile will benefit from a greater appreciation of their own mental opposites and those of others, making it easier to cross the bridge between the different styles.

1.3.4.3 Triple dominant profiles

A high percentage of 34 per cent of the profiles in the database shows a triple dominance. Within this total, 2111, 1121 and 1112 are the most frequent profiles, representing 81 per cent of the triple dominant profiles (Herrmann, 1995; Herrmann International, 2009). These profiles have only one quadrant that is not a primary. The advantage of such multi-dominance lies in the breadth of thinking of the triple dominant profile. It is more expanded than the double dominant profile and allows the individual to process and be able to access the associated language across three quadrants more easily. Interactions with others are thus often easier, as it is most likely that at least one preference will be shared with individuals with whom they interact. The downside of a triple dominant profile is that it can slow down the decision-making process because of the need to engage with all the alternatives available.

1.3.4.4 Quadruple dominant profiles

This profile makes up 3 per cent of the profiles present in Herrmann's database. The 1111 profile is a true multi-dominant profile. The profile expresses primary levels for every one of the four quadrants and offers an enormous potential for highly integrated, varied thinking processes. This gives the profile a unique advantage through the ability to move seamlessly from quadrant to quadrant and mode to mode as the situation requires, as it is often able to understand all the thinking perspectives. Individuals with this profile have the ability to develop an extraordinarily balanced view of any given situation, but may find it a challenge to handle internal conflict within themselves because of the easy interaction between quadrants and a possible sense of indecisiveness or unclear focus that is associated with a multi-modal and multi-quadrant preference. The overall tilt (A+B+C+D) of their thinking preference will be influenced by their highest profile score in a specific quadrant or quadrants (Herrmann, 1995; Herrmann International, 2009), and their adjective pair data, which may serve as a tiebreaker, predisposing them to lean toward a certain quadrant or mode in pressured situations.

1.3.5 *Data summary*

Another way to look at individuals' data are derived from the information captured on the data summary sheet. This indicates how each individual's score for each quadrant is determined. The purpose is to remind those taking part of their responses to many of the questions on the HBDI® survey and to clarify which elements in each quadrant they prefer. It is a representation of a profile using a sequential, linear detailed and quantified mode format. The focus is on analysing the key descriptors and work elements on the data sheet (see Tables 1.1, 1.2, 1.3 and 1.4).

There are four columns in the data sheet sorting the individual's responses into the four quadrants. The first column corresponds to the A-quadrant, the second to the B-quadrant, the third to the C-quadrant and the fourth to the D-quadrant. An 'X' appears next to individuals' selection in the columns relating to the quadrant to which they belong, while the asterisk (*) denotes the most descriptive of the selected key descriptors chosen by the individual. On the HBDI® Survey, eight key descriptors must be selected from a total of 25 and the most descriptive one must be indicated with an asterisk (Herrmann International, 2009).

Selecting 'Work elements', the individual needs to rank the work elements from 1 (work that you do least well) to 5 (work that you do best). The rankings are sorted into the four quadrants. The work preferences are the indicators of thinking preferences™ that are most accessed in a work environment. The latter are influenced by training, preferences, opportunities and challenges that the working environment provides. In analysis of the data sheet it is also important to note that work elements and key descriptors indicated by the individual as high (5 or 4) or low (1 or 2) can perhaps reveal situational work preferences that have developed. These are perhaps somewhat different from the overall more general key descriptor preferences (Herrmann International, 2009).

From Herrmann's own research and backed by studies and publications around the world, the aggregate total of all profiles results in a 1111 profile and is true of most groups if there are at least 100 individual profiles (see Figures 2.1 and 2.2). This implies that taken as a whole the world is a composite of 'Whole Brain'® Thinking (Herrmann, 1996).

An HBDI® profile provides scientifically validated information to understand one's own learning strengths and learning avoidances (Herrmann, 1995). However, it should be mentioned that the instrument does not measure competencies, but thinking preferences (and only that). To prefer something is to be drawn to it, while competency has to do with *inter alia* acquired knowledge, skills and professional experience. True mastery in a specific domain can only be achieved in the area that converges with one's natural preferred mode.

In order to minimise confusion for the reader who is not familiar with interpreting an HBDI® profile, we discuss the single dominant quadrant's preference in more detail, and show how a single dominant profile might relate to a preference for learning opportunities and methods of facilitating learning. The reader should keep in mind that only 5 per cent of the population actually has only one primary preference, most having two or more.

1.4 HBDI® profiles

In this section and consequent subsections real examples of single dominant profiles that are typical of the four quadrants are visually represented and explained. Each explanation and visual representation is rich with quantitative data. The wording, interpretation and visual representation on the other hand offer qualitative data that perfectly fits a mixed-methods approach towards studying the application of Whole Brain® principles in the context of learning and facilitating learning in higher education.

1.4.1 HBDI® single dominant profile example indicating a strong A-quadrant preference

In this section a sample profile with a preference code representing single dominance indicating a strong preference for thinking in the A-quadrant is discussed and visually displayed (Figure 1.2). This is followed by an explanation of the characteristics of the profile.

The preference code of this profile example is 1222 (single dominant), with the most preferred thinking preference being for the upper left A-quadrant with a numerical value of 126 (strong preference of 100+) (Herrmann, 1995). By quite a margin, the next most preferred is the B-quadrant, with a numerical value of 65; although this is a high secondary preference, the sample profile is still representative of singular dominance because the difference in scores between A and B is 59 points. Then follows the D-quadrant with a numerical value of 59, and the least preferred thinking preference is for the C-quadrant with a numerical value of 42.

The adjective pair distribution in this profile between the A-, B-, C- and D-quadrants is respectively 10-3-5-6. This implies 42 per cent of the adjective pair responses registered in the A-quadrant, 13 per cent in the B-quadrant, 20 per cent in the D-quadrant and 14 per cent in the C-quadrant. This is indicated on the profile grid by a broken line. The dotted line profile is also referred to as the individual's stress profile. Although the stress profile is not perfectly aligned with the profile, it is not radically out of alignment either. When interpreting the profile and stress profile it is suggested that the individual under pressure shifts slightly towards the C-quadrant.

The data summary sheet (Table 1.1) highlights the key descriptors and work elements selected by the individual and registered in four columns:

Quadrant:	A	B	C	D
Preference code:	1	2	2	2
Adjective pairs:	10	3	5	6
Profile scores:	126	65	42	59

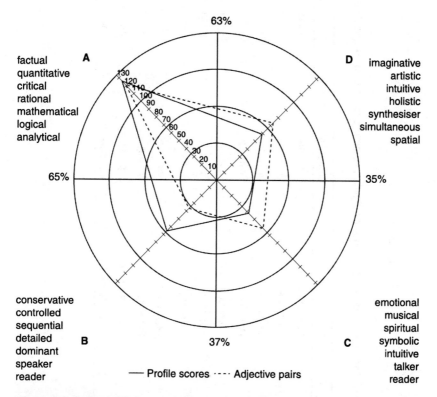

Figure 1.2 HBDI® single dominant sample profile indicating a strong preference for A-quadrant thinking

the A-quadrant first, next the B-quadrant, third the C-quadrant and the last column representing the D-quadrant.

Based on the qualitative data gathered, the key descriptors selected in the A column are *Factual, Quantitative, Critical, Mathematical* and *Logical. Analytical* was selected as being the most descriptive of the individual and marked with an asterisk (*). The work elements selected

Table 1.1 Examples of key descriptors and work elements of a sample single dominant A-quadrant profile

	A-quadrant	B-quadrant	C-quadrant	D-quadrant
Key descriptors	Factual x	Conservative	Emotional	Imaginative
	Quantitative x	Controlled	Musical	Artistic
	Critical x	Sequential	Spiritual	Intuitive
	Rational	Detailed	Symbolic	Holistic x
	Mathematical x	Dominant	Intuitive	Synthesiser
	Logical x	Speaker x	Talker x	Simultaneous x
	Analytical *	Reader	Reader	Spatial
Work elements	Analytical	Organisation 5	Teaching 3	Integrating 5
	Technical	Planning 4	Writing 5	Conceptualising 5
	Problem solver	Administrative 4	Expressing 1	Creative 3
	Financial	Implementation 2	Interpersonal 4	Innovating 3

* Most descriptive

in column A are *Analytical* (5), *Technical* (4) and *Problem solver* (4). The next preferred thinking style is that of the B-quadrant. *Speaker* was selected as the key descriptor while work elements identified as work that the individual does well include *Planning* (5) and *Implementation* (4). The next preferred mode is for the D-quadrant, and *Holistic* was selected as the key descriptor while work elements identified as work the individual selected as done well include *Integrating* (5) and *Conceptualising* (5). The least preferred quadrant is that of the C-quadrant and the key descriptor selected is *Talker*. Looking at the data selected in the 'Work element' column, *Interpersonal* is ranked as a preferred work element (4).

Students with a single A-quadrant preference:

- prefer a cognitive and rational approach to executing tasks and approach problem-solving in a logical manner
- appreciate approaches that reduce the complex to the simple, the unclear to the clear, and the cumbersome to the efficient
- prefer logical, analytical and rational thinking, as well as engaging in feasibility studies, critical assessments and any task that requires focused quantitative research and rigorous discussions
- prefer financial, mathematical and technical matters.

Learning opportunities that students from the A-quadrant would appreciate, according to Herrmann's research (1995) and confirmed by Lumsdaine and Binks (2003), include:

- formalised lectures
- data and information searching through reading textbooks, searching websites and doing library searches
- applying scientific methods in research projects and working through technical and financial case studies
- analysing and studying examples of problems and solutions and building case studies based on facts
- judging ideas based on facts, criteria and logical reasoning
- knowing how things work (the technical aspects) and the cost implications
- always seeking to answer the 'what' question
- challenging debates and robust discussion
- programmed learning.

1.4.2 HBDI® single dominant profile example indicating a strong B-quadrant preference

In this section a sample profile with a preference code representing single dominance in the B-quadrant is discussed and visually represented in Figure 1.3. This is followed by an explanation of the characteristics of the profile of the student with such a preference. The preference code is 2122, indicating a single dominant profile with the most preferred thinking for the lower left B-quadrant.

The profile score with a numerical value of 123 for the B-quadrant is an indication that this is the most preferred thinking preference and that it is characterised by *Controlled, Planned, Organised* and *Structured* modes of processing. There would be a tendency to pay close attention to detail and the implementation of activities. By quite a margin, the next most preferred is for the A-quadrant, with a numerical value of 65, followed by the D-quadrant with a numerical value of 63 and although these are both high secondary preferences, the sample profile is still representative of singular dominance because the difference in scores is 58 points and 60 points respectively. The least preferred preference is for C-quadrant thinking, indicated by a numerical value of 45.

The adjective pair distribution (into A-, B-, C- and D-quadrants) is 7-9-5-3 as indicated by the dotted line (or stress profile). An analysis of these results shows that 38 per cent of the adjective pair responses fall into the B-quadrant, 29 per cent in the A-quadrant, 21 per cent in the D-quadrant and 15 per cent in the C-quadrant. The stress profile is not perfectly aligned, nor radically out of alignment with the profile. Although the preference for the B-quadrant remains under pressure, there is a slight change in the person's thinking style under pressure, towards the A- and C-quadrants. They become slightly more dominant, while the D-quadrant under pressure becomes the lesser thinking preference of all four.

According to the data summary sheet in Table 1.2, the key descriptors selected in the A-quadrant are *Mathematical* and *Logical*, while for the B-quadrant *Detailed* and *Reader* are registered. For the C-quadrant, *Spiritual*, and for the D-quadrant *Imaginative, Artistic* and *Simultaneous* were selected. *Reader* is selected as being most descriptive of the key descriptors and is registered in both the B- and C-quadrants. Although there were more key descriptors selected in the D-quadrant, the most descriptive was selected in the B-quadrant. Both A- and B-quadrants have the same number of selections – this can be explained because the profile is derived from a wide array of data across all 120 questions, which may

Quadrant:	A	B	C	D
Preference code:	2	1	2	2
Adjective pairs:	7	9	5	3
Profile scores:	65	123	45	63

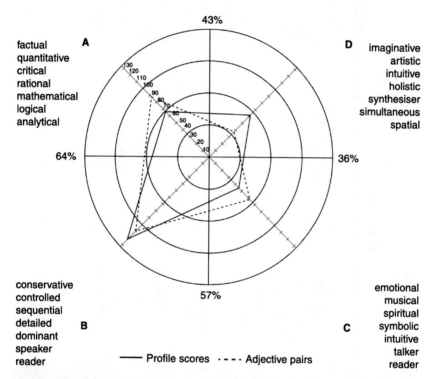

— Profile scores · · · · Adjective pairs

Figure 1.3 HBDI® single dominant sample profile indicating a strong preference for B-quadrant thinking

not all reflect a singular preference. The profile represents the overall trend tile of the profile data, which in this case indicate the most preferred overall is in the B-quadrant.

Work elements selected as work done well in the A-quadrant are *Analytical* (5) and *Problem solver* (4), while in the B-quadrant *Planning* (4), *Administrative* (5) and *Implementation* (4) were selected. These

Table 1.2   Examples of key descriptors and work elements of a sample single dominant B-quadrant profile

	A-quadrant	B-quadrant	C-quadrant	D-quadrant
Key descriptors	Factual	Conservative	Emotional	Imaginative x
	Quantitative	Controlled	Musical	Artistic x
	Critical	Sequential	Spiritual x	Intuitive
	Rational	Detailed x	Symbolic	Holistic
	Mathematical x	Dominant	Intuitive	Synthesiser
	Logical x	Speaker	Talker	Simultaneous x
	Analytical	Reader *	Reader *	Spatial *
Work elements	Analytical 5	Organisation 5	Teaching 2	Integrating 3
	Technical 1	Planning 1	Writing 4	Conceptualising 1
	Problem solver 4	Administrative 4	Expressing 5	Creative 2
	Financial 1	Implementation 1	Interpersonal 4	Innovating 3

* Most descriptive

reflect mental preferences preferred at work. In the D-quadrant, *Conceptualising* (4) was the strongest work element selected, while the least preferred quadrant was the C-quadrant. Notably none of the work elements was selected in the C-quadrant as work that the individual does well, although *Teaching* (3) and *Interpersonal* (3) were selected as work they are comfortable in doing.

Students with a single B-quadrant preference:

- commonly prefer structure and procedure; show a natural inclination towards organisation, efficiency, order, discipline and reliability
- have a strong tendency to prioritise tasks, approach them in a systematic and sequential manner and complete them within a given time frame
- are often mindful of logistical constraints, methodical in their approach to problems and attentive to detail.

Learning opportunities that B-quadrant students would appreciate, according to Herrmann's research (1995) and confirmed by Lumsdaine and Binks (2003), include:

- carrying out detailed written work neatly, timely and conscientiously
- attending lectures that are structured and learning that is facilitated in a sequenced way
- undertaking experimental work to be carried out step-by-step and the acquisition of skills through repetition, drill and practice
- frequently asking the 'how' question
- planning projects and execution according to a set plan and dates
- assembling an object according to detailed instructions in a manual
- setting up an own filing system and using it regularly
- case studies focusing on organisational structures and administrative issues.

1.4.3 HBDI® single dominant profile example indicating a strong C-quadrant preference

In this section a sample profile with a preference code representing single dominance for thinking in the C-quadrant is discussed and visually represented in Figure 1.4.

The preference code for this profile is 2212. The profile score with the most preferred thinking preference is for C-quadrant thinking, with a numerical value of 122 (Herrmann, 1995). This is followed by the D-quadrant with a numerical value of 66 followed by the B-quadrant with a numerical value of 62. Again, although both D- and B-quadrants are high secondary preferences, the sample profile is still representative of

Quadrant:	A	B	C	D
Preference code:	2	2	1	2
Adjective pairs:	3	5	12	4
Profile scores:	44	62	122	66

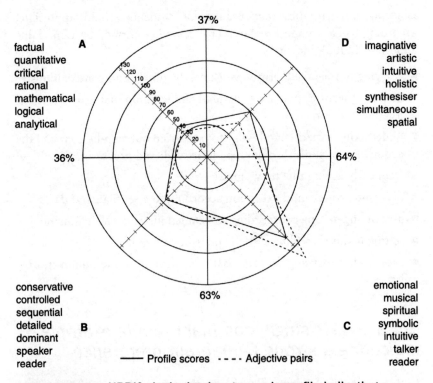

Figure 1.4 HBDI® single dominant sample profile indicating a strong preference for C-quadrant thinking

singular dominance because the difference in scores is 56 points and 60 points respectively. The least preferred thinking preference is for the A-quadrant with a numerical value of 44.

The distribution of the adjective pair questions (into the A-, B-, C- and D-quadrants) is 3-5-12-4 and indicated by the dotted line (stress profile) with 50 per cent of the adjective pair responses registered in the C-quadrant, 17 per cent in the D-quadrant, 21 per cent in the B-quadrant and 13 per cent in the A-quadrant. When under pressure, the C-quadrant becomes even more dominant, with little shift in A and B and a slight decrease in the D-quadrant.

The following quantitative data are of significance: key descriptors selected for the A-quadrant are *Critical* and *Logical*. For the B-quadrant they are *Speaker* and *Reader*, and for the D-quadrant *Holistic* and *Simultaneous*. For the C-quadrant they are *Spiritual, Talker* and *Reader*, with *Emotional* the most descriptive of the key descriptors. In the column 'Work elements' in the A-quadrant *Problem solver* (4) was selected; in the B-quadrant, *Organisation* (4), *Administrative* (4) and *Implementation* (4) were selected and all the work elements in the C-quadrant were selected as work that the individual does well (Table 1.3).

Students with a single C-quadrant dominance:

- prefer to be in tune with and sensitive to others' needs; are naturally attracted to people-related tasks and the ability to relate to others and express themselves easily; they are sensitive to moods, attitude, energy level and the atmosphere in a room where people are gathered
- may have good interpersonal skills, an awareness of the feelings of others and easy communication; they may give credence to sensory intuition in the form of gut feeling
- may display emotive thinking and be highly sensitive, while spiritual aspects play a key role in the lives of some C-quadrant students
- are often open to contributions from team members to attain a set goal; people focus constitutes the bottom line for C-quadrant students.

Learning opportunities that students with a strong C-quadrant profile would prefer, according to Herrmann's research (1995) and confirmed by Lumsdaine and Binks (2003), include:

- listening and sharing ideas during group interactions and discussions
- being emotionally involved and motivating self by asking the 'who' question
- learning through sensory input, movement, smelling and tasting
- hands-on learning by touch and using tools and objects
- keeping a personal journal to record feelings and values
- studying with background music
- making up a song or using music as a memory aid or to express feelings
- learning by means of facilitated learning at a more personal level
- using people-orientated case studies.

1.4.4 HBDI® single dominant profile example indicating a strong D-quadrant preference

This section sets out the quantitative and qualitative data using an example of a single dominant profile indicating a strong preference for the D-quadrant, which is visually represented in Figure 1.5.

This single dominant profile with a preference code of 2221 indicates the most preferred preference for the D-quadrant with a numerical value of 116. The characteristics associated with this quadrant include *Creative, Imaginative, Holistic* and *Integrative* processing. The three remaining quadrants are functional, yet secondary. The next preferred thinking preference is for the B-quadrant with a numerical value of 63, followed by the C-quadrant with a numerical value of 60 and the least preferred thinking style preference is for the A-quadrant with a numerical value of 53. Even though these three quadrants are high secondary preferences, the sample profile is still representative of singular dominance because the difference in scores is 53 points, 56 points and 43 points respectively.

The 1-4-8-11 adjective pair distribution (in the A-, B-, C- and D-quadrants) is indicated by the broken line (stress profile) and noticeably different from the profile in the percentage comparisons. The profile indicates a marked shift to D- and C-quadrant thinking when under pressure, and a lesser preference for A- and B-quadrant thinking. This suggests that there might be a quite different response when under pressure than at other times. Nearly half, 46 per cent, of the adjective pair responses fall into the D-quadrant, 17 per cent in the B-quadrant, 33 per cent in the C-quadrant and 4 per cent in the A-quadrant.

Examples of key descriptors and work elements of a sample single dominant C-quadrant profile

	A-quadrant		B-quadrant		C-quadrant		D-quadrant	
Key descriptors	Factual		Conservative		Emotional	*	Imaginative	
	Quantitative		Controlled		Musical		Artistic	
	Critical	x	Sequential		Spiritual	x	Intuitive	
	Rational		Detailed		Symbolic		Holistic	x
	Mathematical		Dominant		Intuitive		Synthesiser	
	Logical	x	Speaker	x	Talker	x	Simultaneous	x
	Analytical		Reader	x	Reader	x	Spatial	x
Work elements	Analytical	3	Organisation	4	Teaching	5	Integrating	2
	Technical	1	Planning	2	Writing	5	Conceptualising	2
	Problem solver	4	Administrative	4	Expressing	5	Creative	3
	Financial	2	Implementation	4	Interpersonal	5	Innovating	3

* Most descriptive

Quadrant:	A	B	C	D
Preference code:	2	2	2	1
Adjective pairs:	1	4	8	11
Profile scores:	53	63	60	116

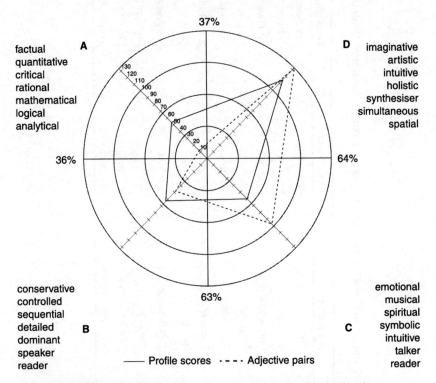

— Profile scores   · - - · Adjective pairs

Figure 1.5   HBDI® single dominant sample profile indicating a strong preference for D-quadrant thinking

Based on the quantitative data gathered, the following is of significance. Key descriptors (Table 1.4) selected within the D-quadrant are *Intuitive* and *Holistic*, while the most descriptive selected is *Imaginative*. In the B-quadrant, *Conservative* and *Sequential* were selected, followed by the C-quadrant where *Emotional* and *Intuitive* were selected as descriptors. The least preferred quadrant is A, and *Logical* and *Analytical* were selected as key descriptors.

Table 1.4 Examples of key descriptors and work elements of sample single dominant D-quadrant profile

	A-quadrant		B-quadrant		C-quadrant		D-quadrant	
Key descriptors	Factual		Conservative	x	Emotional	x	Imaginative	*
	Quantitative		Controlled		Musical		Artistic	
	Critical		Sequential	x	Spiritual		Intuitive	x
	Rational		Detailed		Symbolic		Holistic	x
	Mathematical		Dominant		Intuitive	x	Synthesiser	
	Logical	x	Speaker		Talker		Simultaneous	
	Analytical	x	Reader		Reader		Spatial	
Work elements	Analytical	4	Organisation	3	Teaching	3	Integrating	2
	Technical	4	Planning	5	Writing	3	Conceptualising	5
	Problem solver	4	Administrative	2	Expressing	3	Creative	4
	Financial	1	Implementation	1	Interpersonal	5	Innovating	5

* Most descriptive

In analysing the data sheet and looking at work elements, *Conceptualising* (5), *Creative* (4) and *Innovating* (5) were selected as indications of work that the individual does well and that relate to the D-quadrant. The work element selected in the B-quadrant is *Planning* (5), and in the C-quadrant *Interpersonal* (5). Although the least preferred quadrant was the A-quadrant, work elements selected as work that the individual does well are *Analytical* (4), *Technical* (4) and *Problem Solver* (4).

Students with a single D-quadrant preference:

- are able to handle several mental inputs simultaneously, make rapid connections and work with abstract constructs
- think laterally in a way that inspires imagination; hence innovative and original ideas may stimulate this mode (the D-quadrant can be described as the catalyst for the creative process; strategic thinking and the fact that people with this profile welcome positive change and transformation create opportunities for taking risks and experimenting)
- have an initially holistic approach to problem-solving, as well as the assessment of various facets of a construct or situation and simultaneous execution of tasks
- reach conclusions in a spontaneous rather than a structured way, thus making this individual intuitive in an intellectual sense.

These are the learning opportunities that students with a D-quadrant dominant profile would prefer, according to Herrmann's research (1995) and confirmed by Lumsdaine and Binks (2003):

- exploring hidden possibilities with a strong focus on self-discovery
- synthesising content and ideas to come up with something new
- asking the 'why' question and doing things simultaneously
- making use of visuals and mind maps; preferring pictures to words
- addressing open-ended problems and finding several solutions
- making use of experimental opportunities and playing with ideas
- conducting futuristic-orientated case studies and discussions
- trying different ways (not prescribed procedures) to do something, just for the fun of it
- making sketches to visualise a concept, problem or solution.

1.5 The construct Whole Brain® learning

The basic building blocks of our adult self are the DNA of our inherited genes and chromosomes, but aspects of socialisation, parenting, teaching, life experiences and cultural influences are considered to have a greater influence than genetic inheritance alone. Herrmann states unequivocally that his research into the brain has led him to firmly believe that:

> we were designed to be whole; that the normal, ordinary everyday brain is specialised and interconnected in ways that position it to develop as a balanced, multi-dominant brain capable of accessing and using all of its mental options (1996, 35).

The construct 'Whole Brain'® learning therefore includes genetic influence. This does not imply that we are the product of our genetics and nothing else. Herrmann in his research explicitly states that we are not on a genetically programmed path determined by our genes and chromosomes, but a product of both nature (genes) and nurture (development): 'It's not nature OR nurture. It's nature AND nurture' (1996, 34).

And it is the nurture aspect that has the major influence on who we are and who we become. Herrmann (1996) emphasises that if it was only genetic inheritance, the opportunity to develop into our own unique person would be limited and any learning during our maturing process would have no effect.

The physiological brain is designed to make connections that allow for direct interaction between the different specialised areas. Thus students have access to Whole Brain® learning, which means that any given aspect of designing for learning, such as a learning task and learning material, will have the potential to 'reach' them in some way, even if not in their preferred style. This implies that lecturers can effectively plan for a very diverse audience and look for blended options to provide different platforms for learning and for accommodating the diversity of their students.

Whole Brain® learning provides the basis for bridging the gap between the unique learning needs of the individual student and the appropriate methods of facilitating quality learning.

1.6 Challenges for lecturers

Most people choose occupations where they can exercise their preferred modes of thinking, and for this reason occupational categories have been documented as *pro forma* profiles that contain typical profiles for certain kinds of jobs (Herrmann, 1995). Lecturers need to understand that for each group of students there is an array of thinking style preferences that represent a composite profile. Moreover:

> There is also an equal distribution of learning avoidances distributed across the four quadrants. And learning avoidances are even more significant than learning preferences because they turn people off. A turned-off learner is a waste of educational time and effort as well as corporate time and effort (Herrmann, 1996, 152).

Herrmann goes on to make the reasonable assumption that 'every classroom represents a complete spectrum of learning style preferences' (1996, 152).

Our knowledge of the brain and its inherent uniqueness clearly indicates that a student has unique learning experiences, preferences and avoidances that will be different from those of other students. If we are serious about improving the quality of learning, we need to be aware of this. Each mode and quadrant of the brain is optimised when aligned with an appropriate task. However, as our school systems, and consequently our university systems, concentrate heavily on sequential and fact-based learning, creative abilities have become completely overshadowed and are often discouraged not only by teachers, but also by well-meaning parents, managers and lecturers. The following remark by Herrmann is apt in this regard:

> Principals, superintendents, deans, or college presidents [armed with information on Whole Brain® learning] need to radically change the curriculum development and teaching processes in their institutions if they don't currently deliver the learning product with equal effectiveness across the full learning spectrum (1996, 151).

Therefore learning opportunities must be designed in such a way that they somehow factor in the uniqueness of the individual student. An immediate implication for higher education in particular and education in general is that our assumptions about learning should take into account that our unique learning similarities and differences become part of the learning design and experience, and are thus made visible. As a result, learning is no longer one-dimensional but rather includes the notion of multiple intelligences (interests). This is demonstrated by Howard Gardner's (1993) work, which advocates that the subject matter should be understood by all participants, not just by those whose learning is supported by the method of facilitating learning used by the lecturer. In the context of our book and proposed learning theories, we would like to adapt this notion by promoting the idea of *inter alia* constructing meaning by employing the principles of self-regulated learning, opposed to mere understanding of subject matter.

The challenge is that if lecturers do not facilitate learning in line with students' preferred thinking preferences, students often find themselves laden with study work that demands them to spend large blocks of time operating in tasks of lesser preferences or even avoidance (Herrmann, 1995). The advantage of applied Whole Brain® technology is that it can be learned and is therefore transferable (Herrmann, 1996). The application of this technology within the higher education arena will ensure a more learning-centred approach (Du Toit et al., 2011).

1.7 The advantage of understanding thinking preferences

Research has proved that students who know more about their own strengths and weaknesses will be more motivated to learn. If lecturers can respond to individual students' strengths and weaknesses, then retention of the learning material and performance rates in formal programmes are likely to increase (Coffield et al., 2004). However, the argument in our book is that learning is not only about the retention of learning material, but also about establishing processes of deeper learning that allow students and lecturers to construct new meaning and to apply the principles of self-directed learning – as is discussed in the applicable sections below.

To develop the full potential of students, it is imperative for lecturers to be aware of their own thinking style preference and the implications it has for their preferred style of facilitating learning. Felder suggests:

> If professors teach exclusively in a manner that favors their students'
> less preferred learning style modes, the students' discomfort level
> may be great enough to interfere with their learning. On the other
> hand, if professors teach exclusively in their students' preferred
> modes, the students may not develop the mental dexterity they need
> to reach their potential for achievement in school [university], and
> as professionals (1996, 18).

Educational activities that implement an approach using Whole Brain® Thinking will ensure that students' preferred learning modes are accommodated and that less preferred learning modes are developed. For the purposes of our book, we have adopted the four-quadrant model of learning preferences and avoidance, and through the lens of Herrmann's Whole Brain® Model we have created a comprehensive Whole Brain® Model for learning and facilitating learning (Figure 6.5), which can assist lecturers to enhance the quality of their teaching practice.

Figure 1.6 summarises the expectations of students in the four quadrants and the struggles they encounter in the various quadrants if the lecturer's facilitating of learning is not in accordance with an approach using Whole Brain® Thinking.

The planning and preparation of learning opportunities, as well as the applicable methods of facilitating learning as adapted from Herrmann (1995), are highlighted in Figure 1.7.

Noting all the data in this chapter, Figure 1.7 outlines the way ahead for facilitating of learning to accommodate all students in their preferred thinking modes using the Whole Brain® Thinking methodology.

1.8 Herrmann's expanded Whole Brain® Model for Learning and Facilitating Learning

Herrmann's original idea was to use the Whole Brain® Model for a teaching and learning Walk-Around™ process. This would imply that the key learning points needed to be presented to the students in all four quadrants. Acknowledging the breakthrough research that Herrmann (1995; 1996) left us with, we offer in our book a comprehensive model to not only facilitate Whole Brain® learning, but also incorporate designing of learning opportunities using Whole Brain® technology and Whole Brain® assessment opportunities that would promote deep and constructivist learning. It is a tool to assist lecturers to formulate key learning outcomes in as many ways as possible with a view to reflecting on the different quadrants. Using the comprehensive Whole Brain® Model for learning and facilitating learning, lecturers can learn how to use and integrate all four learning modes to accommodate the uniqueness of individual students and develop their areas of lesser preference.

Designing learning opportunities and learning material in this way must be done to not overwhelm students by providing a deluge of methods of facilitating learning. Instead, the Walk-Around™ Model creates a method that can be used to move back and forth on the Whole

Students' Expectation

A   **D**

Thinkers

- Precise, to the point, information
- Theory and logical rationales
- Proof of validity
- Research references
- Textbook reading
- Quantifiable numbers, data sets, problems
- Opportunity to ask challenging questions
- Subject matter expertise

Struggles with:
Expressing emotions
Lack of Logic
Vague, imprecise concepts or ideas

Innovators

- Fun and spontaneity
- Playful, surprising approaches
- Pictures, metaphors, overviews
- Discovering of the content
- Freedom to explore
- Quick pace and variety in format
- Opportunity to experiment
- New ideas, concepts

Struggles with:
Time management and deadlines
Administration and details
Lack of flexibility

Organizers

- An organised consistent approach
- Staying on track, on time
- Complete subject chunks
- A beginning, middle and end
- Opportunity to practice and evaluate
- Practical applications
- Examples
- Clear instructions/expectations

Struggles with:
Risk
Ambiguity
Unclear expectations/directions

Humanitarians

- Group discussion and involvement
- To share and express feelings/ideas
- Feeling-based
- Hands-on learning
- Personal connection with lecturer/group
- Emotional involvement
- A user-friendly learning 'experience'
- Use of all the senses

Struggles with:
Too much data and analysis
Lack of personal feedback
Pure lecture, lack of participation

B   **C**

 Figure 1.6   Students' expectations in the four quadrants, and potential struggles

Preparing and facilitating learning

A

D

Thinkers

Lecture: facts, details
Research findings
Higher order reasoning
Critical thinking
Textbooks, reading
Case studies
Use of experts
Apply logic
Metacognition
Theories
Thinking strategies

Brainstorming
Mental pictures
Metaphors
Active imagination
Creativity
Illustrations/pictures
Pretending
Mind mapping, synthesis
Holistic exercises (big picture)
Painting/drawing
Patterns/designs

Innovators

Organisers

Outlining
Graphic organiser
Checklists, worksheets
Number sequences
Policies, procedures
Organisation, summaries
Who what why where when
Exercises with steps
Problem solving with steps

Co-operative learning
Group discussions
Body language
Sharing personal experiences
Listening and sharing ideas
Musical and rhythmic
Interviews
Physical activities
Hands-on

Humanitarians

B

C

Figure 1.7 Planning learning opportunities and methods of facilitating learning

Brain® Model by implementing learning activities in each of the four quadrants.

The expanded Whole Brain® Teaching and Learning Model (Figure 1.8) has the Whole Brain® Teaching and Learning Model as baseline and centre. It also focuses on the culture in which the learning process is applied and highlights an array of aspects that have an influence such as *Ethnic, Family, Social* and *Organisational*. The expanded model also highlights the surrounding environment in which the culture exists namely the *Physical, Geographical, Economic, Temporal* and *Motivational*.

In Herrmann's expanded Whole Brain® Teaching and Learning Model (Herrmann, 1995, 417) (see Figure 1.8), the environment in which learning takes place is important. In his model Herrmann highlighted the fact that the environment can also be incorporated into the four-quadrant model. Formal academic lecture halls or downloadable audio or video files of a lecture are often conducive to the learning of A-quadrant students, who are achievement-driven. They offer an environment where these students can listen efficiently to the academic specialist empowering them with skills to acquire new knowledge. The best environment for B-quadrant students is often more traditional, such as the conventional type of classroom setting. This is where they experience normalcy of 'back to basics' and can perform their tasks to the best of their abilities. An opposite type of environment is the learning stimulus of the C-quadrant student who prefers to learn in an environment resembling a student lounge, which allows students to get together and interact with one another on subject matter. D-quadrant students prefer an even more stimulating and yet relaxed learning environment. They have a preference for a 'playground' type of environment where ideas can be brainstormed and creativity is stimulated. These different environments are illustrated in Figure 1.8.

1.9 Learning style theories

Students have different thinking styles, which are characterised by strengths and preferences in the ways they process information and construct new meaning. Some students tend to focus on facts and data, while others are more comfortable with information from pictures and diagrams. Some gain more from written and spoken explanations, while others learn actively through interactive engagements with other individuals (Felder, 1996).

Apart from the HBDI® profile, Felder examines three other learning style models that have been used effectively in engineering education (his field of interest): the Myers-Briggs Type Indicator Model, Kolb's Learning Style Model and the Felder-Silverman Learning Style Model.

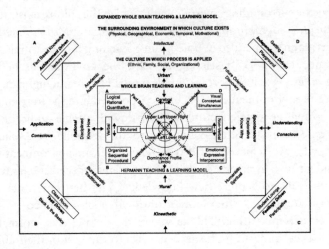

EXPANDED WHOLE BRAIN TEACHING & LEARNING MODEL

Figure 1.8	Herrmann's expanded Whole Brain® Teaching and Learning Model

Source: Herrmann (1995, 417)

1.9.1 The Myers-Briggs Type Indicator Model

This model classifies students according to their preferences on scales derived from psychologist Carl Jung's theory of psychological types. The Myers-Briggs Type Indicator Model can combine 16 different learning style preferences. According to Felder (1996), students may be classified as:

- extraverts (who try things out, focus on the outer world of people) or introverts (who think things through, focus on the inner world of ideas)

- sensors (who are practical, detail-orientated, focus on facts and procedures) or intuitors (who are imaginative, concept-orientated, focus on meanings and possibilities)

- thinkers (who are sceptical, tend to make decisions based on logic and rules) or feelers (who are appreciative, tend to make decisions based on personal and humanistic considerations)

- judgers (who set and follow agendas, seek closure even with incomplete data) or perceivers (who adapt to changing circumstances, resist closure to obtain more data).

1.9.2 Kolb's Learning Style Model

Kolb is widely credited for launching the modern learning styles movement during 1984 with his scene-setting publication *Experimental Learning* (Kolb, 1984). It summarises 17 years of research, claiming that an appreciation of different learning styles can benefit teamwork, conflict solution, communication and the choice of a career (Coffield et al., 2004). Kolb postulates that 'learning is the process whereby knowledge is created through the transformation of experience. Knowledge results from the combination of grasping experience and transforming it' (1984, 41).

Figure 1.9 shows a simplified version of Kolb's Learning Style Model.

Coffield et al. (2004) explain Kolb's model as one that classifies students to have a preference for one of four different types of learning styles.

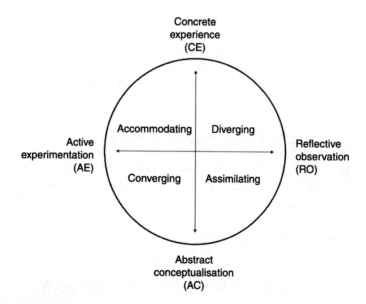

Figure 1.9 Kolb's Learning Style Model

Source: Coffield et al. (2004, 61)

1.9.2.1 Type 1: Converging style

The attributes of this style are abstract and active. Students falling in this category respond well to abstract conceptualisation and active experimentation. They prefer the 'how' question and opportunities to work actively on well-defined tasks, as well as learning by trial and error in an environment that allows them to fail in a safe way. Lecturers should function as mentors to students with a converging style.

1.9.2.2 Type 2: Diverging style

Students with this style of learning like concrete experience and reflective observation as part of their learning. They view concrete situations from many perspectives and adapt by observation rather than action. They are aware of meanings and values and have an interest in people, which tends to make them feeling-orientated.

1.9.2.3 Type 3: Assimilating style

This style was initially referred to in the literature as abstract reflective. Students respond well to abstract conceptualisation and reflective observation by focusing on the 'what' explanations. They like to reason inductively and create models and theories. They are more concerned with ideas and abstract concepts than with people. Lecturers should function as experts in order for students to be activated.

1.9.2.4 Type 4: Accommodating style

This learning style can be described as concrete active. Primarily, students with this style respond well to 'what-if' questions and welcome the opportunity to apply learning in new situations in order to solve problems. Lecturers should 'stay out of their way' but should create opportunities for them to maximise discovering.

1.9.3 *The Felder-Silverman Learning Style Model*

This model distinguishes between the following types of students:

- sensing students (who are concrete, practical and orientated toward facts and procedures)

- intuitive students (who are conceptual, innovative and orientated toward theories and meanings)

- visual students (who prefer visual representations of presented material – pictures, diagrams, flow charts)

- verbal students (who prefer written and spoken explanations)

- inductive students (who proceed from the specific to the general)

- deductive students (who go from the general to the specific)

- active students (who learn by trying things out, working with others)

- reflective students (who learn by thinking things through and working alone)

- sequential students (who are linear, orderly and learn in small incremental steps)

- global students (who are holistic, system thinkers; they learn in large leaps).

1.9.4 Summary of learning style models

Numerous learning style models have been used in education and training. Coffield and his research team (2004) contributed to the scientific validation of what we know about current learning style models when they were commissioned by the Learning and Skills Council in England to investigate the wide range of learning style instruments designed to make learning a more successful process for students.

After evaluating the main theories, they concluded that the field of learning styles is extensive and conceptually confusing. In order to make a contribution to the understanding of learning styles, they not only divided the field into three linked areas of activity, but also identified 71 models of learning styles that are available.

After reviewing and assessing the theoretical robustness of each model, they concluded that only 13 major models offer reliable and valid evidence and clear implications for practice based on empirical findings. They emphasised that it matters fundamentally which instrument one uses.

Of the 13 major models, only six were identified that met some of the set criteria. The rest of the models were disregarded as they failed to meet these criteria and could not be considered for use (Coffield et al., 2004).

The Herrmann Brain Dominance Instrument® (HBDI®) was one of the six recommended models for education and training. The measures used in the HBDI® Survey are more closely related to those used in the Myers-Briggs Type Indicator, but less related to those in the learning style inventory of Kolb. Coffield and his team found that the HBDI® as an instrument is especially useful in further education because it throws light on group dynamics, and encourages awareness and understanding of the self and others (Coffield et al., 2004). They concluded that the instrument not only measures preferences of learning for specific quadrants, but actually highlights a low or even an avoidance preference for a specific learning mode. The latter is perhaps the most significant information for lecturer and students in the learning process, because the key to promoting quality learning and facilitating learning by means of appropriate strategies should be to address those low preferences, some of which may be essential to success in a particular subject or career (Coffield et al., 2004).

1.10 Learning theories for adults

A scholarly conversation position is taken in this section analogue to Haigh's (2006) work on academic staff development. It invites the reader to engage the aspects addressed and to reflect on them using self-conversation or 'intra-reflection' – typical of the C-quadrant of Whole Brain® learning. The learning theories discussed pertain to student learning and the professional learning of lecturers, and they include formal academic staff development, informal peer mentoring (see Section 3.4) and conversations about practice fitting the notion of community of practice referred to by Orlikowski (2002). Any community of higher education practice draws from applicable literature, which in turn is informed by practice. Literature and practice combined promote continuous meaning making. Meaning making includes the notion of unlearning traditional language that Harris (2004) alludes to. Unlearning contributes to working towards a radical transformation (Harris, 2004) based on experience and reflecting on it. Studying literature, gaining experience, having discussions with colleagues and the consequent constructing of meaning collectively form part of Huber and Morreale's (2002) scholarship of teaching and learning (see Section 3.3). Neave urges scholars of teaching and learning in higher education to 'inspire others to join together to form a sustainable and mutually sustaining community of discourse, discovery and mutual learning' (2008, 268).

One should change one's conception of learning and construct new meaning about learning from the following three-dimensional point of view:

- the high quality of learning that lecturers expect of students
- what students expect of lecturers regarding high quality facilitating of learning
- what lecturers involved in staff development activities and peer mentoring expect of one another regarding professional learning.

Similar notions of expectations are highlighted by the comprehensive Whole Brain® Learning Model proposed at the end of our book. Expectations of the learning environment are an important aspect to consider. Regarding new meaning making in learning and facilitating learning, we propose in our book that Whole Brain® learning and the application of the principles become an integral part of our thinking.

The construct 'adults as learners' is preferred to 'adult learning'. Learning is a life-long process; students need to develop their potential to become matured adults who learn. No attempt is made to differentiate between forms of learning for adults and for children.

The discussion of learning theories in the next sections demonstrates that no learning theory can be implemented in isolation. Moreover, we cannot include all existing theories in our book and can only work with examples. The idea is ultimately that one should construct one's own meaning by applying the applicable principles in an integrated fashion.

1.10.1 Theories informing epistemology

Specific learning theories inform the epistemological and ontological grounding of the case studies discussed in our book. They may be considered by lecturers who research their teaching practice (see Section 3.2). The 'way of knowing' proposed stems from constructivist learning and Whole Brain® learning. The ontological stance emanates from combining the construct Whole Brain® Thinking, which forms the epicentre of our book, and the construct 'living theory' (McNiff and Whitehead, 2006), from which the construct 'Whole Brain® living' is coined. However, no learning theory can exist or be studied in isolation.

Collectively they should contribute to the realisation of the aims of higher education. One such aim is fostering a culture of authentic learning.

Authentic learning is described by Slabbert, De Kock and Hattingh as a learning process that needs 'to be initiated by an incessant challenge to the learners' [students'] living of real-life as a whole, so much so that uncertainty is provoked and anxiety not necessarily excluded' (2009, 94).

To make authentic learning possible, students should be immersed in their own learning at a deep level with a view to ensuring the highest quality of learning. Constructivist learning contributes to such quality and is essential for academic learning. Constructivist learning is not prescriptive, and students as independents should take responsibility for their learning. Lecturers should design meaningful tasks and engage students by challenging them to construct new meaning while confronted with a real-life situation. O'Connor (2009, 49) maintains that individuals create or construct their own understanding or knowledge through the interaction of what they already know and believe with the ideas, events and activities with which they come in contact and with knowledgeable people.

According to Driscoll (2000), this is the essence of constructivist learning. Although she uses the construct 'activity', the construct 'task' (Slabbert, De Kock and Hattingh, 2009; Gravett, 2005) is preferred. Task means that students are challenged to get intrapersonally immersed in executing a task imbedded in a real-life context. This defuses the intrinsic–extrinsic motivation dichotomy, whereas activity simply means an activity arranged by someone else (external locus of control) that a student can or cannot take part in. However, executing a task that requires a constructivist and metalearning approach does not always involve an individual in isolation, but more often than not an individual in relationship with others as a social process (typical of the C-quadrant).

Constructivist learning is underscored by learning-centredness (Donche, 2005; Du Toit et al., 2012; Gravett, 2005) – an educational value that should be nurtured according to McNiff and Whitehead (2006). Another value is having respect for students' point of view. Promoting constructivist learning is evidence of transformational teaching practice and learning. Learning and teaching becomes transformative when a shift is made in how one sees the self, others and the world around one, and when the revised perspective is actually acted on (Cranton, 2010) – therefore it becomes the practice of facilitating learning instead of teaching. One transforms one's learning or teaching practice (externally) and the inner-self through self-formation (Strong-

Wilson, 2009). In the context of our book, facilitating learning is considered a practice that includes assessment of student learning. All types of assessment (being diagnostic, formative or summative) and methods of assessment (being self-assessment, peer assessment or assessment by the lecturer of written, oral or practical work) are an integral part of the process of facilitating learning. It implies assessment of learning and assessment for learning. Assessment should be authentic and aligned with real-life challenges that are considered authentic. When challenging students to engage in authentic learning and authentic problems (Slabbert, De Kock and Hattingh, 2009, 69) the

> process of learning about the self from the self has to be a continual process of feedback. . . a process of continually learning to learn in order to enhance the quality of learning, all with the aim of maximising human potential which is the responsibility of each individual human being.

This is a guiding principle for facilitating and assessing constructivist learning. Students should identify the problems that they would want to address and that are relevant. Proponents of authentic learning and assessment propose that students work with innovative ideas and data sets occurring in authentic settings, for example service learning (Ash and Clayton, 2004), other forms of community engagement, experiential education in the workplace (Phuthi, 2012) and 'place-based and experiential initiatives' (O'Connor, 2009, 54).

Characteristics of a holistic constructivist learning environment demonstrate the unlearning of the traditional (pedagogical) language that Harris (2004) alludes to. Lecturers should construct their own pedagogical language. When constructivist learning, action learning, service learning and other theories are merged, a multi-dimensional theory is created that complements the multi-dimensional nature of facilitating learning in higher education. Such a holistic pedagogical philosophy can be considered pedagogy using a Whole Brain® approach.

Pursuit of student questioning is highly valued and serves as another educational value (McNiff and Whitehead, 2006). Developing an inquiring mind is a value-adding attribute (Lee, 2004). Lecturers should be the ones asking facilitative questions as the role of the lecturer has shifted to that of facilitator or mediator of learning (cf. Wilkie, 2004). Questioning as an integral part of the learning process shifts from a one-way to a multi-way questioning approach. All students contribute to asking questions during contact or virtual sessions. They learn how to formulate questions that would promote deep learning and construct new meaning. This underscores the argument for promoting scholarly discourse and conversation, as highlighted by Haigh (2006). Another construct used is 'dialogue', which entails engaging participants in a social relationship in a co-operative process of 'reciprocal inquiry through questions, responses, comments, reflective observations, redirections and building statements that form a continuous and developmental sequence' (Gravett, 2005, 41).

Students are considered more than critical thinkers with emerging theories about the world. Linked to the idea of developing inquiring minds, action learning creates opportunities to think constructively. From this stance new theory is constructed, based for example on what students have learned from studying literature, experience, scholarly discourse and feedback from others.

Scholarly discourse can be aligned with Haigh's (2006) idea of everyday conversation that contributes to learning. Constructing meaning from such conversation and discourse becomes authentic learning, for example during a community-based project, as the community engagement setting is authentic. The notion of conversation as a means of learning is evident in co-operative learning (appreciated by students who prefer C-quadrant learning). Socio-constructivist learning opportunities as the 'fulfilment of an important social function can also enable learning' (Haigh, 2006, 11). Conversation forms an important part of reflective learning. Reflection as conversation can take the form of self-conversation (self-talk) or can be interpersonal – with others (also C-quadrant preferences).

Donald's (2004) ideas of independent knowing are closely related to constructivist learning. The aspects she refers to, such as independent knowing and creating one's own opportunities for experience, are the underpinning premises for constructing new meaning. Constructing new meaning is a holistic act that contributes to finding and constructing one's own space in the formal learning environment and in the world. Complementing this idea, O'Connor refers to the importance of offering students the opportunity to become involved in 'the process of learning about themselves and their place in the natural world' (2009, 54). Donald (2004) points out that individual students construct their own understanding of larger public bodies of knowledge.

Action learning as process for student learning and action research as process for the professional development and learning of lecturers are closely related (see Section 3.2 for a discussion on action research as part of professional development).

Different constructs such as 'self-regulated learning', 'self-directed learning', 'metalearning' and 'action learning' are closely related. These constructs form part of the theoretical framework for the action research projects (reported in our book) that promote deep learning (see Chapter 4). The origin of these theories can be traced back to the original fruitful work of Kolb (1984).

The basic elements of the strategies applicable to all the theories mentioned revolve around the planning of learning and research actions to be taken, execution of the plan by taking action, and monitoring of the execution and learning and research process by different means. Critical reflection (C-quadrant) and assessing the outcome of the learning process and end product (A-quadrant) are important in this regard. Critical reflection is considered an intrapersonal act (Du Toit, 2009), which reflects the principal idea of the position students or lecturers take when taking care of their learning with a view to improving what they are doing. Although the construct 'critical reflection' is used in the literature, we support in our book Du Toit's (2012) idea that 'scholarly reflection' should rather be used, especially in the case of research.

Action learning is the original idea of Revans (Teare and Prestoungrange, 2004) and closely related to action research. Action learning and research create an opportunity for students and lecturers to test accumulated knowledge (Marquardt, 2002).

The basic difference between action learning and action research is that action learning is usually executed by students, while action research is executed by lecturer or practitioner researchers. The same steps are taken during a spiral of learning that consists of different cycles, each consisting of different steps. Different ways of making the final outcome known are the most significant difference. The outcome is not made public for students who have to execute an action learning task. It is documented in the form of a portfolio (for example) and serves the purpose of *inter alia* final grading (see our case study focusing on professional portfolios in Section 3.2). With action research executed by a professional such as a lecturer, the outcome is made public by means of articles or conference papers. Should the lecturer be enrolled for a formal education qualification such as the Postgraduate Certificate in Higher Education (PGCHE) (see Section 4.2.1) and should formal assessment be carried out, writing a journal or conference paper is considered authentic assessment.

To the background of the theory on Whole Brain® learning specifically and multiple intelligences (Gardner, 1993), critical reflection in essence has to do with emotive thinking of the C-quadrant and intrapersonal intelligence. The different intelligences distinguished are dominantly closely related to one or more of the different quadrants. In authentic learning no quadrant can operate in isolation, but it must function in a synchronous way with the other quadrants. In the same way, no intelligence can function in isolation but needs to be integrated with others. The following eight intelligences (Gardner, 1993) are listed as examples of multiple intelligences:

- intrapersonal intelligence (self-smart)
- interpersonal intelligence (people smart)
- musical intelligence (music smart)
- naturalistic intelligence (nature smart)
- linguistic intelligence (word smart)
- logical-mathematical intelligence (logic smart)
- bodily-kinaesthetic intelligence (body smart)
- spatial intelligence (picture smart).

We acknowledge the fact that further research on multiple intelligences has brought to the fore additional intelligences such as intuitive intelligence and transcendental intelligence (Slabbert, De Kock and Hattingh, 2009).

Constructing meaning regarding the learning theories discussed below should be done against the backdrop of one's understanding, experience and scholarly discussion of the four quadrants and multiple intelligences.

The term action learning is used to describe the initiative students take to execute a learning task at the highest quality of learning (Slabbert, De Kock and Hattingh, 2009), when they are proficiently matured and weaned from inquiry-guided learning as promoted by Lee et al. (2004). It implies moving from dependent learning to independent learning or self-inquiry. As an alternative, Boud (2006, 24) refers to self-directed learning as 'negotiated learning', while Straka (1997) describes self-directed learning as an initiative taken by the individual. Diagnostic self-assessment serves as a substantiated point of departure for deciding on the appropriate learning strategies and methods to apply in executing a specific task; this is aligned with Biggs's (1999) idea of metalearning, which as a process starts with a presage phase. This phase consists of aspects pertaining to student attributes and the learning environment. Student attributes include personality, historicity, learning style, meta-cognitive knowledge and study background. The learning environment consists of the subject, the lecturer (personality, teaching style), time for or on task, task requirements, libraries, laboratories, and so on. This is followed by executing a task, which involves a metalearning experience, action learning, deep learning, and so on. The end product or outcome reflects achievement. According to Biggs (1999), reflecting on the end product would include cognitive (A-quadrant) and affective (C-quadrant) aspects, but for the Whole Brain® Model the student should also reflect on the sequence (B-quadrant) to execute the task and adopt a holistic (D-quadrant) approach.

A significant attribute of action learners or researchers is the ability to become flexible. This is not acquired by osmosis, but should be nurtured. In the Whole Brain® Model it is the nurturing of becoming flexible that is nested in the D-quadrant. Students and lecturers who are willing to take risks and who observe the advantages of flexibility in others (students and peers) may be adaptable to such an extent that they influence the learning environment in a positive way. Flexible learning is considered a new way of learning that should be promoted in higher education (Garrick, 2000). Another dimension of flexible learning is divergent thinking. Authentic problems cannot be solved in the same way as others. Each problem has unique complexities and requires different approaches to solving it, as is evident from a Whole Brain® Thinking perspective. Such complex problems are to be found in authentic learning settings, for example in community engagement such as service learning.

Ash and Clayton (2004) consider engagement with the community as the context for inquiry learning. A deeper dimension to inquiry learning is evident when students enact solving the real-life problems they are faced with in collaboration with the community in question. Apart from the community offering the opportunity to students to deliver a service, learning from the community in a reciprocal fashion is yet a deeper dimension added to authentic service learning. As is typical of participatory action research (Zuber-Skerritt, 2000), which is common in service learning, 'participatory action learning' is an appropriate construct to use in the case of student learning where the outcome of the learning is not made public.

Positive influences may bring about free choices for students, peers and lecturers. Students decide to what extent they are willing to be controlled by others or other things – whether abstract such as learning culture, or tangible such as learning material. The same goes for peers. Lecturers have the free choice of promoting action learning, or staying in the rut of their old paradigm of lecturing and language.

All the learning and other theories pertaining to learning at university level (e.g. co-operative learning) inform curriculum development. Consequently, simple and practical guidelines for curriculum development are proposed. This is followed by a discussion of action research that is used for assessing one's application of the curriculum aspects, such as assessment, for which one is responsible as lecturer.

1.10.2 Curriculum development for Whole Brain® learning

We acknowledge that curriculum development *per se* is a specialised field with its own theoretical underpinning. However, it is included here with a view to indicating the position learning theories take in the curriculum. Learning theories inform curriculum development. In turn, curriculum development informs the application in practice of pertinent principles of learning theories as evident in different methods of facilitating learning. Moreover, the process of curriculum development *per se* reflects a constructivist approach.

Curriculum development takes different forms at different higher education institutions such as universities. Moreover, as higher education institutions differ vastly, they each would have their own curriculum development model that expects different actions when designing a curriculum, implementing it, evaluating it in a formative fashion, adapting it and eventually evaluating it summatively. It is a continuous iterative process and reminds one of the action research process discussed in Section 3.2. As curriculum development is a scholarly act, action research is promoted as a useful process to design, implement, monitor and evaluate the curriculum. The entire process of steps taken includes continuous scholarly reflection. The responsibility of participating in curriculum development activities is, *inter alia*, to be found in the roles stipulated by the Norms and Standards for Educators (Republic of South Africa, 2000), which include design and implementing of programmes, courses or modules, or interpreting curricula. The latter is specifically applicable where a curriculum is mainly prescribed by a professional body, such as a body for the professional development of chartered accountants, or a body for the professional development of medical practitioners. In our book, and contextualised for the South African higher education landscape, the construct 'module' is most often used. Another construct used is 'learning programme' or 'programme'. Such a programme consists of several modules. For the purpose of discussions in our book, the construct 'module' is used. Readers should change this designation according to their own context, as we acknowledge that different higher education systems and different countries use different and context-specific constructs such as 'course'.

The curriculum development model (the so-called cone model) that has been in use at the University of Pretoria (Kachelhoffer, Malan and Knoetze, 1990) for several years is currently revisited. It has since been adapted by a university of technology (Masebe, 2007) to suit its specific context. Three levels of curriculum development activities are distinguished: the macro-level, meso-level and micro-level. Instead of meso-level, we prefer to use the construct 'mid-level' or 'middle level'. The contribution the lecturer makes occurs at the micro-level and is informed by curriculum development activities at mid-level. Mid-level curriculum development activities are informed by activities on the macro-level. At this level, curriculum development activities by a constituted curriculum development committee revolve around needs analyses executed by a faculty, such as Health Sciences, by looking into relevant policies of a Health Sciences Council. In the case of the professional development of medical practitioners, other similar health sciences programmes at local and international level can be studied. Applicable qualification frameworks and other policies should be adhered to. Facilities, human resources and cost implications should be kept in mind, as well as the duration of studies for a qualification.

At mid-level, the responsibility becomes that of the constituted curriculum development committee of a specific academic department or academic unit. The department is responsible for refining the needs analysis and for identifying and formulating overarching learning outcomes. This would inform the selection of modules. Decisions regarding an overarching schedule and approaches to be included, such as service learning, should be stipulated and made.

The micro-level curriculum development activities to be conducted by the individual lecturer include taking cognisance of the module expectations. Learning outcomes are refined and inform the division of the module into different study units, while complementing assessment opportunities are identified. Based on the intended assessment practice, appropriate learning opportunities are planned. These include practicals and co-operative learning that would not only foster deep and authentic learning, but would also complement the learning outcomes. All aspects are combined and documented as a study manual per module – to promote communication between the lecturer and student. For each module a purpose statement is communicated. In the case of modules that are integrated (which we advocate since the world of work is integrated and not compartmentalised), one might find that a study manual consists of guidelines for more than one module. Again, depending on the specific context of a higher education institution, other types of learning material and documentation may be appropriate. Principles of Whole Brain® learning should be kept in mind, as well as the principles of other learning theories. The process starts with the formulation or re-formulation of learning outcomes that should ensure the promotion of deep, authentic learning. This can be achieved by including challenging learning outcomes that would expect students to demonstrate that they have followed an appropriate action learning process by documenting it as part of an assignment. It is clear that the applicable learning theory in question here is action learning. When action learning is combined with constructivist learning, the formulation of the learning outcomes should reflect this. In some way students should be assessed on constructing new meaning while executing the action learning process, as the construction of new meaning builds on one's experience.

The study guide serves as communication document to students about what is expected of them and as a contract between the lecturer and student. In brief, such a manual may include the following structure:

- an organisational component:
  - □ vision of module
  - □ motivational aspects, such as a welcoming letter
  - □ lecturer information
  - □ tutor and assistant lecturer information
  - □ schedule and programme
  - □ section on assessment opportunities and grading
  - □ section on philosophy of facilitating learning and approaches, approaches to learning, expectations of students
  - □ guidelines for plagiarism
  - □ grievance procedures
  - □ guidelines for online learning
- a study component:
  - □ overview of module (preferably in the form of a visual or mind map)
  - □ a purpose statement
  - □ introduction to Whole Brain® learning (all tasks to be executed accordingly)
  - □ each study unit documented as a subsection indicating:
    - – learning outcomes

- self-study tasks
- collaborative tasks
- online tasks
- problems to be solved (problem-based learning)
- assignments
- assessment criteria
- rubrics
- list of references, and so on.

It is specifically when it comes to assessment that the learning theories alluded to in our book should be kept in mind. The overarching outcomes should reflect expectations for Whole Brain® learning, constructivist learning, metalearning and action learning, and so on. Biggs' SOLO taxonomy comes in handy when the attributes of these theories need to be assessed (Biggs and Telfer, 1987).

These overarching outcomes should be refined as learning outcomes that each reflects the refining of learning for (constructed) knowledge (Whole Brain® Thinking) competencies, and so on. Learning tasks that would create opportunities for quality learning should be aligned with these learning outcomes. Arguments such as the one of Clayton and Kimbrell (2007) in favour of developing creative problem-solving skills inform curricula. Other so-called soft skills, such as communication skills, working as a member of a team, and leadership are pervasive skills that need to be included. This will contribute to designing a curriculum that will provide students the opportunity to develop in a holistic way.

When assessing one's practice using action research, the study manual in use should also be assessed as part of one's curriculum development responsibility. It might entail developing a new module or transforming an existing one. Against the background of the learning theories discussed, the assessment of one's study manual and curriculum development skills should offer substantive evidence (McNiff and Whitehead, 2006). Such evidence should include the application of the principles of Whole Brain® learning, constructivist learning, and so on, which become the criteria for assessment of the manual.

1.11 Conclusion

From the aforementioned theories, it becomes clear that people think differently, with stronger and lesser preferences for certain styles of thinking. This characteristic of the human brain therefore also has an impact on the thinking of individuals. It is therefore evident that lecturers need to know how to accommodate the various Thinking Styles™ of students while facilitating learning and assessing students with a view to enhancing quality learning. Moreover, lecturers need to know how to challenge students to learn how to think beyond their comfort zone or preferred way of thinking. As the world of work demands of every employee to be flexible when thinking, communicating and solving problems, every person should become more whole brained. The same goes for students as prospective employees, including lecturers. Apart from facilitating learning in a Whole Brain® fashion, lecturers as specialists in their field are responsible for ensuring that curricula, assessment opportunities and so on reflect accommodating and promoting the notion of Whole Brain® Thinking.

In the next chapters we endeavour to provide evidence of the practical application of the principles of Whole Brain® Thinking and other theories pertaining to higher education. It includes illustrations of how action research can be used as an applicable research design to investigate one's own teaching practice, especially regarding the application of the principles of Whole Brain® Thinking. The exemplars, from an array of fields of specialisation such as medicine, engineering and information science, typically show how experimenting with novel ideas in one's practice, such as Whole Brain® Thinking, and linking it to other learning theories for adults in an integrated way can bring satisfaction to lecturers and enhance the quality of every aspect of one's teaching practice.

2

Baseline data – determining thinking preferences

Abstract: Most lecturers take a traditional view of students being a homogeneous learning group and assume in their teaching that 'one fits all'. In this chapter the focus is on the data collected over the past 15 years from 1000 university students and 312 lecturers in various faculties. Each group's data is presented in a figure highlighting the group average, the composite profile of the group and a preference map.

Our analysis of the data confirms the statement made by Herrmann in 1995 that every classroom represents a complete spectrum of learning style preferences and avoidances. We conclude that it is not necessary to profile each and every student, but rather to adapt your style of facilitating to embrace Whole Brain® learning.

Keywords: empirical data, samples, group average, composite profile, preference map.

2.1 Introduction

Although interest in learning styles started already during the twentieth century, it is still growing and research activities are increasing. The latter do not only add new ideas to existing knowledge but also explain the growing number of instruments designed to measure learning styles.

Our aim with the baseline data was to evaluate the thinking style preference of a wide range of students and lecturers across diverse faculties. We used the same instrument to provide empirically validated findings on:

- understanding how students prefer to learn
- understanding how lecturers prefer to facilitate learning
- creating a comprehensive model for learning and facilitating learning that can enhance teaching practices and develop student potential.

2.2 Empirical data

The empirical data obtained at the University of Pretoria spans 15 years. A research grant from the University of Pretoria enabled the researchers to conduct a pilot study in 1998 in which students were requested to complete the HBDI® Survey online voluntarily. The initial sample of students who participated counted to 1004. The rest of the data collected over the past 15 years includes more than 2000 profiles of lecturers and students from diverse disciplines.

Since individual profiles were described in Chapter 1 (mainly for explanation purposes), the baseline data collected describes the data from diverse faculties and departments. The data presented in this chapter reveal three sets of information:

- The first graphic in every figure labelled 'Average' represents the group average, which is expressed as a generic profile for the group in relation to the A-, B-, C- and D-quadrants. A code 1 indicates a strong preference, while a code 2 indicates intermediate preference and usually signifies comfortable usage when the situation requires it. A code 3 indicates a tertiary preference for or even a potential avoidance of the respective quadrant.

- The second graphic in the figure labelled 'Composite' represents a composite profile of the group. This is determined through superimposing individual profiles on top of one another, giving an overall picture of the group.

- The last graphic in the figure labelled 'Preference map' is a visual display of the distribution of the individual profile preferences across all four quadrants. For easy understanding and for the sake of uniformity, all three visuals have been combined into a single figure for the specific group.

2.2.1 Samples of lecturers' profiles

The sample in Figure 2.1 summarises 312 lecturers from various disciplines at the University of Pretoria.

The generic average profile of the group indicates a multi-dominant profile preference with a 1111 preference code. This represents the equal distribution of profiles in all four quadrants. The composite profile reveals a highly diverse but well-balanced distribution across all four quadrants. There are individuals in this group that have very strong preferences for A-, B-, C- and D-quadrant thinking (as indicated in the last two circles that represent a strong preference value of 67–99 and a very strong value of 100+). The preference map confirms the results of the composite and group average – a well-balanced group with balanced representation across all four quadrants.

Our data confirm the results of Herrmann who argues that if the sample is large enough (for instance 250, 500 or 1000), the composite of individual profiles represents a highly diverse, but well-balanced distribution across the four quadrants of the Whole Brain® Model (Herrmann, 1996, 47).

2.2.2 Samples of student profiles

The sample collected represents 1000 students from diverse faculties and various disciplines within the faculties at the University of Pretoria. Although our baseline data include 1004 students, the maximum number of profiles that can be grouped together for meaningful results is 1000.

The generic profile of the 1000 students across all faculties represents a preference code of 1111, with an equal distribution of profile preferences in all four quadrants (Figure 2.2). The composite profile confirms the equal distribution of profiles among the four quadrants. The preference map further confirms the results by Herrmann for large groups of 1000 participants (1996). Since this large group of students inevitably comprises a composite whole, lecturers must adjust their assumptions about who is in the classroom or auditorium (Herrmann, 1996, 150–1).

The data of the lecturers and the students confirm the major finding from Herrmann's work that, taken as a whole, the world is a composite of Whole Brain® Thinking with an extraordinarily well-balanced distribution of individual preferences across all four quadrants. The same can be said for smaller entities like businesses, universities and schools (Herrmann, 1996, 150).

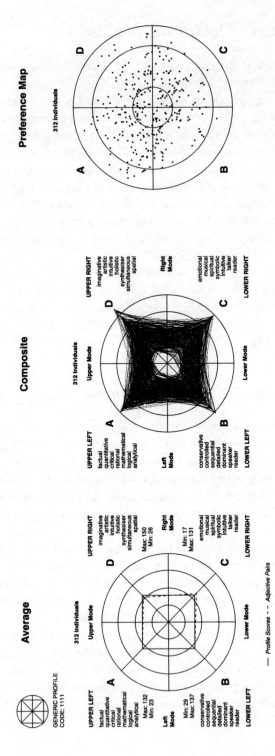

Figure 2.1 Sample of lecturers' profiles across faculties at the University of Pretoria

The four-quadrant graphic is a registered trademark of Herrmann Global and is reproduced under written contract for display in this text. © 2012. All rights reserved.

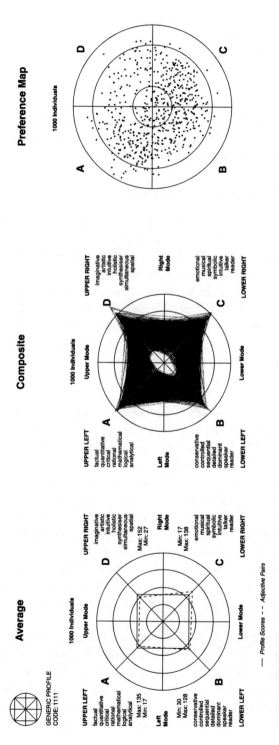

Figure 2.2   Sample of students' profiles across faculties at the University of Pretoria

The four-quadrant graphic is a registered trademark of Herrmann Global and is reproduced under written contract for display in this text. © 2012. All rights reserved.

2.2.3 Humanities

The data presented in the next few pages represent students enrolled for specific courses in the human sciences. Some of the groups are relatively small because of the number of students or lecturers that participated in the study. In one instance the data reflect only seven students' profiles, while the largest group in the study, postgraduate engineering students, reflects the data of 661 students.

2.2.3.1 Undergraduate students

The generic profile of 75 students enrolled for an arts degree at the University of Pretoria (Figure 2.3) reveals a preference code of 2111. This is a triple dominant profile for B-, C- and D-quadrant thinking. The composite profile represents individual profiles.

Although some individuals have a preference for the A-quadrant, the stronger preference is for B-, C- and D-quadrant thinking. The preference map indicates that the least preferred thinking mode for this group is for A-quadrant thinking. The generic profile (Figure 2.3) of the group average reveals a preference code of 2111. This implies a triple dominant profile, with stronger preferences for C-, D- and then B-quadrant thinking.

The composite group, which represents 34 students enrolled for a degree in drama, tilts towards a strong preference for D- and C-quadrant thinking (Figure 2.4). The preference map reveals less preference and possibly avoidance of A-quadrant thinking.

The generic average profile of 74 students enrolled for a degree in communication pathology shows a preference code of 2111 – a triple dominant profile for B-, C- and D-quadrant thinking. The composite profile represents the individual profiles and shows preferences in all four quadrants with a stronger tilt towards B-, C- and D-quadrant thinking (Figure 2.5). The preference map of the group indicates a stronger preference for C- and B-quadrant thinking and less preference, and for many possible avoidance, of A- and a low preference for D-quadrant thinking.

The generic profile of the group average for a degree in social science shows a preference code of 2111. This is a triple dominant profile with the most preferred quadrant the C-quadrant, followed by the B- and then the D-quadrant (Figure 2.6). The lowest preference of social workers is almost always for the A-quadrant (Herrmann, 1995). This occupation, which epitomises the helping professions, would typically have the

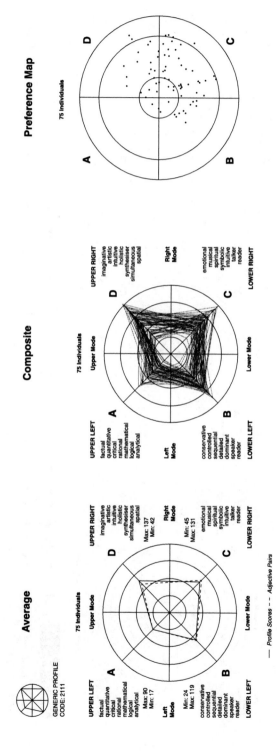

Figure 2.3 Profiles of students enrolled for a degree in arts at the University of Pretoria

The four-quadrant graphic is a registered trademark of Herrmann Global and is reproduced under written contract for display in this text. © 2012. All rights reserved.

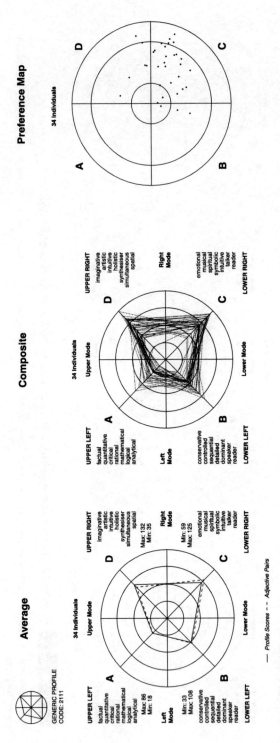

Figure 2.4   Profiles of students enrolled for a degree in drama at the University of Pretoria

The four-quadrant graphic is a registered trademark of Herrmann Global and is reproduced under written contract for display in this text. © 2012. All rights reserved.

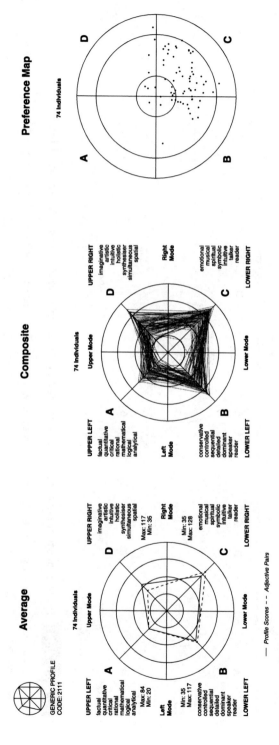

Figure 2.5 Profiles of students enrolled for a degree in communication pathology at the University of Pretoria

The four-quadrant graphic is a registered trademark of Herrmann Global and is reproduced under written contract for display in this text. © 2012. All rights reserved.

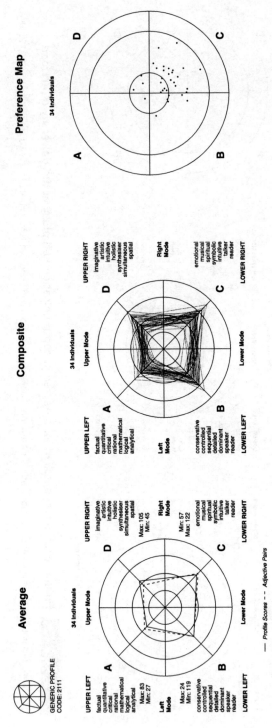

Figure 2.6 Profiles of students enrolled for a degree in the social science at the University of Pretoria

The four-quadrant graphic is a registered trademark of Herrmann Global and is reproduced under written contract for display in this text. © 2012. All rights reserved.

strongest preference in the C-quadrant. Our data collected from students enrolled for a degree in social work support this assumption. The B-quadrant reflects a preference for administrative aspects and greater success of social workers can be predicted if they also have a strong preference for B-quadrant thinking (Herrmann, 1995). The composite profile is based on the profiles of 34 students enrolled for a degree in social work. Their most preferred Thinking Styles™ are for C- and B-quadrant thinking. From the data on the preference map it is clear that there is low preference and potential avoidance of the A-quadrant mode, which also supports the findings of Herrmann.

The generic average of 40 students enrolled for a degree in human movement science displays a preference code of 2111. The triple dominant profile is for B-, C- and D-quadrant thinking with a good understanding and the ability to function on many levels (Figure 2.7). The composite profile confirms the triple dominance average profile. The preference map indicates a stronger preference for the B-, C- and D-quadrants, and low preference and potential avoidance of A-quadrant thinking.

The generic profile of 51 students enrolled for a degree in music and musical education (Figure 2.8) has a preference code of 2211. This is a double dominant profile with strong preferences for D- and C-quadrant thinking. The composite profile represents individual profiles. Although there is representation across all four quadrants in the composite map, the preference map tilts towards preferences for the C- and D-quadrants. The preference map also indicates a low preference for A-quadrant thinking – a pattern that is repeated in this faculty.

The generic group profile from 75 students enrolled for a degree in psychology represents a preference code of 2111. This is a triple dominant profile for B-, C- and D-quadrant thinking, and is typical of many professionals whose occupation requires an understanding and ability to function on many levels. Work that is considered most satisfying includes working with people, integrating ideas, bringing about change. The composite profile reveals a distribution of thinking preferences in three quadrants (Figure 2.9). The preference map confirms the stronger preference for the C- and D-quadrants of thinking and low preference for, or even an avoidance of, A-quadrant thinking.

Although the data shown in Figure 2.2 display a balanced preference across the Whole Brain® Model, the data and information gathered from analysing individual departments in the humanities highlight the following:

- Students enrolled for undergraduate programmes in the human sciences have a strong preference towards C- and D-quadrant thinking.
- The data reveal a lack of A-quadrant thinking. Curriculum development should focus on developing the A-quadrant thinking of these students because if this is not done in their undergraduate studies, it could be to their disadvantage at postgraduate level and in their professional careers.

2.2.3.2 Lecturers

The data presented are from academic staff from the humanities faculty, who voluntarily took part in the study. They wanted to understand their own thinking preferences and wished to improve their teaching practice to be able to better accommodate and develop the skills of their students.

The generic profile of 20 lecturers from the Department of Modern European Languages represents a preference code of 2111. This is a triple dominant profile, with preferences for B-, C- and D-quadrant thinking. This multi-dominant profile reflects a balance and ease to understand and implement mental diversity because of the three primary quadrants. The composite profile indicates the individual profiles, with representation across all four quadrants (Figure 2.10). The preference map indicates a tilt towards the C- and B-quadrants, but with some very strong D- and A-quadrant thinking preferences as well.

The generic profile represents 26 individual profiles from lecturers in the Department of Communication Pathology and indicates thinking preferences in all four quadrants (Figure 2.11). The preference code of 2111. This is a triple dominant profile with a strong preference for the B-, C- and D-quadrants. The composite profile represents. The preference map indicates a stronger preference for B- and C-quadrant thinking, while the lowest preference is for the A-quadrant thinking mode. Similar findings have been observed from the students.

Although a very small group of lecturers from the Faculty of Humanities participated in the study aimed at establishing baseline data, the information obtained in Figures 2.10 and 2.11 shows that they prefer C- and D-quadrant thinking and that some also display a preference for the B-quadrant. There is a clear lack of A-quadrant thinking preferences.

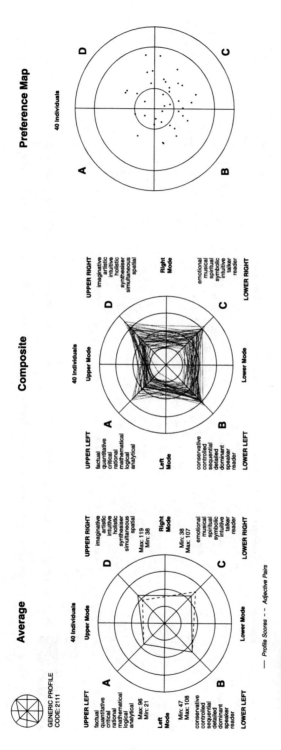

Figure 2.7 Profiles of students enrolled for a degree in human movement science at the University of Pretoria

The four-quadrant graphic is a registered trademark of Herrmann Global and is reproduced under written contract for display in this text. © 2012. All rights reserved.

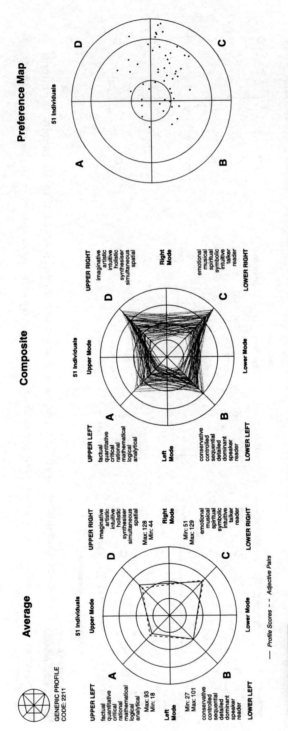

Figure 2.8 Profiles of students enrolled for a degree in music and musical education at the University of Pretoria

The four-quadrant graphic is a registered trademark of Herrmann Global and is reproduced under written contract for display in this text. © 2012. All rights reserved.

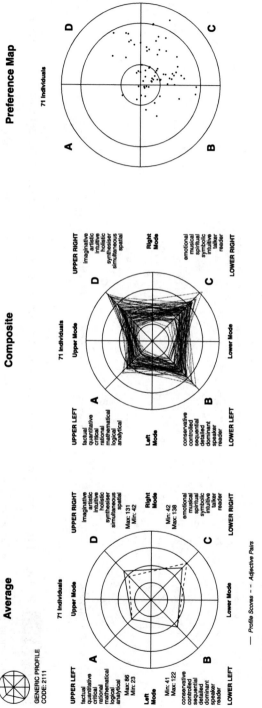

Average

GENERIC PROFILE
CODE: 2111

71 Individuals

UPPER LEFT

A

factual
quantitative
critical
rational
mathematical
logical
analytical

Left
Mode

Min: 41
Max: 122

B

conservative
controlled
sequential
detailed
dominant
speaker
reader

LOWER LEFT

Upper Mode

D

UPPER RIGHT

imaginative
artistic
intuitive
holistic
synthesiser
simultaneous
spatial

Max: 131
Min: 42

Right
Mode

Min: 42
Max: 138

C

emotional
musical
spiritual
symbolic
intuitive
talker
reader

Lower Mode

LOWER RIGHT

Composite

71 Individuals

UPPER LEFT

A

factual
quantitative
critical
rational
mathematical
logical
analytical

Left
Mode

B

conservative
controlled
sequential
detailed
dominant
speaker
reader

LOWER LEFT

Upper Mode

D

UPPER RIGHT

imaginative
artistic
intuitive
holistic
synthesiser
simultaneous
spatial

Right
Mode

C

emotional
musical
spiritual
symbolic
intuitive
talker
reader

Lower Mode

LOWER RIGHT

—— Profile Scores - - - Adjective Pairs

Preference Map

71 Individuals

A   D

B   C

Figure 2.9 Profiles of students enrolled for a degree in psychology at the University of Pretoria

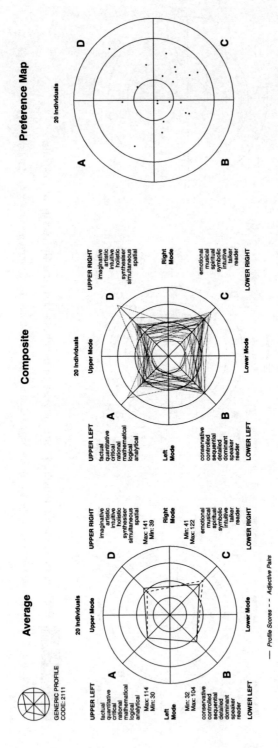

Average

GENERIC PROFILE
CODE: 2111

20 Individuals

UPPER LEFT

A
factual
quantitative
critical
rational
mathematical
logical
analytical

D
UPPER RIGHT
imaginative
artistic
intuitive
holistic
synthesiser
simultaneous
spatial

Max: 114
Min: 30

Right
Mode

Max: 141
Min: 39

Left
Mode

B
conservative
controlled
sequential
detailed
dominant
speaker
reader

C
emotional
musical
spiritual
symbolic
intuitive
talker
reader

Min: 32
Max: 104

Min: 41
Max: 122

Lower Mode

LOWER LEFT   LOWER RIGHT

— Profile Scores   - - Adjective Pairs

Composite

20 Individuals

Upper Mode

UPPER LEFT

A
factual
quantitative
critical
rational
mathematical
logical
analytical

D
UPPER RIGHT
imaginative
artistic
intuitive
holistic
synthesiser
simultaneous
spatial

Right
Mode

Left
Mode

B
conservative
controlled
sequential
detailed
dominant
speaker
reader

C
emotional
musical
spiritual
symbolic
intuitive
talker
reader

Lower Mode

LOWER LEFT   LOWER RIGHT

Preference Map

20 Individuals

D   C

A   B

Figure 2.10 Profiles of lecturers from the Department of Modern European Languages at the University of Pretoria

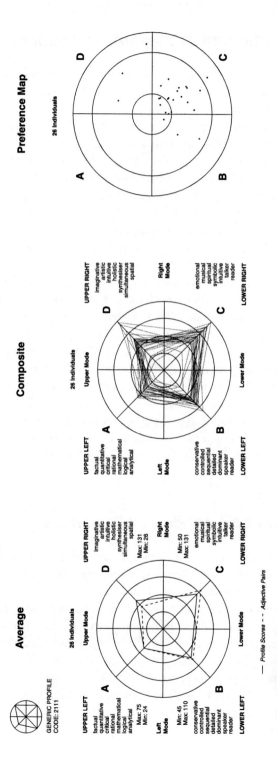

Average

Preference Map

Composite

26 Individuals

GENERIC PROFILE
CODE: 2111

UPPER LEFT
A
factual
quantitative
critical
rational
mathematical
logical
analytical

UPPER RIGHT
D
imaginative
artistic
intuitive
holistic
synthesiser
simultaneous
spatial

Max: 75 Min: 26
Min: 24 Max: 131
Min: 131

Left Mode

Right Mode

Min: 50 Min: 45
Max: 110 Max: 131

LOWER LEFT
B
conservative
controlled
sequential
detailed
dominant
speaker
reader

LOWER RIGHT
C
emotional
musical
spiritual
symbolic
intuitive
talker
reader

— Profile Scores - - Adjective Pairs

Figure 2.11 Profiles of lecturers from the Department of Communication Pathology at the University of Pretoria

2.2.4 *Economic and management sciences*

The only students from the Faculty of Economic and Management Sciences who participated in our study were undergraduate students enrolled for a degree in accounting.

The generic group profile represents a preference code of 2111. This is a triple dominant profile with two primaries in the B- and C-quadrants and the third lowest primary in the D-quadrant. The group's composite profile represents the individual profiles of 48 students, and indicates a distribution across all four quadrants (Figure 2.12). The group preference map indicates a tilt towards B- and C-quadrant thinking preferences, which supports the nature of an accounting work environment – working with check lists, worksheets, procedures and detail and possibly an interest in serving internal and external customers (C-quadrant).

The preference map also indicates a lower preference for A- and D-quadrant thinking. In an article on thinking preferences as diagnostic and learning tools for managerial styles and predictors of auditor success, Clayton and Kimbrell (2007) report on their findings that partners in public accounting firms usually exhibit a Whole Brain® Thinking style, while lower levels of management (staff auditors and managers) usually exhibit left-brain Thinking Styles™. Their findings indicate that universities need to create creative problem-solving experiences for undergraduate students as part of curriculum design. Based on these findings a few schools have already adopted this approach by adding a creative problem-solving course to their programme to stimulate A- and D-quadrant thinking during undergraduate studies (Clayton and Kimbrell, 2007).

2.2.5 *Natural and agricultural sciences*

Students enrolled for a degree in anthropology take subjects in the human sciences and natural and agricultural sciences, and the data collected from this undergraduate group are displayed in Figure 2.13.

The generic profile of the group represents a preference code of 2111. This is a triple dominant profile with dominance or primaries in the B-, C- and D-quadrants. The composite profile of eight students indicates a stronger preference for D- and C-quadrant thinking. The strong D-quadrant indicates a preference for the exploratory, synthesising and predicting nature of the work, while the strong C-quadrant represents a preference for topics related to the study of human social systems, team work and team support.

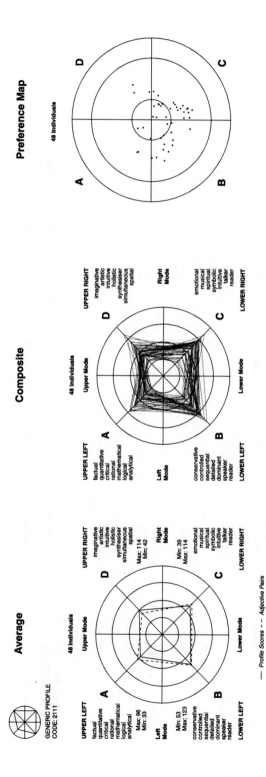

Figure 2.12 Profiles of students enrolled for a degree in accounting at the University of Pretoria

The four-quadrant graphic is a registered trademark of Herrmann Global and is reproduced under written contract for display in this text. © 2012. All rights reserved.

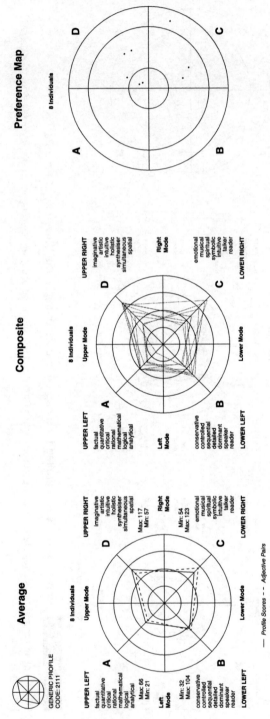

Figure 2.13 Profiles of students enrolled for a degree in anthropology at the University of Pretoria

The four-quadrant graphic is a registered trademark of Herrmann Global and is reproduced under written contract for display in this text. © 2012. All rights reserved.

A lack of A-quadrant thinking is visible in the preference map and not a single profile is represented in this quadrant as the strongest primary (several students have secondary preferences in the A-quadrant). Admittedly, the size of the group is small and this could explain why it does not show preferences for A-quadrant thinking. Furthermore, perhaps the students selecting anthropology as a specialisation were exactly lured in their selection of the study field by the stronger tendency towards the human sciences, which does not prefer A-quadrant thinking.

The generic profile of 38 students admitted for the extended degree programme in natural sciences indicates a representation across all four quadrants (De Boer and Steyn, 1999) and the group average shows a preference code of 1112. This triple dominant profile for A-, B- and C-quadrant thinking is relatively balanced. The composite profile of the group. The preference map tilts strongly towards A-, B- and C-quadrant thinking, with a lower preference for D-quadrant thinking (Figure 2.14).

For the general undergraduate degree in natural sciences, the profiles seem to match the requirements of the course content. However, taking note of the lack of preference for thinking in the D-quadrant, it becomes clear that the development of holistic, integrating and synthesising abilities is essential to ensure the individual's success in postgraduate studies as well as in a professional career.

2.2.6 Health sciences

The first group of students represented from this faculty consisted of 16 undergraduate students enrolled for a general degree in medicine. The generic group average indicates a multi-dominant profile with even distribution preferences in all four quadrants – a preference code of 1111.

The composite profile, although a very small sample, indicates thinking preferences distributed across all four quadrants. Looking at the composite map, it is clear that the tilt is stronger towards the combined primaries of A- and D-quadrants and A- and C-quadrants (Figure 2.15).

The documentation supplied with the HBDI® (Herrmann International, 2009) shows that occupations associated with this profile are those that require effective processing in all four quadrants. Work that is considered most satisfying includes dealing with and incorporating many different aspects of work. An opportunity to engage in multiple types of activity would be important. Results obtained in two specific case studies within the health sciences are discussed in Chapter 4, in the case studies in Sections 4.6.1 and 4.6.3.

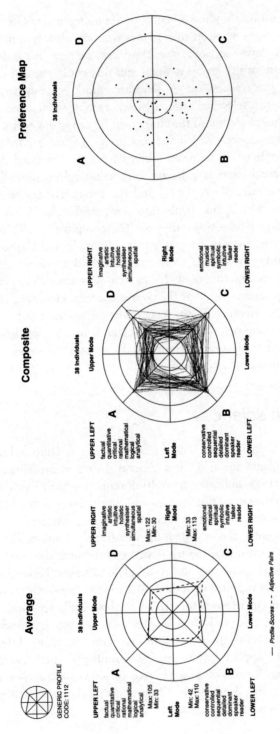

Figure 2.14 Profiles of students enrolled for a natural sciences degree at the University of Pretoria

The four-quadrant graphic is a registered trademark of Herrmann Global and is reproduced under written contract for display in this text. © 2012. All rights reserved.

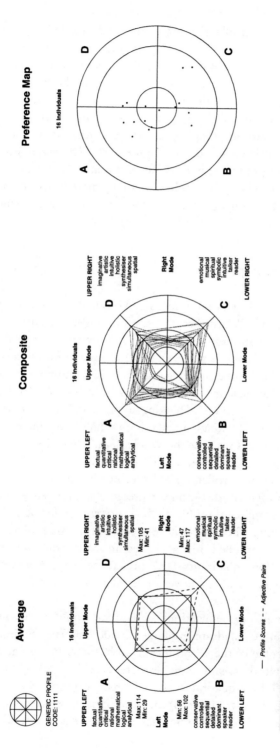

Figure 2.15 Profiles of students enrolled for a general degree in medicine at the University of Pretoria

The four-quadrant graphic is a registered trademark of Herrmann Global and is reproduced under written contract for display in this text. © 2012. All rights reserved.

The generic profile displays a preference code of 2111 – a triple dominant profile for the B-, C- and D-quadrants. The generic profile is characterised by its multi-dominant and generalised nature, fairly balanced amount of understanding and ease of using the three primary quadrants. The composite profile, which represents 62 students enrolled for a degree in occupational therapy, is dominated by female enrolment and demonstrates strong thinking preferences for the C-, B- and D-quadrants in a fairly balanced way (Figure 2.16). The preference map indicates a stronger preference in the C-quadrant and a lower preference for the D-quadrant thinking mode. In developing more learners who use the Whole Brain® Thinking methodology, the curriculum needs to include aspects to develop A-quadrant thinking even further.

2.2.7 *Education*

If we want to change the education focus and create the mind shift that is necessary to facilitate Whole Brain® learning, undergraduate students seeking a career in education need to be made aware of the role that thinking preferences have on performance and non-performance in the various subjects. The existing curricula must be adjusted to embrace Whole Brain® Thinking. Curriculum writers need to learn how to develop the content using a Whole Brain® Thinking approach. Lecturers need to facilitate Whole Brain® Thinking content using a Whole Brain® methodology to accommodate learners who use the Whole Brain® technology.

The profiles represented in Figure 2.17 are the data collected from the final-year students who enrolled for a degree in education.

The generic profile of the group represents a preference code of 1112 – a triple dominant profile with a preference for A-, B- and C-quadrant thinking. The composite map represents the profiles of 15 final-year students enrolled for a degree in education, and shows preference in all four quadrants. The preference map, however, tilts towards the B-quadrant with a lower preference for C- and D-quadrant thinking.

The challenge for the education curriculum would be to include stronger A-, D- and C-quadrant thinking in undergraduate studies.

The generic profile of the 18 profiles from lecturers in the Faculty of Education is multi-dominant with a preference code of 1111, thus preferences in all four quadrants. The composite profile represents a diverse but balanced distribution of thinking preferences across all four quadrants (Figure 2.18). The preference map confirms the results and

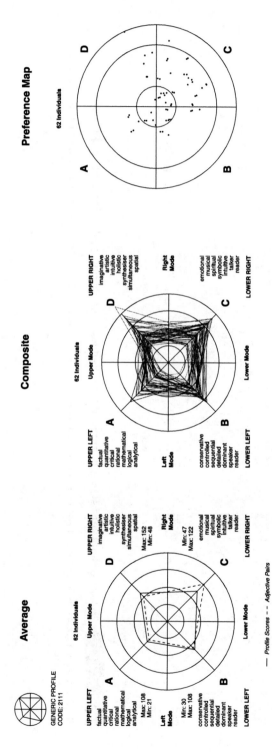

Figure 2.16 Profiles of students enrolled for a degree in occupational therapy at the University of Pretoria

The four-quadrant graphic is a registered trademark of Herrmann Global and is reproduced under written contract for display in this text. © 2012. All rights reserved.

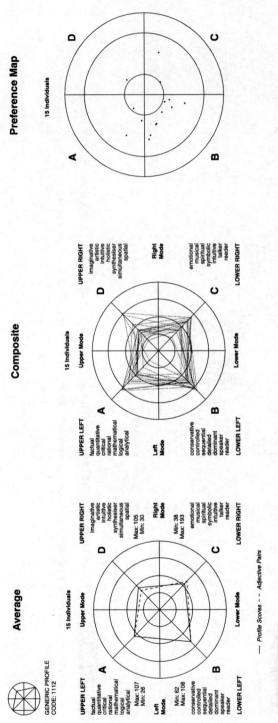

Figure 2.17 Profiles of final-year students enrolled for a degree in education at the University of Pretoria

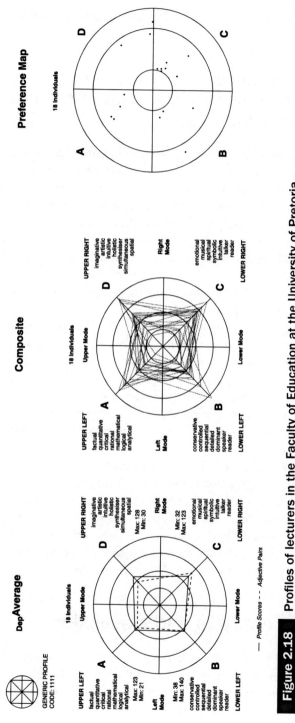

Figure 2.18 Profiles of lecturers in the Faculty of Education at the University of Pretoria

The four-quadrant graphic is a registered trademark of Herrmann Global and is reproduced under written contract for display in this text. © 2012. All rights reserved.

although this is a small group of lecturers, it confirms the findings in our baseline data (see Figure 2.1).

2.2.8 *Professional educators attending short courses at the university as part of continued education programmes*

The generic profile of 52 lecturers from a technical college who enrolled for a professional development course represents a balanced multi-dominant preference for all four quadrants, with a preference code of 1111. The composite profile indicates a diverse but balanced distribution of thinking preferences across all four quadrants (Figure 2.19).

The preference map indicates a stronger preference for A- and B-quadrant thinking and a lower preference for the C- and D-quadrant thinking mode.

The data in Figure 2.20 confirm the data in Figure 2.1 collected from lecturers across all disciplines.

Once again the generic profile of 42 university lecturers from diverse disciplines who enrolled for a course in innovation represents a multi-dominant profile, with a preference code of 1111 and preferences distributed in all four quadrants. The composite profile is made up, indicates a diverse but well-balanced distribution across all four quadrants. The preference map indicates a stronger tilt towards the D-quadrant and the C-quadrant, and a lower preference for B-quadrant thinking modes.

Once again the data reveal a balanced profile and preference for all four quadrants as highlighted at the outset of the study in Figure 2.1.

The focus of the case studies discussed in Section 4.2 is on the professional development of academic staff. The case studies report in detail how academic staff can and have been stimulated to develop Whole Brain® Thinking. Lessons learned from these case studies can be incorporated into undergraduate curricula to facilitate Whole Brain® learning.

2.3 Data analysis and discussion

Our data confirm the research findings of Herrmann – that there is a diversity of thinking preferences across the various faculties and that 'every classroom represents a complete spectrum of learning style preferences' (Herrmann, 1995, 151).

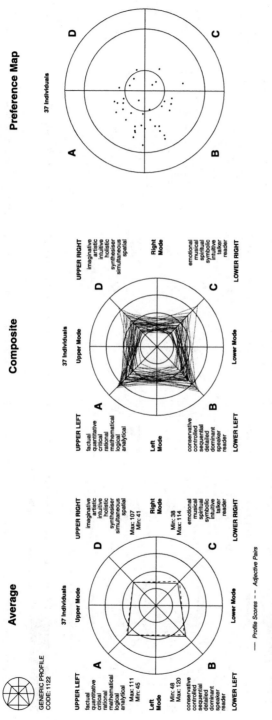

Average

GENERIC PROFILE
CODE: 1122

37 Individuals

Upper Mode

UPPER LEFT

A

factual
quantitative
critical
rational
mathematical
logical
analytical

UPPER RIGHT

D

imaginative
artistic
intuitive
holistic
synthesiser
simultaneous
spatial

Right Mode

Max: 107
Min: 41

Left Mode

Min: 48
Max: 120

B

conservative
controlled
sequential
detailed
dominant
speaker
reader

LOWER LEFT

C

Min: 38
Max: 114

emotional
musical
spiritual
symbolic
intuitive
talker
reader

LOWER RIGHT

Lower Mode

— Profile Scores - - Adjective Pairs

Composite

37 Individuals

Upper Mode

UPPER LEFT

A

factual
quantitative
critical
rational
mathematical
logical
analytical

UPPER RIGHT

D

imaginative
artistic
intuitive
holistic
synthesiser
simultaneous
spatial

Right Mode

Left Mode

B

conservative
controlled
sequential
detailed
dominant
speaker
reader

LOWER LEFT

C

emotional
musical
spiritual
symbolic
intuitive
talker
reader

LOWER RIGHT

Lower Mode

Preference Map

37 Individuals

D

C

A

B

Figure 2.19 Profiles of technical college lecturers enrolled for a course in professional development at the University of Pretoria

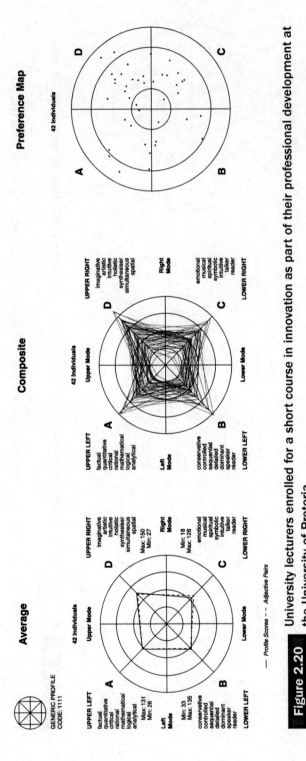

Average

GENERIC PROFILE
CODE: 1111

42 Individuals

Upper Mode

UPPER LEFT

A

factual
quantitative
critical
rational
mathematical
logical
analytical

Left
Mode

Min: 33
Max: 135

conservative
controlled
sequential
detailed
dominant
speaker
reader

B

LOWER LEFT

Lower Mode

D

UPPER RIGHT

imaginative
artistic
intuitive
holistic
synthesiser
spatial

Right
Mode

Max: 150
Min: 27

Min: 18
Max: 126

emotional
musical
spiritual
symbolic
intuitive
talker
reader

C

LOWER RIGHT

— Profile Scores - - Adjective Pairs

Composite

42 Individuals

Upper Mode

UPPER LEFT

A

factual
quantitative
rational
critical
mathematical
logical
analytical

Left
Mode

conservative
controlled
sequential
detailed
dominant
speaker
reader

B

LOWER LEFT

Lower Mode

D

UPPER RIGHT

imaginative
artistic
intuitive
holistic
synthesiser
simultaneous
spatial

Right
Mode

emotional
musical
spiritual
symbolic
intuitive
talker
reader

C

LOWER RIGHT

Preference Map

42 Individuals

A

D

C

B

Figure 2.20

University lecturers enrolled for a short course in innovation as part of their professional development at the University of Pretoria

The data also show that people are 'distributed throughout the teaching and learning model in terms of their mental preferences and the profiles represent a highly diverse, but well-balanced distribution across the four quadrants' (Herrmann, 1996, 47). We can therefore no longer ignore the data gathered around the world through many publications and in this robust study – we must acknowledge the uniqueness of the students.

Each individual is a unique student with learning experiences, preferences and potential avoidances that are different from those of other students. By gaining insight into how we prefer to think, process information and learn, we will be able to formulate learning strategies and implement flexible learning across all four quadrants to improve performance (Lumsdaine and Lumsdaine, 1995).

We must start using different design and delivery approaches to improve and facilitate the learning experience of our students. By moving back and forth with techniques and activities representative of each of the four specialised quadrants, we can ultimately provide learners with different options for critical learning points in the learning process (De Boer, Bothma and du Toit, 2011).

Our data also confirm that most people are not singular in their preference and have at least two or three primary quadrants. No group revealed a single dominant profile.

2.4 Conclusion

The school system concentrates so heavily on sequential reasoning skills that creative abilities have become completely overshadowed and are often discarded not only by teachers but also by well-meaning parents. In contrast, Ornstein (1997, 96) rightfully states that both hemispheres 'contribute to everything, but they contribute differently'.

In most instances lecturers will not have access to information on their students, or they will at best have a guess. However, they can expect many students in their class to have opposite learning preferences than their own, and for this reason important constructs must be taught in all four quadrants for optimised learning to take place. As facilitators of learning, we need to create an environment that provides opportunity for all students to strengthen all four of their thinking modes.

When we understand our own preferences and appreciate the diversity of Thinking Styles™ that our students possess, we can ensure that students understand what we are teaching, even if they have Thinking Styles™ that differ greatly from our own. A teaching approach of 'one size fits all' does not optimise learning for all. The most successful approach is to design learning opportunities that creates a Whole Brain® Thinking experience for a Whole Brain® learning group.

Incorporating activities that reach all thinking styles will make students more receptive and greatly enhance their learning experience. Although each person is a unique coalition of all four thinking modes, different occupational groups exhibit characteristic generic profiles:

- For the humanities the focus should be on including stronger A-quadrant thinking in the curricula to develop their students.

- For the economic and management sciences the focus should be on including stronger A- and D-quadrant competencies in the curricula.

- In the natural and agricultural sciences the focus should fall more strongly on developing D-quadrant thinking in the curricula.

- For the health sciences, to continue to implement and practise Whole Brain® Thinking for students using the Whole Brain® methodology.

- For the Faculty of Education, the challenge is to embrace Whole Brain® Thinking so as to facilitate Whole Brain® learning from the undergraduate to the continued education level.

- For all the engineering disciplines, the focus needs to continue on developing more C-quadrant competencies in the curricula.

When students become more independent in their learning as a result of knowing their strengths and weaknesses, negative effects from contact between lecturers and students will be counterbalanced because students will develop more effective learning strategies that they can use outside formal contact time (Coffield et al., 2004).

3

Professional development

Abstract: This chapter explores ideas on what professional development entails and how to go about one's development as lecturer. The notion of transforming one's practice by applying the principles of innovative ideas forms its core. Professional development includes an array of related areas, such as peer mentoring, scholarly reflection and scholarship of teaching.

Keywords: professional development, action research, scholarly reflection, peer mentoring, multiple intelligences, scholarship of teaching.

The key words for this chapter are included in the form of the following poem, which is made up of haikus. It demonstrates our claim in the prologue to our book that we advocate Whole Brain® communication. The haikus are typical of D-quadrant communication.

Seasons of Action Research
(Haikus)

Action Research
Needs an Agent of Change

Just as the Four Seasons Change
Designing of plans
Promises of Improvement
Blossoming of Spring

The Time for Action
Execution of Designs
Summer – Great Works Done

Data Gathered

Evaluations Commence
Collect, for Autumn
The Need to Reflect
Crucial to One's Improvement
Closing for Winter

The Cycle Repeats
Infinite Loops of a Life
Thus – Action Research
By Coligny Nel

3.1 Introduction

De Jager (2011) highlights the fact that there is no agreed definition or shared understanding of the construct 'professional development'. This is not surprising when keeping in mind that the notion of a constructivist epistemology and practice theory is fertile ground for professional development. Practice theory is a construct used by scholars such as Korthagen (2001) and Slabbert, De Kock and Hattingh (2009). A constructivist approach towards professional development (Greyling and Du Toit, 2008) allows all participants involved in professional development the freedom to construct their own meaning, based on their study of scholarly work, experience (practice) and scholarly discourse. Such an approach would contribute to self-directed scholarship of professional development. Part of this scholarship is constructing one's own practice theory about professional development within the context of one's own practice. De Jager (2011) also proposes a Whole Brain® Thinking approach to professional development. We would therefore consider the construct 'Whole Brain® Thinking practice theory' as a contribution to the current body of knowledge on the scholarship of 'Whole Brain® Thinking professional development'.

Whole Brain® Thinking professional development of lecturers forms part of the quest for building universities as learning organisations, especially with regard to human capital development. It calls for all stakeholders to contribute as leaders and critical thinkers. This would mean that any mentor or leader should become knowledgeable about what mentoring constitutes, what new innovative ideas about mentoring have been developed and how to implement these ideas in a mentorship practice. One such innovative idea that has been coined by Du Toit (2012) is 'constructivist mentoring', and it is in strong contrast to most traditional models of mentoring that consider mentoring as receiving information (Le Cornu, 2005). Mentoring now includes reflection, which we interpret as an integral part of 'scholarly reflection', 'Whole Brain® Thinking reflection' or 'Whole Brain® Thinking scholarly reflection'.

According to the latest trends in university leadership, lecturers are viewed as leaders who should promote scholarly capacity building towards the integration of thinking and acting. We refer to the latter as Whole Brain® Thinking professional conduct, and view lecturers as leaders and promoters of scholarly capacity building. Rooke and Torbert (2005) consider a leader as someone who needs to be developed. In the context of our book, this would mean that leaders in higher education institutions should be developed as Whole Brain® Thinking leaders and thinkers who should be able to enact Whole Brain® Thinking leadership attributes.

This stance represents a shift away from the traditional models of mentoring, as alluded to earlier, and brings to light the influence of constructivism and social constructivism on mentoring and the professional development of lecturers. Social constructivism suggests that the professional learning of lecturers should be participatory, communal and collaborative (Le Cornu, 2005). This is one of the trends that prompt universities to move towards becoming learning organisations. Our re-constructing of constructivism creates the construct 'Whole Brain® Thinking professional constructivism'. The need for creating Whole Brain® Thinking constructivist learning environments and promoting the establishment of Whole Brain® learning communities substantiates a shift in focus.

3.2 Action research as a process of professional learning

This section should be read in conjunction with the sections on professional development, also referred to as professional learning of academic staff and mentoring. Action research is a scholarly process that lecturers should use for monitoring their professional learning. It includes gathering evidence of one's practice in a scholarly way and contributing to the creation of 'evidence-knowledge', as Taylor and Colet (2010, 147) call it. The same researchers argue that such 'evidence ranges from learning and teaching theory to academic, culture, [educational] leadership and change theory' (Taylor and Colet, 2010, 147).

The basic principles of action research should be converted to contexts in which lecturers apply the principles of action learning as an approach to promoting deep learning. Action learning that pertains to students is self-governed and uses aspects of action research. Executed in tandem, action learning and action research become a synchronous process (Du Toit, 2009). While lecturers execute their action research aimed at having a deeper understanding of their teaching practice, students execute their action learning processes to have a deeper understanding of the 'what' and 'how' of learning. As a quality teaching procedure (Lovat et al., 2009, 56), action research that infuses action learning and deep learning becomes a pedagogy in its own right.

Scholarly reflection (Du Toit, 2012) – in the literature referred to as critical reflection – constitutes an integral part and an essential principle of action research. Scholarly reflection cannot occur effectively without an accountable theoretical background (literature review) and experience of practice. Clement and Frenay (2010, 95) support this notion: 'Making the connection with published literature emphasizes that education is a subject for research, and that the results of this research can inspire one's practice.' One's constructs or meaning making changes over time and reflects living theories (McNiff and Whitehead, 2006). What is important is that one needs to give evidence of one's claims. An example is evident in one of the case studies discussed. It is claimed that lecturers involved in professional staff development activities actually transform their practices and monitor them by planning and executing action research. By transforming teaching (into facilitating learning) learning would also be transformed (Donche, 2005).

The process of continuous reflexive practice, also referred to as 'reflexivity' (Burton and Bartlett, 2005), has its roots in learning theories such as self-regulated professional learning and constructivism, which promote high levels of intellectual quality. Lovat et al. comment on intellectual quality:

> Intellectual quality refers to pedagogy focused on producing deep understanding of important, substantive concepts, skills and ideas. Such pedagogy treats knowledge as something that requires active construction and requires students to engage in higher-order thinking and to communicate substantively about what they are learning (2009, 56).

This quotation does not explicitly reflect meaning making and focuses on the fact that pedagogy 'treats knowledge'. It also refers to 'what [students] are learning' without making a link to how they are learning. The 'how' of learning, be it facilitated by professionals such as lecturers, is an essential ingredient of deep learning that cannot be ignored. When taking the ideas of Lovat et al. (2009) into account, it is evident that one has to 'unlearn' as Harris (2004) urges one to do.

As a result of its long history and global acceptance as a worthy and proven way of practitioner research (Burton and Bartlett, 2005; McNiff, 2002), action research is the most appropriate way for lecturers to examine their teaching practices and to reflect in a scholarly way on how they facilitate learning. It empowers lecturers to take responsibility for their teaching practice as a measure of quality assurance from within (a bottom-up approach), as opposed to quality assurance measures that are enforced externally from management (a top-down approach).

Practitioner research and self-reflective practice cannot be divorced from intellectual work (Huber, 2004). Huber raises a question about the professionalism of lecturers who do not recognise their own profession as one embedded in a rich and rigorous scholarship and as 'serious intellectual work'. A question arises, as chartered accountants are seen as professionals: how can the profession of higher education practitioners (lecturers) be promoted to that of 'chartered lecturers' or 'chartered academics' (Du Toit, 2012)?

When undertaking action research practitioners conduct research by gathering data applicable to their own life or practice in context. In action research the focus is on self-inquiry. The individual is both practitioner and researcher at the same time. The practitioner becomes the intra-researcher (intrinsic motivation). Rather than using the outdated idea of 'intrinsic motivation', we prefer to refer to the construct 'intrapersonal motivation' as the dominant aspect of 'Whole Brain® Thinking motivation'. Practitioners as researchers ask questions about what they do, why they do it in a specific way and why they operate in a specific way. O'Connor promotes the idea of 'the use of a narrative self-study methodology . . . to uncover some of the fundamental values [he or she finds] true to [his or her] identity' (2009, 56).

Self-inquiry is systematic and follows a process in which one continuously learns through doing and monitoring by means of intrapersonal quality assurance. The purpose of self-inquiry is to gain a better understanding of oneself as a person and as a professional. A holistic approach to professional development is promoted. Although the lecturer is part of a bigger teaching-in-context picture where other people, their preferences and developing their potential are an issue, developing the lecturer's own full potential is equally important. According to McNiff (2002), action research is educational. For the lecturer undertaking the action research and colleagues involved, it offers numerous opportunities for professional learning and contributes to creating a learning organisation. The term 'education' includes self-education, which comes in many forms. De Beer's (2009) clay figures and poems, which represent the metaphors of her emotions and experiences, assisted her self-exploration and the subsequent transformation of her identity. Transforming one's teaching practice would inevitably include transforming one's identity (De Beer, 2009) as part of developing the whole person. Any new meaning derived from holism including Whole Brain® learning contributes to constructing one's own practice theory (Korthagen, 1993; Østerlund and Carlile, 2005).

The action research process is systematic, vigorous and open-ended. It is a developmental process of starting with an idea, implementing the idea and checking continuously if what one is doing and how it is done is what one had initially planned. It is simply a lens for looking into one's living based on one's educational values and what one believes in, and for ensuring that one does not 'live a lie' (McNiff, 2002). One should come up with supportive, validated evidence for any claim one makes. If one of the values a lecturer holds is to respect diversity in others (as, for example, reflected in the notion of Whole Brain® learning), what evidence is there to confirm that this specific educational value is played out in that lecturer's teaching practice? If the evidence supports this, the lecturer's integrity can be viewed as solid; if the evidence is contradictory, questions arise about the lecturer's integrity and claim to 'live the truth' (as Whitehead puts it: living contradictions) (McNiff, 2002).

Different approaches to action research can be observed. Sometimes the focus is on technical aspects. Action researchers who would be inclined to attend to the technical aspects of a project would rather want to get the method(s) right (B-quadrant). Others, for whom a value-driven practice is important, might like to focus on living out their values (C-quadrant). For example, the lecturer who believes in the value of promoting self-directed learning in students might expect them to take control of what they do and how they do it, while acting as a role model in this regard. Alternatively, a practitioner or action researcher might claim success based on theoretical substantiation and data (A-quadrant). Another might be more visionary and would like to experiment with innovative ideas (D-quadrant). In the end, the action research process becomes educational, as one learns from experience. However, when a holistic view is taken of professional development – making provision for developing one's full potential – one needs to develop in a multi-dimensional way. A balance between technical, visionary, value and theoretical aspects is important. This approach is aligned with Gardner's (1993) view of multiple intelligence and the notion that human beings are made up of an array of different characteristics. Since the concept 'intelligence' is multi-dimensional (Knowles, 1990), it cannot be reduced to a single number on paper (such as an IQ). Knowles remarks that

> the assumptions about the student [lecturer] must now be completely reconsidered. Intelligence is no longer one-dimensional, but rather includes the notion of multiple intelligences. Each individual [lecturer] is now being thought of as with learning preferences [preferred ways of facilitating learning] and avoidances [different from other students (lecturers)] (1990, 241).

Regarding one's own professional development, the professional development of one's colleagues and the development of students, lecturers should keep in mind that it is 'of the utmost importance that we recognize and nurture all of the varied human intelligences, and all of the combinations of intelligence' (Gardner, 1993, 12).

The model for action research explained below is useful for lecturers. The proposed model is representative of the actions a lecturer would typically take and is based on the work of Zuber-Skerritt (2000) and McNiff (2002), as adapted by Du Toit (2009). Instead of 'planning for change' (the term that is generally used) or 'planning to improve', the construct 'planning for innovation' or 'planning for transformation' (Du Toit, 2009) is proposed.

Most scholars of action research refer to problem identification (Zuber-Skerritt, 2000; Burton and Bartlett, 2005) or identifying a concern (McNiff and Whitehead, 2006) as one of the steps in or the point of departure for an action research project. Identifying a problem and formulating a so-called research problem is typical of traditional research and a deficit-based approach to action research. Instead, it is proposed that the assets and attributes of the lecturer or learning environment, or the identification of a new, innovative idea, be used as baseline. This would change action research to become an asset-based approach (Du Toit, 2009). Especially within a visionary model one would rather work with innovative ideas. It is more about experimenting with new ideas than solving existing problems.

In the action research process discussed later, the example of assessment practice is used. It is closely linked with the case study on portfolio assessment discussed in the case study section (see Section 4.2.1) but the fact that problems regarding assessment exist and should be taken care of should not be negated. Since action research is research in action while the practitioner is in action, the process of reflecting on what one does could start at any time. One could, for example, start with experimenting with a new idea and during the course of executing the action research encounter some problems. This might force the lecturer to give immediate attention to a specific problem that was identified, so the action researcher has to continue with the initial cycle of action research (which has the experiment as focus), while another cycle might start in the middle of the initial cycle, taking the action researcher in another direction. In other words, action research can take many turns. At the same time, critical reflection is multi-dimensional and also takes many directions and turns. Reflection is a scholarly skill that lecturers need to acquire. Skills of reflection, according to Senge, 'concern slowing down our own thinking processes so that we can become more aware of how we form our mental models and the ways they influence our actions' (McGill and Beaty, 1992, 195).

The multiple cycles that most action research projects consist of are depicted in Figure 3.1. This visionary action research model illustrates that action research is not a clear and neat one-way cyclical process as one usually finds depicted in the work of action research scholars. Action research is most of the time a complex and somewhat messy process. The

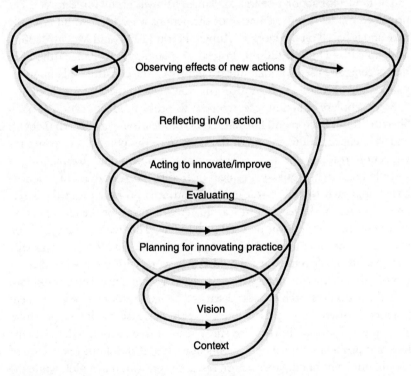

Observing effects of new actions

Reflecting in/on action

Acting to innovate/improve

Evaluating

Planning for innovating practice

Vision

Context

Figure 3.1 A visionary action research model for transforming one's assessment practice

Source: Du Toit (2009)

notion of the multi-dimensional turns that are characteristic of action research is confirmed by Burton and Bartlett (2005) and McNiff (2002). The example used in the action research model below (Du Toit, 2009) (adapted from McNiff, 2002, and Zuber-Skerritt, 2000) highlights a single aspect of teaching practice – assessment of students' work. The focus on assessment is aligned with the focus on portfolio assessment in the case study on the PGCHE (see Section 4.2.1).

Since the steps to be followed in this sequential, cyclic model are obvious, they are not discussed here. Rather, their application is outlined as an example in the context of a lecturer's teaching or assessment practice. The de-routing cycles are included to indicate the complexity of the action research process. One might have started the action research process with a focus on one aspect of assessment, such as peer assessment, while for a de-routing cycle there might be a need to focus on reformulating an assignment. Again, these cycles are not discussed here. Most de-routing cycles follow the same phases:

- planning for innovation and transformation
- acting to innovate and transform
- observing effects of new actions
- reflecting before, during or after action (Schön, 1987)
- assessing.

An in-depth study of relevant literature on assessment and related aspects should form the basis of any accountable action research project to be undertaken – documented as the theoretical framework for one's action research or scholarly reflection. Qualitative feedback obtained from colleagues involved in assessment, moderators and students, as well as through self-assessment, could be used for triangulation purposes. Then different sets of data and data from different sources can be compared to validate one's claims. Pithouse and colleagues support the view that instead of 'peer review', the term 'constructive peer feedback' should be used to promote the idea of 'collaborative scholarship' (Pithouse, Mitchell and Moletsane, 2009a). This should greatly enrich the action research process and outcome.

3.2.1 Action research with a focus on assessment practice

The action research model discussed below implies leadership and visionary thinking.

3.2.1.1 Step 1: Planning for innovating and transforming assessment practice

The lecturer responsible for the assessment practice could decide to improve, innovate or transform a current examination practice that is not conducive to self-regulated and deep learning. It could be the case that a written examination paper should be changed from being content-based to being outcomes-based, or from being too focused on assessing lower-level thinking (such as knowledge and comprehension) to assessing higher-level thinking (such as synthesising and evaluating). Alternatively, the main reason for making a change might be that the questions asked do not satisfy the need for assessment according to the multiple intelligence or Whole Brain® Thinking theory. If self-regulated learning is to be assessed, the assessment innovation could be to expect from students to compile a professional portfolio that includes reflection reports and evidence of action research or action learning, instead of sitting for a written examination. In this way, the portfolio becomes a process and product for scholarly reflection and deep professional learning.

Lecturers might view self-regulated Whole Brain® learning (Du Toit, 2012) as a novel idea that was not implemented in their assessment practice in the past. Du Toit (2012) calls this an asset-based approach. What should always be kept in mind is the curriculum design and development. The curriculum, which sets the expected learning outcomes to be achieved and assessed, informs the form of assessment, be it formative or summative, or the types of assessment – as found in the assessment of written, practical and oral work. If lecturers need to change their assessment practice, they surely should do so by taking account of the philosophy behind the assessment practice, the outcome of the curriculum development and the way in which learning is facilitated. These three areas cannot be transformed in isolation.

Processes that would introduce new assessment instruments that need to be aligned with the portfolio must be planned for. In the case of a written examination where the focus is on the end product, one usually has a more objective approach to assessing answers based on a detailed memorandum. When assessing a portfolio, one needs to design scoring rubrics for assessing both the end product and the process. When self-regulated learning and the openness of action learning are considered, one might give students the opportunity to design the scoring rubric themselves – an example of how students can be expected to take responsibility for their own learning.

Portfolio assessment is an appropriate method for assessing deep learning. A portfolio is a developmental process that is sequential and needs thorough planning. Portfolio building based on the principles of action learning is reflective and very personal. No meaningful portfolio can be built without basing one's evidence on facts and data. A portfolio should also give proof of visual and holistic thinking. The steps involved in this type of assessment therefore require that the principles of each of the four quadrants of the Whole Brain® Model be applied.

Another example of transforming one's assessment practice is to expect lecturers participating in the PGCHE (see Section 4.2.1) to write an innovative test, challenging them at a very high level of learning to demonstrate teaching scholarship. The test is based on their competence when assessed and their mastery of learning outcomes applicable to the PGCHE. The test consists of two simple requests:

- Set a test consisting of questions at different levels on each of the topics you had to study for the PGCHE with a final grading of 100 per cent. Indicate the mark allocation for each question.

- Answer the questions you have asked yourself according to the mark allocation, thus not as a summarised memorandum, but in detail as the marks require.

3.2.1.2 Step 2: Acting to transform

In this second step, the lecturer should implement the strategy for replacing the written examination by portfolio assessment. This may imply that instead of the examination paper being set towards the end of a learning programme or module, the portfolio assignment is included in the study material that students receive when the programme or module commences.

Together with the students' continuous development of their portfolios, formative assessment opportunities and learning opportunities that complement the learning process should be implemented and managed. Using the scoring rubrics as planned in Step 1 comes into play. Proof of peer assessment should be included, as well as evidence of improvement, innovation or transformation, based on the feedback from peers. Provision should be made in the rubrics for this. In some cases portfolio work is carried out in collaboration with other students, which implies that provision should also be made for the assessment of group work.

When the aim is to promote authentic, deep learning, students should be expected to draft their own rubric and decide on the criteria against which they would like to be assessed – a deeper dimension of self-regulated learning.

3.2.1.3 Step 3: Observation

For the purpose of observation, different partners should be involved. Cohen and Manion's notion of multiple method triangulation (Zuber-Skerritt, 1992) could be used to obtain a more holistic perspective on what an assessment practice entails.

The responsible lecturer should obtain as much feedback as possible, especially from other stakeholders. As a secondary way of learning about one's assessment practice, feedback from students could be obtained by means of different questionnaires. For instance, a questionnaire could be designed for obtaining feedback from students about their experience of portfolio development. Another questionnaire could be used to gain general feedback on a learning programme or module as a whole. Qualitative feedback can be obtained by analysing narratives in portfolios. Specialists could include the following partners:

- the external examiner or moderator
- colleagues at national and international level.

The lecturer's observation is multi-faceted. The lecturer is in the prime position to observe own growth at first hand. Monitoring assessment opportunities provides the lecturer with an array of observation possibilities. Different observation sheets and tick lists can be used to observe student engagement. Since assessment should be an integral part of facilitating learning, video recordings and other photographic material might come in handy as methods of data collection. The visual material can be used for the qualitative analysis of assessment opportunities. The focus is on monitoring the formative assessment process, the way different assessment opportunities are integrated and how they contribute to compiling the portfolio.

3.2.1.4 Step 4: Scholarly reflection

Reflection is an integral part of self-regulated assessment practice and essential for professional development and monitoring one's assessment practice. Scholarly reflection on the novel implementation of portfolio assessment and managing the implementation process can be undertaken before, during and after action. Scholarly reflection *before* action is envisioning what the innovative idea holds for promoting deep learning in students. Scholarly reflection *in* action takes place during the process of students building the portfolios and assessing this process for formative purposes. Scholarly reflection *after* action is twofold: it focuses on the process and on the end product. It also includes taking a retrospective view of the attitudes and experiences of all stakeholders. The reflection step includes using a scholarly lens to reflect on the new assessment strategy and the execution of the action research process.

3.2.1.5 Step 5: Assessment (evaluation)

The whole process of portfolio assessment as the assessment innovation should be evaluated to ensure that the necessary adjustments have been made. The assessment phase consists of two dimensions – the structural and affective. These two dimensions fit the construct of self-regulated learning as described by Biggs (1985) and alluded to in Section 4.2.1.

The structural dimension includes aspects such as organisational ability, scientific accountability of the assessment practice, the execution of the assessment tools, and the contribution mentors might make. The affective dimension focuses on the psychological and emotional effect that taking responsibility for the assessment practice has on the lecturer. This implies that lecturers may be satisfied or dissatisfied with the implementation of their assessment innovation, or only partially satisfied with the new idea. Hence they need to replan for yet another cycle of implementing innovations until they are convinced that the specific use of portfolio assessment is of a high quality and that the implementation is accountable.

The process of action research outlined above and the outcome can be documented and disseminated in different ways – whether as a professional portfolio, a journal or conference paper, a chapter for a scholarly publication or a monograph. These options are discussed next.

3.2.2 *Documenting and disseminating the outcome of one's action research*

Using the term 'scholarly reflection', Du Toit (2012) intends to align the scholarship of teaching with the idea that action research is currently transforming the traditional thinking about scholarship of teaching and learning into the so-called 'new scholarship'. Traditional research still dominates the research landscape and action research scholars are often confronted by traditional ways of judging research (see Section 3.3). The criteria used to evaluate research are still traditional and focus on technical aspects of research such as quantitative data gathering, analysis and interpretation. The importance of these aspects is not negated in action research, but complemented by a rich qualitative component.

Ultimately the person carrying out the action research is responsible for assuring the quality of the research report. As practitioner–researcher one has to set the criteria for judgement. According to McNiff (2002), it might be helpful to consider whether you show:

- that you are trying to live according to your beliefs
- that you can hold yourself accountable for your claims to knowledge
- how you have changed your own thinking and practice, and how this has possibly influenced others' thinking and practice.

By setting criteria such as these, one is able to make professional judgements about what one has intended to change, improve, innovate or transform – all of which are about one's understanding, productive work and relationships. Neave concurs with McNiff's (2002) ideas:

> Scholarship, however, goes hand in hand with scepticism – until evidence has been provided that allows the weighing up of and thus the judgement as to whether the claim made is sustained or 'is found wanting' (2008, 273).

One's own professional judgement needs to be validated by others to ensure that it is not seen merely as one's opinion. According to McNiff (2002), a critical friend and a validation group are needed in this regard – people whose opinion one values and who are able to critique one's work.

A professional portfolio could consist of different sections that report one's enacting of curriculum development activities, the implementation of learning programmes and modules, or innovating and transforming one's assessment practice. Depending on the context, a portfolio could include sections on research and community engagement. The professional portfolio of the lecturer should be based on action research and provide proof of scholarly reflection – it should be a scholarly work that moves beyond the general notion of a portfolio that is a file of evidence only. Scholarly reflection forms an integral part of professional portfolio development. It includes self-assessment and peer assessment. Analogue to the view of Kimeldorf (1996), lecturers empower themselves by taking control of their professional growth and building their professional development portfolios.

3.3. Scholarship of teaching

The underlying problem regarding the scholarship of teaching and learning is highlighted by Huber (2004). Teaching at higher education level is considered a practice enacted by lecturers, purely for the sake of having students learn. More often than not, learning is seen as a reaction (stimulus–response) of students to a lecturer's lecture. In our book, learning is seen as a constructive and self-directed action that students should take in order to maximise the quality of their own learning.

The dichotomy between facilitating learning and research in the context of higher education has been the topic of discussion for many years – to such an extent that it has become an archaic argument. Yet, the battle has not been decided. In 2013 (the year of publication of our book) the debate continues. As research has become the ultimate measure of being an academic, the gap between teaching and research remains. Actually it has become wider and deeper, especially in the context of higher education in South Africa. However, we cannot blame the university system *per se*. For many years, lecturers have taught in a way that caused learning to take place at a very low (parrot) level. In most cases it was about teaching the facts and expecting students to recall and regurgitate them in a test or an examination. It has never been clear to us what the term 'imparting knowledge' means. We can hardly call it a construct as we do not see any constructivist thinking behind it. However, it is sad that it happened in the past and is still happening while the world of work needs employees who can think using a Whole Brain® approach. Why then our concern regarding the scholarship of teaching and learning? It is in part imbedded in young lecturers' realisation that they are not appointed as lecturers but as researchers. They are perplexed by this idea when they realise they do not have the appropriate research skills and that they would rather teach. In many cases they have actually left their professional practice (that of auditor or accountant for example) because they 'want to work with people'.

We have argued for many years in our staff development and mentoring practices that if we want the gap to be filled, we would have to take responsibility for creating opportunities or interventions for young lecturers to develop the necessary competence for the scholarship of teaching and learning and so should those involved in such interventions and established communities of practice. This principle is argued in the sections on action research and learning theories for adults. As for students, the application of the principles of learning theories (such as constructivist and self-regulated learning) should be applied for the sake of professional learning and development.

Professional learning can be accomplished by transforming one's teaching practice (as was highlighted in the section on action research). Such transformation would demand that one starts with oneself. In our book we explore numerous examples of lecturers who are transformed when they get to know themselves better by means of the Whole Brain® Model. Supporting this notion is the application of the principles of Whole Brain® learning in their practices. They can no longer ignore the fact that balance in how students learn and in how lecturers should facilitate learning is of utmost importance. But it is not enough to only transform. In addition, one should also in some way give evidence of the transformation that has taken place in one's teaching practice. This cannot be done in isolation, and one's field of specialisation (also referred to as discipline) should form an integral part of this evidence. Immediately when one raises the construct 'evidence', researchers would want to know how one will come up with scientific evidence. Often, especially in the case of young and inexperienced lecturers, such a reaction from researchers makes them think that they are not in a position to respond to a seasoned academic and researcher in a way that would satisfy the latter. This is where the scholarship of teaching and learning should come to their rescue. This vital point highlights the importance of academic staff development and mentoring.

However, the practice of staff development and mentoring should also be research-based in order to be convincing in the research landscape. These research-driven practices are not something specialists in academic staff development and mentoring as role models can ignore. Moreover, as Huber and Morreale (2002) accentuate, it is (as any other field of research would be) underpinned by a specific field of specialisation. For teaching and learning, the field of specialisation is higher education.

We are aware of many transformative-orientated lecturers who would rather offer their students, even at undergraduate level, the opportunity to participate in conferences. If only lecturers who consider their teaching to be part of the professional development of their students would realise what such an experience would mean for any student. We do not refer to conferences in fields of specialisation such as medicine or engineering; the focus is on teaching and learning in such a field. It would put the student who has to present at ease if the lecturer as co-author introduced the context of that student's transformed practice of facilitating learning. Such a presentation cannot be anything different to a well-researched topic. In the context of our book, we consider action research as the appropriate process since it allows for participatory interventions of which the student becomes part and by which the student learns about research methodologies and the execution of applicable methods. As we suggest in Section 3.2, on action research, a suitable research design would be based on a mixed-methods approach. This is linked to the idea highlighted by Carr and Kemmis (1986) – that students become a reflective and self-reflective community of participant-researchers.

In the end, research is about becoming critical. The same applies to becoming critical about one's teaching practice. Carr and Kemmis (1986) alert us to this important matter, which should be kept in mind when research about one's teaching practice is at stake – in other words the scholarship of teaching. They refer to a number of aspects to be investigated that form part of any curriculum. We adapted these in the context of our book – realising that there are numerous others – as the lecturer's teaching practice is multi-dimensional and the lecturer is teaching practitioner and research practitioner at the same time:

- different levels of educational enquiry, such as at faculty or departmental level, and especially at the level where lecturers are responsible for their teaching practice, and, for example, service learning
- different perspectives on the character of educational contexts, especially the lecturer's own teaching practice
- different views of educational interventions as units of analysis, such as facilitating learning and assessment
- different degrees of emphasis on higher education as a distinctively human and social process in which adults are involved
- different degrees of emphasis on interventions by practitioner-researchers such as studying their practice by incorporating others as a community of practitioner–researchers and students as part of a participatory research design – a collective effort.

In the context of our book, researching one's practice is all about constructing new meaning and contributing to the current body of knowledge. If it is about one's professional development as lecturer and researcher, one's critical stance should be made public. Different means could be deployed for this purpose, such as journal and conference papers, as suggested by Clement and Frenay (2010) and Kember (2000). Even contributing to a chapter or part of a chapter (as co-author) in a scholarly work promotes the scholarship of teaching. The fascinating book *Making Connections* by Pithouse, Mitchell and Moletsane (2009b) addresses the importance of collaborative scholarship and aptly demonstrates it by including a chapter that has as main focus reflecting on a collaborative self-study on processing the book, which we would consider meta-reflection. The core of this collaboration when getting the book published – implied in its focus – is peer mentoring and is addressed next.

3.4 Peer mentoring

Mentoring is an umbrella term for a range of activities (Fringe, 2012) organised by different stakeholders. In the field of higher education the term has been used with varying models of lecturer induction (see Section 4.2.2). It facilitates the transition from studying at university level to obtaining a qualification that will give access to higher education as a career. A professional teaching practice that forms an integral part of higher education is considered an authentic context for professional work-based learning. Drawing on the work of Seminiuk and Worral and Hargreaves and Fullan, Fringe (2012) contends that mentoring has two benefits: first, the possibility for a more skilled lecturer to provide help, guidance and support to a novice or less competent practitioner, and second, pressure to make the lecturing practice less private and less isolated. In the context of our book we would rather see that the benefits of mentoring involve being a competent (rather than skilled) lecturer so as to align the teaching practice of a lecturer with attributes that promote the scholarship of teaching and professionalism in higher education. As the focus of our book is on the scholarship of teaching and learning, we do not negate the fact that the same applies to research scholarship.

Mentoring comes in different forms. Professionals involved in academic staff development may act as mentors and offer an academic induction programme (see Section 4.2.2). A senior, more experienced academic may be assigned to mentor a young(er) lecturer. Peers could mentor one another in a reciprocal one-on-one situation, or mentoring may occur in a group, as propagated by Darwin and Palmer (2009). This is considered a co-operative professional learning group of mentees in which each member makes a contribution. Participants act as co-learners or co-constructors of meaning (Le Cornu, 2005). Becoming an independent lecturer should be the outcome pursued in any mentorship relationship and process. The role of conversation (Haigh, 2006) is evident. Contributions might come in the form of professional learning that is facilitated by peers or a professional support group, as adapted from

Mullen (2000). Such a collaborative group of professionals offers mentees a safe environment in which they can learn independently from others at a professional level. At the same time the mentor is a co-learner. An important aspect of peer mentoring is self-assessment, which we would call intrapersonal assessment, and peer assessment at a professional level, which to us would be assessment at an interpersonal level. In some instances the construct 'peer review' is used, which seems to be an unpopular construct. Review is often experienced in the context of publications as a hard and unfriendly professional world with its own rules and a daunting endeavour for newly appointed lecturers (see Section 4.2.2) and established academics alike.

As alluded to in previous paragraphs, peer mentoring involves the mentoring of newly appointed academic staff and the mentoring of one another as established academics. It might include lecturers who have been newly appointed but are experienced as they come from another university. Mentees usually attend an induction programme to become acquainted with the culture ('ways of doing') of the new institution. They may also be involved in peer mentoring – as mentor and as mentee. The epistemological perspective on mentoring can be found in the theoretical framework in Chapter 1.

Peer mentoring should involve role modelling the different roles of educators. The most dominant role in peer mentoring is that of leader. Mentors take a leadership position and apply the principles of the different theories discussed in their mentorship practice. Constructs such as mentoring using the Whole Brain® Thinking methodology (Du Toit, 2012), 'constructivist mentoring' and 'facilitative mentoring' are used. For example, if mentors introduce the idea of Whole Brain® learning to mentees, the principles of Whole Brain® learning should be applied in their mentorship practice. Then fact-based learning (A-quadrant) should be part of the mentoring, for example by sourcing mentees with knowledge as to how the (new) workplace functions, and the typical forms to be used in the (new) workplace so as to enable them to analyse and know them, and by informing the mentee about procedures. In constructivist mentoring the mentee would be allowed to learn from experience and new ideas (concepts, literature, and so on) to construct own meaning (new facts). A procedural (B-quadrant) approach may help both the mentor and mentee to structure the mentoring process in such a way that regular meetings be held. It may also assist with the continuous monitoring of the process. At an emotive level (C-quadrant), the mentor should take a supportive position. Knowledge of self as the point of departure could be determined by identifying the learning style of both the mentor and mentee. As the D-quadrant represents holistic thinking, mentors should challenge mentees to construct a holistic view of their new practice, as it is multi-dimensional in nature. A holistic view of the university as organisation is also required. When keeping a learning-centred approach in mind that is critical in the context of learning and facilitating learning, the same principles apply in the context of mentoring. Therefore mentee-centred mentoring is of essence. The notion of being flexible is equally important. This notion is also encountered in the work of Harrison, Dymoke and Pell (2006).

As mentoring is enacted within a socio-constructivist context, we see mentoring as a mutually reciprocal scholarly activity that promotes professional learning for all involved in a mentoring intervention. No longer is mentoring seen as a top-down relationship, but rather as a relationship of accepting mutual responsibilities and a collective effort. In this regard, several scholars such as Hargreaves and Fullan (2000) and Klasen and Clutterbuck (2002) refer to this shift as establishing peer mentoring as authentic.

Kember (2000) refers to the important point that lecturers should become involved in educational research projects to enhance the quality of teaching and learning. In the same way, (peer) mentors should become involved in research on mentorship. Thus, the scholarship of mentoring (Du Toit, 2012) can be promoted in a constructivist way.

Using our Whole Brain® Thinking lens, we support the notion that a professional constructivist approach to mentoring is a two-way approach where professional meaning is created personally at an intrapersonal level (C-quadrant) (adapted from Klasen and Clutterbuck, 2002). Adapted from Le Cornu's (2005) work, the notion of professional learning communities that was alluded to earlier highlights that the professional learning cultures at higher education institutions are subject to change. This implies a move from individualist to collaborative cultures, involving commitment to shared goals, interdependency, participatory decision-making processes and team work – all executed against the background of promoting professionalism. This does not negate the fact that an academic should be able to work independently when a task so requires.

The case studies discussed in the next chapter are in some way built on the ideas of peer mentoring discussed in this section. Our construction of new meaning for peer mentoring ultimately creates a new professional space for considering it as a constructivist Whole Brain® Thinking endeavour that is enacted in an authentic context and at a level of high quality.

3.5 Conclusion

Professional development of academic staff is no luxury, but an imperative. If everyone concerned wants to see higher education practices of facilitating learning being transformed, be they managers or lecturers as practitioners, there is no other way to take a collective position. Interventions initiated to work towards learning of the highest quality are not the responsibility of one person. Ultimately each lecturer is responsible for transforming their own practice and constructing new meaning about this practice in a scholarly way. However, working with other lecturers in a community of practice and as peer mentors promotes the notion of becoming independent through a process of interdependence. By means of action research scholarly independence is promoted – an important ingredient of the scholarship of teaching. Lecturers should implement the principles of action research with a view to enhancing their competence in designing curricula, facilitating learning and assessing student performance, to name but a few.

Employing the principles of action research should be aligned with the expectation that students should follow the same process by applying the principles of action learning. In this way both the lecturer and students become constructivist thinkers, which is necessary in the context of Whole Brain® learning. In the end the focus is on developing higher education institutions as learning organisations. This can only be accomplished by people who take responsibility for transforming their own teaching practices and those of their peers.

4

Evidence-based practice – case studies

Abstract: In chapter 4 the focus is on the application of Whole Brain® facilitating of learning. This chapter shows the evidence-based practice the authors were engaged with over the past 15 years. The case studies were selected in order to enrich the reader with practical tools to embark on the process of Whole Brain® facilitating of learning.

Keywords: Creative Problem-Solving Model, Whole Brain® learning, Whole Brain ® facilitating of learning

4.1 Introduction

Numerous applications of Whole Brain® learning at the University of Pretoria complement the theories explored and baseline data explained. Examples of these applications are contextualised and reported as case studies. The contexts vary from an academic staff development perspective and formal academic modules to informal further development of practitioners outside the University by means of short courses.

The reporting of the case studies takes different forms. Some that are investigated by means of action research are discussed in greater depth and a more scientific way. Most of these case studies are lengthy. Others are explained more in practical terms and may not be as lengthy. Depending on the context of each case study, a case study may focus specifically on the HBDI® profile. In another it may focus on a combination of the HBDI® profile (or HBDI® profiles) and examples of how the principles are applied, substantiated by qualitative data such as feedback and photo evidence. In some case studies the application of the principles of Whole Brain® learning is integrated with the application of principles of some of the learning theories discussed in our book.

In most cases the professional development of academic staff is the key unit of analysis (Mouton, 2001).

4.2 Application of Whole Brain® principles in professional development

A spectrum of professional development opportunities in the application of Whole Brain® principles are employed to advance learning. Many formats are implemented, such as a structured certificate programme, formal induction workshops, workshops within academic departments and support services, multi-disciplinary work sessions for the execution of Whole Brain® principles in learning and facilitating of learning, as well as the coaching of individuals.

The cases described are examples of what took place at the University of Pretoria. Although multiple workshops were conducted, only a few examples are discussed for illustration purposes, such as a case study from a university in Mozambique (see Section 4.6.5) and a European one (see Section 4.6.4).

The aim of the examples described in the case studies, and the wealth of practical application from the literature, is to provide readers of our book, who may not have formal opportunities for personal development in the use of the Whole Brain® principles, an opportunity of self-education.

Some of the examples have been written in the first person because they are based on action research, while others are simply descriptive.

4.2.1 *Postgraduate Certificate in Higher Education*

As a specialist in teaching and learning in higher education, I constantly endeavour to develop my full potential and to instil the same desire in my colleagues – hence my quest to be a role model to all my students and colleagues. The programme in question, the PGCHE, is a formal higher education qualification that focuses on the professional development of lecturers. I consider them my student colleagues. I use action research in a continuous fashion as it substantiates my epistemological stance to construct new meaning about my practice and contribute to the current body of knowledge on higher education. In becoming more and more constructivist in my thinking and doing, and holistic as a practitioner, my ontological stance is that of being a Whole Brain® Thinking person, but never complete. As I am multi-dimensional, whole and incomplete, action research is multi-dimensional, whole and incomplete – evidence of the multi-dimensional practice I am involved in. It is multi-dimensional *inter alia* in its research, community engagement, teaching practice, assessment practice, curriculum development, mentorship, academic staff development and postgraduate supervision. In my multi-dimensional practice as an integrated whole, the focus is on the PGCHE, for which I act as programme co-ordinator and offer several modules. As our book has Whole Brain® learning as focal point, combining the construct Whole Brain® learning and the construct action research has contributed to my process of scholarly meaning making. It has made sense to me to coin the construct 'Whole Brain® Thinking action research' (Du Toit, 2012).

The PGCHE is a 120-credit programme that consists of nine modules: Mediating Learning, Professional Development, Curriculum Development, Assessment Practice, Educational Technology, Leadership and Management, Community-based Learning and two electives (to be chosen from a possible four) constitute the programme. In this section I touch on some of the modules and the related theories that are applicable – as included in the theoretical framework.

4.2.1.1 Research questions

The longitudinal nature of my action research and the multi-dimensional nature of my practice as an integrated whole do not allow me to list and address all the relevant research questions. However, the following serve as examples and in each case reference is made to the research method questions by means of which data were collected to illustrate how I reached conclusions:

- What are my thinking preferences?
- What are the thinking preferences of my student colleagues who are enrolled for the PGCHE? (Only some are included as examples.)
- What did my colleagues include as critical reflections of the programme for which they enrolled? (At the time of formulating the research questions, the construct 'Whole Brain® scholarly reflection' was not yet coined. The nature of action research is such that the focus and therefore the research questions will continuously change.)

Some theories that informed these questions and navigated my research stem from the learning theories for adults are discussed in Section 1.10, and some theories on action research are discussed in Section 3.2. The principles of action research serve as a process for promoting the professional learning of academic staff. Although a rich body of knowledge that is applicable to my study is documented in the literature, reference is made only to those sources addressed.

As stated earlier, I am responsible for the elective module on mentorship, which has become a vital element of academic staff development. The theoretical underpinning for this module and for my own mentorship practice is discussed in the section on mentoring (Section 3.4). Action research, again, is the process that is used to monitor any professional development activity. My student colleagues who were enrolled for the PGCHE established a community of practice in which they could share their ideas about theory and practice and co-construct new meaning by using action research. Both collegial support and engaging in scholarly reflection were evident from the reports in their portfolios (Du Toit, 2012).

There is a close link between professional communities of practice and professional co-operative learning, which can be closely linked to participatory action research. Peer mentoring becomes an enriching learning experience for everyone when the different thinking styles of the individuals concerned are involved. Eventually the participatory aspect should change to independent or self-directed professional learning through Whole Brain® Thinking. Action research is executed with a view to promoting the notion that lecturers develop their full potential using their entire brain and are life-long learners using the Whole Brain® Thinking methodology.

The PGCHE programme is a work-based programme that offers student colleagues the opportunity to apply the principles of applicable theories in their daily practice as part of a metalearning (Biggs, 1985) approach to their professional development. The innovative and transformational nature of the programme is evident in the assessment opportunities offered. Academic staff who design modules expect student colleagues to write conference papers, journal articles, action research reports, monographs or book chapters, or to submit a professional portfolio as the end product of their action research, rather than to sit for a written examination. Within Biggs' (1985) model of metalearning, which we will call professional metalearning in the context of our book, the following is important. The pre-phase that consists of two 'domains' – the personal and environmental contexts – inevitably would include Whole Brain® Thinking (personal HBDI® profile) and a learning environment that would promote Whole Brain® Thinking (and tasks). Executing the tasks requires the application of principles of action learning and action research or self-regulated learning and so on. The end product should be viewed from a Whole Brain® Thinking perspective. The tasks serve as authentic assessment opportunities. The action research is conducted in the student colleagues' own fields of specialisation, which may be accounting, health sciences, veterinary science, and so on. As I complement their action research by doing action research on my practice, I call this multi-layered action research endeavour a synchronous process (Du Toit, 1995). Action research as theory became the core of the programme as it forms part of the professional learning process and its principles. As reported in Du Toit (1995), I consider the PGCHE curriculum as driven by action research.

As part of my living (or lived) theory (McNiff, 2002), I have come to construct new meaning for the constructs with which I work. Working with Herrmann's (1996) theory on Whole Brain® learning has enriched my own thinking about these constructs and helped me to perceive them from a more holistic, whole and multi-dimensional point of view, underpinned by the epistemology and ontology referred to in a previous paragraph. The Whole Brain® Thinking theory of Herrmann forms part of the scholarship of my multi-dimensional practice referred to above. It enriches my teaching and research, community engagement, assessment, curriculum development, mentoring and research supervision. At the same time it enriches the scholarship and action research of my student colleagues. This fact validates the claim I make – that my student colleagues and I are continuously constructing new meaning. Evidence of constructed meaning is to be found in conference papers presented by student colleagues enrolled for the PGCHE (for example Bender and Du Toit, 2007; De Vries and Du Toit, 2007; Scherman and Du Toit, 2007; Goode and Du Toit, 2010; Pillay, Wolvaardt and Du Toit, 2010; Wolvaardt and Du Toit, 2011). For some it was the first time to read a paper at a conference; for some the first time to attend an educational conference. In this way their scholarly confidence was built and they took the next step in their professional development as lecturers.

Integrating different aspects of my practice, in other words integrating different theories and constructing my own living theory (McNiff and Whitehead, 2006), are typical of my thinking style as determined by the HBDI® profile. Knowledge about my thinking style has become part of the meta-cognitive knowledge (Biggs, 1985) that I need to develop as a self-regulated practitioner. I have come to realise that Whole Brain® learning is the palette that I use to colour my entire academic world.

I know that I should be able to adapt so as to accommodate my student colleagues who have different preferences and that I should be able to challenge them to learn by means of other modes in order to develop their full potential. This would mean that from time to time I, as the lecturer, should 'think out of the box'. Du Toit aptly explains this constructionalisation 'coining' while being a proponent of constructing new meaning as follows:

> Typical of my constructivist stance, I critically evaluated this commonly used slogan, but then realised that what it actually should say is: 'Thinking out of my box!' – keeping the construct of brain profiling in mind. It would be common to expect that the notion of 'thinking out of the box' would imply that as lecturer one should think and do in line with attributes of the D-quadrant. However, those lecturers who are high on the D-quadrant have to challenge themselves to think outside the D-quadrant – 'out of their box'. Lecturers who are strong on the C-quadrant should for example be challenged to put aside their strong C-box and instead, to think and act according to the A- or B-quadrants. These lecturers should therefore learn how to use 'out-of-my-box' thinking and acting to develop their full potential (2012, 1220).

Constructing new meaning as part of a constructivist (Von Glasersfeld, 2001) approach to professional learning has become a challenge, as I expect my student colleagues to construct new meaning from experience, scholarly discourse, and so on. My construct is self-regulated professional learning.

It is evident that action research constitutes an essential part of the programme and its theoretical framework. As my own research is action research-driven, it is not addressed here but in the section on action research (Section 3.2). The example used involves transforming one's assessment practice, which is aligned with the case study in question.

It is through my scholarly discourse with colleagues on the programme over years, self-talk and years of experience and studying the applicable literature that I am able to construct new meaning about what it is that I do and what I claim to be doing while pursuing my educational values (McNiff, 2002). What I have learned from implementing action research is not so much about contributing to the current body of knowledge by adding new facts, but to activate others to do the same.

In the next section I report on evidence to substantiate my knowledge claims.

4.2.1.2 Quantitative data

A mixed-methods approach complements my action research, as I have gathered data by using quantitative and qualitative methods (Du Toit, 2012). Some of the quantitative sets of data obtained by means of the HBDI® Survey are reported as examples of this type of research method.

It is clear that my learning profile serves as a baseline study and point of departure for my professional development. This learning profiling is aligned with the first research question listed above. In the same way, colleagues who could afford to have their profiles determined by means of the HBDI® Survey could use their profiles as a baseline study for their respective action research projects. Collectively these sampled profiles serve as a data set that I used to substantiate the claim made – that it is imperative to adapt one's style of facilitating learning. This statement is aligned with the second research question listed. The quantitative aspects of my own profile are substantiated by means of the Herrmann International scoring system as represented in Figure 4.1. This is followed by a brief qualitative explanation as provided by Herrmann International (2009).

With this profile comes a preference code of 3211, indicating the level of preference for each quadrant. For A-quadrant my preference is tertiary (3) – indicating an avoidance; for the B-quadrant it is secondary (2), and for the C- and D-quadrants it is primary (1), with the highest score on D (numerical value 128).

According to the narrative provided with the HBDI® profile my most preferred thinking style was identified as the D-quadrant. I selected descriptors such as *Synthesiser, Artistic, Holistic* and *Intuitive*, all of which are indicative of my preferred way of dealing with situations in day-to-day life. For work-related situations, I selected descriptors such as *Creative, Integrating* and *Innovative*. The second most dominant quadrant is the C-quadrant. *Musical, Talker, Intuitive* and *Emotional* were the descriptors chosen, with *Emotional* as the key descriptor. Among the array of descriptors, *Emotional* was the one that described me best. For work elements from this quadrant, I selected *Teaching, Writing* and *Interpersonal*. My least preferred quadrant proved to be the A-quadrant.

Regarding communication, especially communication between me and my students, which is essential in my practice, my most comfortable approaches may include allowing time to explore, giving a conceptual framework, establishing rapport, involving others and anticipating how others feel. What may be overlooked during communication are critical

Quadrant:	A	B	C	D
Preference code:	3	2	1	1
Adjective pairs:	2	2	11	9
Profile scores	30	39	108	128

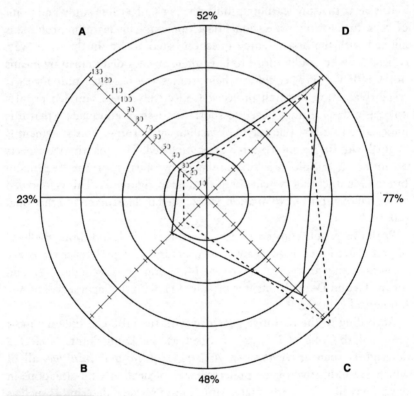

Figure 4.1   Profile of one of the authors

analysis, a written schedule and plan, a step-by-step approach and technical accuracy. Against the background of my profile as described above, it is significant to look at exemplars of my student colleagues' expectations for each quadrant and what they struggle with.

The profiles in Figure 4.2 serve as examples from my colleagues sampled over the past few years. I selected mainly those that differ from my own profile since from the discussion above it can be assumed that I

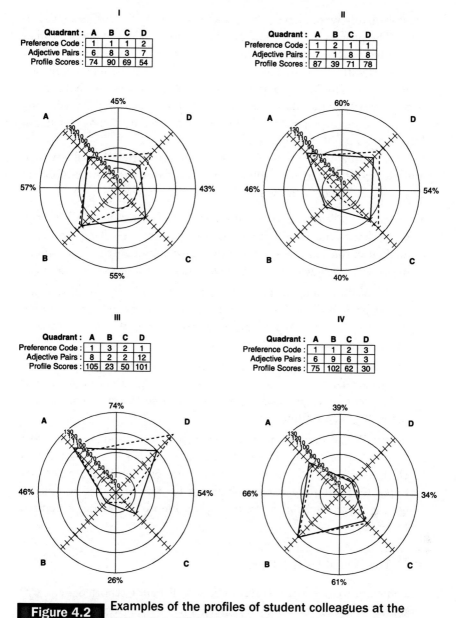

Figure 4.2 Examples of the profiles of student colleagues at the University of Pretoria

most probably would have accommodated those with profiles similar to mine. The profiles are not individually discussed. The sample of profiles is reported merely to show that in my PGCHE programme I have student colleagues with all the possible preferences, thus making up a composite Whole Brain® Thinking group. I am therefore faced with the challenge to become flexible and adaptable when facilitating learning. As with my profile, the quantitative and qualitative data obtained from Herrmann International (2009) is reported.

It is clear that the profiles in Figure 4.2 are very different from my own and each colleague would probably have preferred me to accommodate them in accordance with their specific thinking preference:

- *Profile I* indicates a triple dominant preference for A-, B- and C-quadrants and would most probably present a challenge to me as facilitator, since I need to work hard to accommodate the expectations of student colleagues who have the A- and B-quadrants as a dominance.

- *Profile II* shows a triple dominance for A-, C- and D-quadrants, which I most probably could accommodate, based on the descriptors of my profile. However, I would need to stretch into the A-quadrant to accommodate the needs of this colleague.

- *Profile III* is double dominant in the A- and D-quadrants. The challenge for me would be to stretch into the strong A-quadrant preference of the student colleague, and for both of us to be aware that we do not prefer B-quadrant thinking.

- *Profile IV* has a double dominance for the A- and B-quadrants, with a very strong preference for the B-quadrant and (also of importance) a clear avoidance of the D-quadrant. Our two profiles are directly opposite, posing the biggest challenge to both sides as the student colleague would challenge me to work in a more factual and structured fashion.

4.2.1.3 Qualitative data

The qualitative feedback from student colleagues reported here was obtained by means of personal e-mails and through text analysis. Text analysis was used *inter alia* to gather data from examples in the portfolios of student colleagues. The last three research questions listed earlier are applicable.

Several e-mails were received that mainly demonstrate that student colleagues had a positive experience. The following is an example of such an e-mail as reported in Du Toit (2012, 1226) as it was the most significant one – a single sentence. This is the background of this correspondence:

> I made contact with a former student colleague of mine to make an enquiry. He is a qualified medical practitioner and currently runs a private higher education institution that offers management programmes for health science practitioners. At the end of his e-mail response to me I observed the array of qualifications he holds: MBChB (Pret), MMed (Int) (Pret), FCP (SA), AMP (Manch), PGCHE (Pret). I immediately observed that the PGCHE qualification was now also listed. My response was simply: '*Ek is bly om te sien die PGCHE is nou ook een van jou kwalifikasies*'. [I am glad to see that the PGCHE is now also listed as one of your qualifications.] A single short response was sent to me: '*Dit is die een wat ek die meeste geniet het*'. [That is the one I enjoyed most.] What better feedback could I wish for?

Qualitative feedback was sourced from the portfolios of seven student colleagues on their completion of the PGCHE reported in Du Toit (2012). The feedback demonstrates deep learning, constructivist learning, self-regulated learning and authentic learning by students and colleagues, and it was obtained from the portfolios during text analysis. In addition, the following examples are aligned with the theories for adults as we discuss in our book.

The professional field of expertise Respondent 1 is graphic design. He writes in his 'concluding notes' section:

> I would like to offer some holistic ideas about how the various aspects of this portfolio flow together and become inseparably integrated in the way I function as an educator.

The integration highlighted is further referred to when collaboration with others is brought to the fore:

> OBE assessment strategies are a critical and integral part of each learning opportunity presented in this portfolio. These were facilitated and in some cases co-facilitated through powerful collaborative and cooperative initiatives that played out in partnership with colleagues and students. All the work included some or other evaluation process, either . . . assessment by colleagues or in the process that was made for students to provide feedback on

the learning process. Underpinning this practice . . . a life-giving, energy/knowledge-generating reflection.

Respondent 2's field of specialisation is the health sciences. She stated in her portfolio:

Evident in part of my reflections . . . I also came to realise that I prefer learning a 'whole' of something and not the details . . . The inclusion of a reflective exercise . . . The next phase of this action research cycle should focus on the inclusion of reflection by learners [students] as part of the supervisory facilitation . . . If facilitative supervision is truly like a Piet Mondrian painting, and the devil really is in the detail, then we could do better if we stood closer to the subject!

In her portfolio Respondent 3 describes her approach to her professional learning and student learning, claiming that her living theory (McNiff, 2002) revolves around the notion of critical thinking, co-operative learning and constructivist learning:

Living the theory of action research and learning style flexibility [is about] critical reflection . . . [and] instead of just completing accounting transactions, students had to design them [by means of] cooperative learning for the first time.

My final conclusion (Du Toit, 2012) confirms the claims that I make about the value of the programme. First, my students actually apply in their respective practices the principles of the theories they engaged with during the PGCHE. Second, my student colleagues manage to sustain the construction of new meaning in higher education theory more often than not, through a collaborative effort. This is evident from the large number of conference papers presented in most cases as co-authors.

This case study was discussed in detail as I have been involved in the PGCHE programme for more than 20 years and started my action research project on it more than ten years ago. I will report more briefly on the induction programme and its three related case studies (see Section 4.2.2), as I have only been involved in the induction programme for a little more than five years and have conducted action research on the case studies as such over the past three years or less. (It is significant to see how the different action research processes take shape in the different contexts.)

4.2.2 *Induction programme for newly appointed academic staff*

(We would like to acknowledge the assistance of Professor Wendy Kilfoil, Director of the Department for Education Innovation, for permission granted to include the data referred to in this case study, and Marena Lotriet who has been responsible for the induction programme for many years.)

Newly appointed academic staff in the University of Pretoria are required to attend an informal induction programmes. Two such programmes are presented here to address the specific needs of lecturers: one for full-time lecturers and one for assistant lecturers.

4.2.2.1 Full-time lecturers

The academic induction programme for newly appointed academic staff at the University of Pretoria is an informal one-week programme. It is offered at the beginning of the first semester of the academic year in January and again in July as the second semester commences. Attending the programme forms part of the requirements of the probation period that runs for two years.

Currently an action research project has been registered to investigate the induction programme. The project started only recently and the point of departure (baseline study) is the learning profiles of a sample of newly appointed academic staff who attended some of the induction programmes. The group average and group composite profile, and the group preference map are illustrated in Figure 4.3, which shows that the facilitators responsible for offering the induction programme have to make provision for all thinking preferences. Being one of these facilitators and also one of the authors of this book, I am part of the action research study. Therefore it is important to me to be a role model for the participants attending the induction programme. I make use of different tasks to accommodate all preferences and at the same time I challenge participants to develop other modes of learning as implied by the different quadrants.

For instance, I expect the participants to come up with a metaphor for their practice (D-quadrant learning) as a group task. They have to keep the multi-dimensional and holistic nature of their practice (D-quadrant) in mind. This idea is presented to the whole group by one of the 'specialists' from each small group. A task that expects individuals to analyse a set of learning outcomes accommodates the A-quadrant colleagues. Regular group work provides for those individuals who prefer C-quadrant learning, while the micro-teaching session at the end of the week where participants are expected to demonstrate an attempt to apply the principles of Whole Brain® learning for the first time is a hands-on task that simulates a real-life experience – typical of B-quadrant learning.

Another D-quadrant demonstration by me is introducing the Whole Brain® Model and the different quadrants by means of suitable hats. For the A-quadrant I use a mortar board – visualising the intellectual self; for the B-quadrant I use an army helmet that represents the safe-keeping self. The C-quadrant is represented by a sports cap since it is about interpersonal relations and typical of the emotive self. For the D-quadrant I use a joker hat that reflects the experimental self of the D-quadrant as it includes fun in the class and experimenting with new ideas that can help one transform one's teaching practice. The visuals included in this case study show how I implement these principles and experiment with ideas as part of the educational values and claims that I make.

The session on Whole Brain® learning is offered on the first day of the programme. It sets the scene for what is to come and is promoted as an appropriate approach to be presented at micro-teaching sessions on the last day.

One follow-up session is scheduled within three months and all participants are invited. Those who would like to share their experience of implementing ideas are invited to give a presentation or to lead a discussion. During the event, which serves as a celebration session, participants receive a certificate of attendance, handed over by the vice-principal responsible. The certificate is evidence of their having complied with the requirements of the probation period and can be included in their portfolio and CV.

The induction programme is offered by education consultants and other knowledgeable academics and professionals from across the University. The education consultants are generally responsible for the professional development of all academic staff and each faculty (e.g. Law) is allocated one such a consultant. They reside in the Department for Education Innovation, an independent entity reporting directly to the vice-principal concerned. The induction programme has been offered for more than ten years. It has seen several iterations but the core focus remains the same.

The purpose of discussing this case study is to give evidence of how Whole Brain® learning has become an integral part of the programme. The idea of action research by means of which the implementation of Whole

Brain® learning and other theories can be monitored has also become part of the programme, although not to a large extent. The ultimate aim of the programme is to enable participants to become independent professionals who can take responsibility for their own professional development and for becoming scholars of teaching and learning. As time is limited and prevents the themes from being addressed comprehensively, themes are addressed in detail during follow-up workshops or short courses, which can last up to three days. The workshops are not compulsory – lecturers decide which to attend according to the specific needs of their department – and they include assessment, online learning and so on. In some cases, lecturers choose to enrol for the formal higher education qualification (PGCHE), which is discussed in Section 4.2.1. This decision is more often than not taken by lecturers who see themselves as lecturers in their field rather than specialists in practice. For example, lecturers in accounting and health sciences opt for completing the programme with a view to following it up with a Master's or PhD in higher education. In some cases lecturers who have already obtained a PhD in their field of study enrol for the induction programme as they need (or rather have a passion) to learn more about their new profession.

Clement and Frenay (2010) describe several models of building teaching capacities in higher education, but the constructs used by other universities are different from what we use in our section on learning theories for adults and the opportunities for capacity building are few. Some universities offer an array of such programmes and use constructs that are aligned with the constructs we use. No more than three out of 14 universities refer to 'flexible teaching', 'student-centred learning' and 'autonomous' learning as part of their teaching philosophy (Clement and Frenay, 2010).

Our induction programme at the University of Pretoria is closely linked to the idea of mentoring as is pointed out in the relevant section on peer mentoring (see Section 3.4). At the University it is also linked to a similar programme run for assistant lecturers in information literacy (see Section 4.2.2.2). In the table offered by Clement and Frenay (2010), a great number of the topics on teaching and learning and the philosophies of several universities are aligned with that of the University of Pretoria. The main discrepancy is in the focus on research. The closest that the programme comes to research is by focusing on action research for transforming teaching practice. As an independent separate department for research exists in the University, the stance is taken that research capacity building is the responsibility of such an entity.

The outcomes listed below serve as a general outline of the induction programme at the University of Pretoria and the themes that are usually addressed. The aim of these outcomes is not to describe the entire scope of professional development initiatives at the University, but to give an outline of the objectives of the induction programme. The version of the latest programme, offered in January 2013, lists the following as course outcomes:

- getting to know the University of Pretoria teaching and learning context and culture
- knowing university students and how they learn
- being more sensitive to and accommodating diversity
- handling student discipline in class
- identifying and exploring the strengths, weaknesses and possibilities for application of various teaching methods and modes
- planning and facilitating various and rich learning opportunities within a blended learning environment
- designing, developing and reviewing a curriculum
- planning and implementing accountable assessment
- planning and pursuing your own personal development as a scholar of teaching and learning.

During the weeklong induction programme colleagues are challenged to:

- identify (and discuss and suggest solutions to) problems relating to their own teaching practice
- work together with other lecturing staff as a member of a small group
- identify ways of organising and managing their own teaching responsibilities
- communicate effectively, using education media and language skills to take part in a variety of blended activities
- contribute to the personal and professional development of each participant by actively participating in the activities, sharing their existing expertise and taking part in peer evaluation activities
- reflect on and revisit their own ideas about teaching and learning.

The induction programme caters for colleagues from all quadrants – as it should – to meet the composite group profile of the three groups of HBDI® profiles shown in Figure 4.3.

The generic profile for a group of 101 newly appointed lecturers indicates a multi-dominance with a preference for all four quadrants (1111) and once again confirms research undertaken by Herrmann (1996,

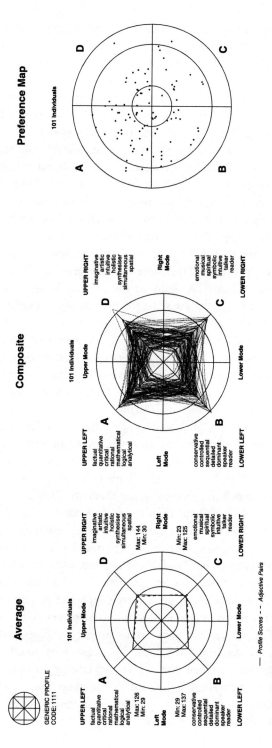

Figure 4.3 Profiles of newly appointed lecturers attending the induction programme at the University of Pretoria

47). The composite and preference maps indicate a diverse but well-balanced distribution of thinking preferences across all four quadrants.

The session on Whole Brain® learning on the first day lasts only one and a half hours, but provides an underpinning theoretical framework for other sessions during the week. A Whole Brain® Thinking approach is followed in which participants are challenged to contribute using the Whole Brain® Thinking methodology. Some tasks accommodate their preferences; others challenge them to work beyond their comfort zone – stretching them to think 'out of their box'. It entails playing games and constructing meaning by discussing the possibilities of applying the principles of Whole Brain® learning and other complementing learning theories in their practices.

Tasks that participants typically need to execute challenge them to think metaphorically (D-quadrant). One such task is to work in groups thinking of a metaphor that will represent their teaching practice while keeping in mind that it is multi-dimensional. This metaphor should be in the form of a colourful visual. As soon as the set time is up, specialists from each group need to go clockwise to the next group to explain their group's construct to the next group. The latter group has to analyse critically the presented metaphor and give constructive feedback. Depending on the time, each specialist reports back to their own group. If time allows, some of the groups are requested to introduce the metaphor to the entire group by means of a presentation. Figure 4.4 shows a typical example of a metaphor for facilitating learning.

As I need to act as role model, I need to apply the principles of quality facilitating of learning. The groups also have to execute an action research task where they have to start as a group inflating balloons – one balloon per group. On these inflated balloons they have to write all preconceived ideas pertaining to research in general that put them off. They have a short discussion in the small group and then share their ideas with the large group. As soon as the ideas are exhausted they are requested to burst the balloons. After the first round the process is repeated. Each group member also gets a personal balloon that needs to be inflated. On this balloon the group member should write down every positive idea that comes to mind when thinking about research, and the research expertise that they would want to acquire. This is first shared among group members and then with the large group. The inflated balloons are then tied to strings and hung around the venue to 'celebrate' research. This task took many of the participating lecturers out of their box, which was exactly my intention as I advocate the notion of developing their full potential (as they should also do with their students). Figure 4.5 shows one step in the execution of this task and strings of balloons celebrating it.

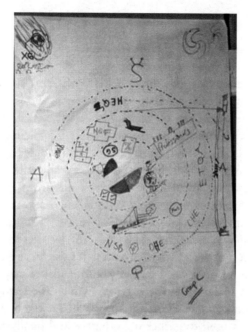

Figure 4.4 Example of a visual representation of a metaphor for facilitating learning

Figure 4.5 Classroom activities

A blended learning approach is followed during the induction programme as the contact sessions in the course of the week are linked to the learning management system of the University, commonly known as clickUP (see Section 4.2.4). The course, which is made active before the induction programme commences, is sustained during the week, especially for 'burning questions', and after the programme, with a view to preparing for the follow-up session.

4.2.2.2 Assistant lecturers

The study revolves around the professional development of a group of assistant lecturers who are responsible for offering a module on information literacy to approximately 8000 first-year students annually. At the beginning of each academic year a new group is employed since most of the lecturers are Honours (4th year), Master's or doctoral students who teach on the programme while completing their studies. Since they usually do not return to present the module the next year, the week's induction programme has to be repeated annually. Apart from the induction programme, regular follow-up sessions are offered by a subject specialist and me. This case study reports on only one specific year's group of assistant lecturers, as a group of 16.

The point of departure for each assistant lecturer is their learning profile, which serves as quantitative data that I use for my action research project. During the semester I gather photo evidence as part of a set of qualitative data to establish the extent to which the lecturer is actually adopting a Whole Brain® Thinking approach. Linked to this, a student feedback form is used to gather quantitative and qualitative data. This feedback is not reported.

Figure 4.6 shows the profile of an assistant lecturer (Lecturer I) who is dominant in both the A- and B-quadrants.

Figure 4.7 shows photo evidence of the lecturer's approach towards facilitating learning and shows a typical stance to his teaching practice. What can clearly be observed is that Assistant Lecturer I remains standing in front of the class and mainly uses PowerPoint slides to teach. He seems to be concerned merely about conveying the facts.

Figure 4.8 shows the profile of another assistant lecturer, Assistant Lecturer II, who offers the same module – they are guided by the same learning material and learning outcomes. It should also be kept in mind that the module has been designed by senior lecturers (subject specialists) who have their own thinking and learning preferences (see applicable baseline data), but this case study clearly shows how one can break through the barrier of this framework. An obstacle to overcome is the fact that the module is offered in a computer laboratory – a venue that often does not encourage quality learning as the computers are aligned in narrow rows. This setup allows little room for executing learning tasks, especially group tasks that are not carried out on the computer. The case of Assistant Lecturer II shows that one can design one's own learning material. Apart from that designed by design specialists, this learning material is used effectively as alternative or additional learning material that promotes quality learning.

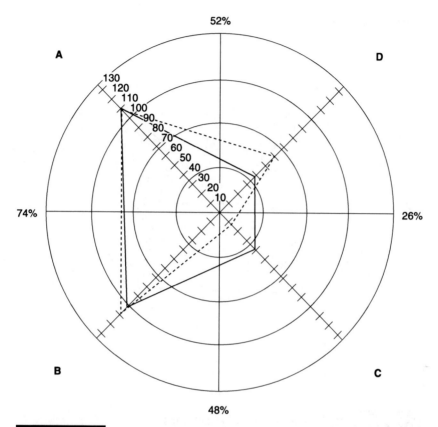

Figure 4.6 Profile of Assistant Lecturer I

Figure 4.7 Assistant Lecturer I teaching

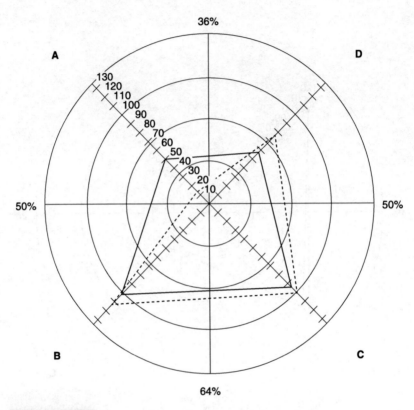

Figure 4.8 Profile of Assistant Lecturer II

The profile of Assistant Lecturer II reflects a preference for the B- and C-quadrants.

In the profile in Figure 4.8, the dominant quadrants depicted are the B- and C-quadrants. It would be expected that Assistant Lecturer II likes to be organised when facilitating learning and focuses on her students and getting them to work in a collaborative fashion. This is exactly what she does – as portrayed in Figure 4.9.

Students experience an open and free approach to learning as they are allowed to sit on the floor in different specialist groups. They are not 'sentenced' to sit in front of the computer as they are used to do. However, the task at hand is executed in an orderly fashion – as would be expected of Assistant Lecturer II who likes to organise her classes. In contrast with the facial expression of Assistant Lecturer I, this lecturer shows that she is enjoying what she has planned and now is implementing. It can also be

Figure 4.9 Classroom activities of Assistant Lecturer II

observed that the students are actively involved in the learning process, but it seems as if the learning material was prepared by Assistant Lecturer II herself, whereas it should have been constructed by the students themselves – in accordance with the notion of learning-centredness. This information would be aligned with our proposed theories discussed. I realise that transforming one's practice takes time and that the professional development of assistant lecturers is short lived as they are involved in offering the module for one year only.

4.2.3 *Learning design professionals*

Learning design professionals formed part of a research project on developing Whole Brain® learning material for first-year information literacy students. The group included an education consultant, instructional designers and a graphic designer. They all possess at least a Master's degree in education or information science, and work in an academic support service. Their knowledge regarding the Whole Brain® Model ranged from one person who included it as part of a PhD study, to others who were not familiar with the model at all.

Development of the learning design professionals' knowledge of the Whole Brain® Model occurred informally and serves as an example of a group constructing meaning through the scholarship of teaching and learning. As an introduction, the whole group attended an orientation workshop on Whole Brain® principles facilitated by a Whole Brain® Thinking expert. Each of the designers received their own HBDI® profile (as explained in Chapter 1) with a complete explanation of how to interpret it. These profiles were debriefed during the workshop and informally discussed with one another to gain a better understanding of the thinking preferences and avoidances of each member of the team.

The application of the Whole Brain® learning principles occurred through informal avenues such as discussions, mentoring and action research. Discussions and debates helped to create a common understanding of the application of the Whole Brain® Model within the group. During the first phase of the information literacy project, the discussions centred on the analysis of existing learning material to determine the degree to which Whole Brain® principles were applied. The team members' appreciation of Whole Brain® learning and facilitating learning in a Whole Brain® Thinking fashion grew further as they were involved in designing and developing additional learning material and strategies that would complement Whole Brain® learning. The professional development of the designers was greatly enhanced through the action research that formed part of the project. Their research resulted in conference presentations (Scheepers et al., 2010a, 2010b; Du Toit et al., 2011; Pretorius, Scheepers and De Boer, 2011; De Boer et al., 2012b) and journal articles (Scheepers et al., 2011; De Boer et al., 2012a; Du Toit et al., 2012), which further contributed to the professional development of members of the team as implied by action research.

Some of the instructional designers who formed part of the information literacy project team are also part of a larger training team responsible for the professional development of university staff in the educational application of the learning management system at the University of Pretoria. The University implemented a new learning management system after the designers started working on the information literacy project. The instructional designers who worked on the information literacy project insisted on using Whole Brain® learning and principles of facilitating learning during the development of learning material and activities for the implementation of the new learning management system. After explaining the use of Whole Brain® principles to the other members of the training team, the whole training team was convinced of the usefulness of the model and in the end the principles were applied to nine

Table 4.1	Qualitative feedback sourced from the learning management system workshops

A-quadrant	D-quadrant
'The Assessment tool summary hand-out' 'Overview of possibilities' 'Having time to think about how I am going to use . . . to add value to my course'	'The fact that it is an overview and we are left to fiddle' 'The time to do things & explore on my own' 'Exploring all the possibilities of assessment'
B-quadrant	**C-quadrant**
'Step-by-step instructions' 'Receiving material on the course that I can access on my own and practise on until I am satisfied that I know my way about the system' 'Being able to do the steps practically' 'Hand-outs and guidance from the instructor'	'The group discussion we had' 'Hands-on activities' 'It was very interesting to hear how other departments/lecturers use . . . some of their ideas could very well be adjusted for my own modules' 'Trying myself but then being able to call an assistant that KNOWS the answers and can help me'

workshops. The success of this decision is reflected in the feedback received from participants in the workshops. Table 4.1 provides some comments received from participants in answer to the question 'What is the most valuable aspect of the workshop?' These comments can be linked directly to the implementation of the Whole Brain® principles.

One of the learning design professionals commented on her use of Whole Brain® learning in her practice of facilitating learning. She said that teaching using the Whole Brain® Thinking methodology:

> is, for me, one of the pieces in the complex puzzle of teaching and learning. The value for me personally, therefore, was in learning more about myself – how I learn and teach. For me it became so integrated with other teaching strategies, tools, methods, concepts and theories, that when I personally do planning of a module, or support other lecturers, or teach students, I would not focus on it alone. However, I see it as a very important cornerstone, and would definitely place emphasis on it, encouraging people to find the experts, find out what it entails and to internalise it into their own approach to learning, teaching, communicating and life in general.

> I think interventions always need to be approached with an open mind – and sometimes Whole Brain® learning will be the main focus, driving the action, but other times there might be another strategy as the key, with Whole Brain® learning one of the supporting strategies.

Two instructional designers describe the impact of the Whole Brain® Model on their practice:

> With better understanding of the Whole Brain® [thinking] concept and different learning styles, I can provide and support lecturers with different approaches in designing and providing their learning material to students. I take the Whole Brain® [thinking] concept into consideration when designing products e.g. clickUP modules, multimedia and training material and try to build in different tools and activities to address all four quadrants.
>
> The knowledge of the Whole Brain® Model, particularly the inner teaching and learning circles, has helped me have a holistic approach to include learning activities from each quadrant in a new workshop the CBT [Computer-based Testing] team developed to train our lecturers to use our new CBT system. The experience of developing a lecturer's toolkit in CIL 121 in 2010 was invaluable in opening my mind to the type of activities that can be built into a learning programme. This has helped me to better advise my lecturers when I meet with them how they can better engage and accommodate their students' thinking preferences and way of learning in their teaching.

The use of the Whole Brain® Model during the information literacy project also proved to have a lasting effect on the graphic designer's practice:

> I try and approach every brief from every quadrant, and try to envision how a person with a preference for a certain quadrant will respond to the design I put forth. Also, I can visually force the reader to use all four quadrants.

Managing the Information Literacy project required that the manager of the instructional designer group apply the principles of Whole Brain® learning and contextualise it as Whole Brain® Thinking management. A Whole Brain® Thinking expert mentored the manager in the use of Whole Brain® principles to manage teams and projects. This resulted in a more successful information literacy project (see Chapter 6). The skill of applying the Whole Brain® Model to the management of teams and projects also brought success in later projects the manager was involved in. She describes it in the following way:

> The use of the Whole Brain® Model is a wonderful tool to understand how people think. It has helped me to understand why certain individuals in different groups I have to manage always are at odds with one another, or why a specific person experiences stress at a particular phase of a project. Just by understanding where each one comes from, I can deal with the conflict (often within myself as well) in a more constructive way than before. I also have a good indication on whom to ask to perform specific tasks during a project to ensure maximum results.

Five other members of the team also found the Whole Brain® Model useful to maintain relationships in the work environment:

> I now have a better understanding of how and why I react to certain situations and personalities in the work environment – why I respond to my manager the way I do; why and how I interact with colleagues and clients. I also have a better understanding that everyone acts in accordance to their own preference – as do I, but that I (and them) can stretch ourselves to some of the other quadrants to make for a better person/employee/team.
>
> I am thankful for the opportunity I had to do the Whole Brain® [thinking] evaluation!
>
> Biggest benefit was that it did teach me to understand myself better. Previously there was a sense of 'there is a right way and there is a wrong way' when it comes to solving problems and thinking. This view has now shifted to 'different ways' or 'different focuses' to use when attempting a goal. Makes one value teamwork so much more.
>
> My own profile and the workshop helped me to understand myself and others better as well as the way we think and learn. I have a better understanding of people's actions and feelings as well as reactions when they are under stress. In the past I've compared myself with others and could not understand why I'm struggling to complete some tasks while it seems to be easy for others. I couldn't understand why I'm different from the 'rest'. I'm now aware of my stronger areas and the less strong areas.
>
> The Whole Brain® Model has opened my mind to a whole new way of thinking and understanding myself as well as others in a variety of groups I find myself in. It has given me a new respect for my colleagues

and what each individual brings to a group and how important it is to have a group comprised of individuals who have strengths in each of the four quadrants of Herrmann's Whole Brain® Model, so at the end of the day, your intervention to students/lecturers is richer and accommodates the thinking preferences of your target audience.

4.2.4 *Development of blended learning competencies*

Blended learning is a strategic focus within the University of Pretoria to support student learning and success. For this reason, the University implemented the Blackboard system as a learning management system. Instructional designers at the University present a number of courses to enable academic and administrative staff to make use of the learning management system to support and facilitate learning. These are all four-hour courses and they are presented at regular intervals during the year in an attempt to accommodate the busy schedules of participants.

Lessons learned through the information literacy project (described in Sections 4.2.2.1 and 4.7 and Chapter 5) led to the decision to ensure that a Whole Brain® Thinking approach was followed in the presentation of the courses and in developing support documentation such as course hand-outs and a help website.

When the courses were designed, it was decided to present different courses for the two different audiences who attend the professional development sessions. Courses for the academic staff follow a workshop approach, while courses aimed at the administrative staff focus on using the learning management system. In the workshop for academic staff, lecturers are challenged with:

- educational theory that underlies the use of the learning management system, offered through narrated PowerPoint presentations viewed via the learning management system (A-quadrant) and discussion among participants (C-quadrant)
- examples of how lecturers use the system to promote learning, provided through presentations by the facilitators (A- and D-quadrant), or through listening to stories that lecturers tell of their experiences via an online 'coffee table book' (A-, C- and D-quadrant)
- exercises with steps to practise only certain important functionalities (B-quadrant)
- planning their own use of the system (A- and D-quadrant)

- building the activities (B-, C- and D-quadrant) that they want to implement in their modules in the learning management system.

Courses for the administrative staff focus on how to use the system to perform basic functions that lecturers require, such as sending out announcements or loading class notes and test marks into the learning management system. Their activities concentrate on repetition of the actions to acquire the necessary skills (B- and C-quadrant).

Learning a new computer system requires the development of specific skills. These skills need regular repetition before they are mastered. As the clickUP courses are too short for participants to practise new skills until they are mastered, and because participants have varying levels of basic computer literacy, these skills cannot be mastered during the course itself. The participants have to practise them in their own time. For this purpose, support material was developed in different formats to accommodate all four quadrants of the Whole Brain® Model. The material is distributed to the participants in the form of course hand-outs, and on a help website, which is available through the Internet (*http://www.click.up.ac.za/new*). The A-quadrant need for facts is accommodated through summarised notes called 'fact sheets' where the purposes and use of a specific tool are described, while terminology is provided by means of the 'glossary' tool, which is available in the learning management system. Tool comparison tables provide facts about how different tools may be used to address specific needs. B-quadrant preferences are addressed through the use of step sheets, where clear step-by-step instructions are provided on how to execute a specific task within the learning management system. The hands-on nature of the tasks while using the support material addresses the needs of participants with a preference for the C-quadrant. Movie clips that simulate the steps one has to follow in the system to accomplish a specific task are used to address the need of participants with a strong D-quadrant preference.

Feedback received from participants on the implementation of Whole Brain® principles is reported in Table 4.1.

4.3 Application of Whole Brain® principles in engineering

The field of engineering has over the past 15 years been the front runner for numerous publications on the value and application of Whole Brain® Thinking for learning and facilitating learning. The information obtained from students in our baseline data for the School of Engineering at the University of Pretoria reveals a balanced distribution of thinking preferences for the Whole Brain® Model. Analyses of case studies of the different departments can further assist curriculum designers and lecturers to ensure that the necessary shift in focus is made and thinking preferences are developed in areas of non-preference.

Throughout the School of Engineering the emphasis is on a demand from industry and professional bodies to develop stronger soft (C-quadrant) skills. Four case studies from the following departments and schools are included in Sections 4.3.1 to 4.3.4: the departments of Civil Engineering, Mechanical Engineering and Mining Engineering, and the Graduate School of Technology Management. All demonstrate how re-engineering the curriculum can support the development of appropriate skills needed in the modern workplace.

Lumsdaine and Lumsdaine (1995) highlight the importance of aligning the curricula of engineering students at universities with the needs of the specific industry and its professional bodies. In the engineering environment, the demand is for a stronger emphasis on soft skills and innovation, without compromising on the hard core technical skills and analytical abilities. According to Lumsdaine and Lumsdaine (1995), the industry is looking for graduates who can think globally (holistically), innovate, work in multi-disciplinary teams, synthesise, optimise designs, and integrate environmental and societal values and ethics into their work, and for entrepreneurs who can start their own companies and create jobs. In a recent study, Liebenberg and Mathews (2012) also accentuate that engineers must be technically competent, globally sophisticated, culturally aware, innovative and entrepreneurial, and life-long students, because of the changing workforce and technology and the dramatically challenging nature of engineering practices.

However, given the already overcrowded curricula, today's engineering students have all too little opportunity for discovery-orientated, interactive and collaborative learning experiences (Liebenberg and Mathews, 2012, citing Duderstadt (2008)). Thus in terms of the Whole Brain® Model (2008) tasks that demand right-brain thinking skills are mainly neglected.

Numerous books (Lumsdaine, Lumsdaine and Shelnutt, 1999; Wysocki, 2002; Lumsdaine and Binks, 2003) and research articles (Lumsdaine and Lumsdaine, 1995; Horak, Steyn and De Boer, 2001; Horak and Du Toit, 2002; Liebenberg and Mathews, 2012) have been published over the past 15 years highlighting the value of the HBDI® Survey as an assessment tool in determining thinking preferences of undergraduate and postgraduate engineering students. The main focus of these publications is to accentuate the diverse thinking preferences of specific engineering students, to create an awareness of one's own and others' preferred way of thinking and to emphasise that heterogeneous thinking is a necessity rather than a burden for team and project work.

The widely published value of the HBDI® Survey as an instrument and the successful incorporation of Whole Brain® methodology in teaching practices could assist engineering faculties to review and renew their curricula so as to incorporate the much needed skills demanded by industry (as illustrated by the success achieved by Lumsdaine and Lumsdaine (1995) and Lumsdaine, Lumsdaine and Shelnutt (1999) in these faculties).

The initial research and work inspired a research project to address shortcomings and apply the Whole Brain® methodology in the University of Pretoria's Department of Civil and Biosystems Engineering (Horak, Steyn and De Boer, 2001; Horak and Du Toit, 2002). The outset of the project involved analysing and interpreting the subject content offered to students using the Whole Brain® Model as described in Chapter 1. The results revealed that 36 per cent of the curriculum fell in the A-quadrant, 35 per cent in the B-quadrant, 8 per cent in the C-quadrant and 21 per cent in the D-quadrant. Although this analysis was not objective, it indicates trends confirming that the curriculum is biased towards the A- and B-quadrants. It also highlights the potential mismatch between what the School of Engineering offers students and what the industry requires from graduates.

Having analysed the curriculum, the academic staff wanted to have their own database for comparison and analysis of trends through assessing the thinking preferences of students and lecturers by means of the HBDI® Survey. The results were then used to position the incorporation of soft and innovative skills in the curriculum.

4.3.1 *Department of Civil Engineering (curriculum renewal)*

Herrmann (1996) argues that thinking preferences can be developed. Development of (for example) more innovative thinking (D-quadrant thinking) can be and has been achieved through curriculum change, specific classroom interventions, consistent practice and positive feedback to the individuals in the desired direction as documented by Lumsdaine and Lumsdaine (1995).

The module Civil Engineering Practical Orientation created the platform for incorporating soft and innovative skills through understanding the thinking preferences of students and lecturers, and allowing students to work as heterogeneous teams. The HBDI® profiles of lecturers in the Department were determined, and all first-year students enrolling for a degree in civil engineering (1999–2001) also completed the HBDI® Survey as part of the course material (Horak, Steyn and De Boer, 2001). The HBDI® Survey was used mainly to give students insight into their own preferred way of thinking, and to create an awareness of the thinking diversity within the group. The research project adhered to the guidelines of the Faculty Committee for Research Ethics and Integrity to ensure that all the participants were informed and fully aware of the nature and objectives of the study. Participation was voluntary (Horak and Du Toit, 2002).

The researchers were curious to determine the possible implications for students whose preference for thinking and learning was more right-brain orientated within civil engineering's left-brain dominant environment and curriculum.

Figure 4.10 shows the combination of profiles of first-year students enrolled for a degree in civil engineering during the period 1999–2001.

A total of 121 students participated in the baseline study. The generic profile of the group was 1121 – in other words a triple dominant profile, with dominant preferences for A-, B- and D-quadrant thinking and a noticeable avoidance of C-quadrant thinking (Horak and Du Toit, 2002; Liebenberg and Mathews, 2012). Similar results were obtained with engineering students in other parts of the world (Lumsdaine and Lumsdaine, 1995). An interesting fact reported by Lumsdaine and Lumsdaine (1995) is that a generic 1122 profile (in Figure 4.10) remains the most prominent profile for first-year students in engineering as long as the curriculum does not make provision for the development of right-brain thinking.

Looking at the composite profile, the preference is for Whole Brain® Thinking, which again confirms Herrmann's results that thinking preferences are distributed across all four quadrants when the group is large enough (Herrmann, 1996).

Looking at the preference map, however, there is a stronger preference towards A-quadrant thinking, as expected (Horak and Du Toit, 2002). Civil engineering students prefer analytical, quantifying and logical reasoning, all of which are prerequisites in the workplace. Despite the strong demand from industry for engineers who can work in teams and communicate well, these are still areas avoided by many engineering students and their lecturers. It seems that the majority of engineering students are being 'cloned' in the dominant A-quadrant profile of the faculty. The preference map highlights that only a few students prefer

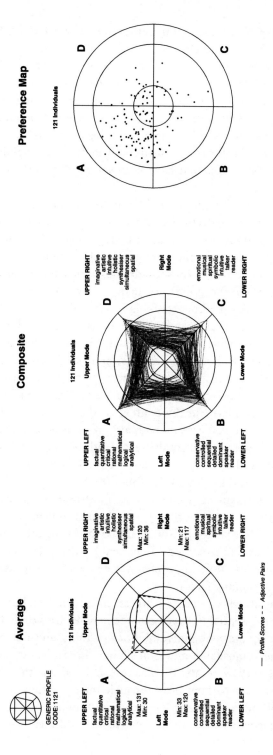

Figure 4.10 Profiles of students enrolled for a degree in civil engineering at the University of Pretoria

C-quadrant thinking (Lumsdaine and Lumsdaine, 1995; Horak, Steyn and De Boer, 2001; Horak and Du Toit, 2002).

The second part of the case study focused on the profiles of the lecturers in the department. All volunteered to participate in the study. Admittedly, the sample of 16 is small, but the typical average engineering faculty profile shown in Figure 4.11 nevertheless confirms the results obtained by Lumsdaine and Lumsdaine (1995) – that there is bias towards the A- and D-quadrant preference of thinking. This trend is in line with engineering faculties at several institutions that have been surveyed with the HBDI® Survey.

The generic profile of this group (1221) favours A- and D-quadrant thinking. It implies that the lecturers prefer the logical, analytical and quantitative thinking of the A-quadrant, and integrating and synthesising creative and holistic aspects of the D-quadrant. The composite profile represents preferences across all four quadrants, with a tilt towards the A- and D-quadrants. On the preference map, a low preference – even avoidance – for B- and C-quadrant thinking is noticeable.

The data from the project also highlighted the tendency for male students in civil engineering to be more left-brain orientated, thus complementing the curriculum requirements, and being aligned to the thinking and learning preferences of the lecturers who facilitate learning. The males' higher academic achievements are noted (Horak and Du Toit, 2002), but must be evaluated in the context of the fact that preferred modes of thinking are aligned with individuals' preferences, and with the curriculum which require less mental energy and are more enjoyable. Female students showed a balanced preference for left- and right-brain orientated interventions (Horak and Du Toit, 2002).

The implications for students who are more right-brain orientated are that they experience a less supportive learning environment than their colleagues with a preference for left-brain thinking. As the attrition rate of engineering students has exceeded 25 per cent over the past years, the possibility of linking low thinking preference or avoidance to attrition rates could be a determining factor.

If the industry needs entrepreneurs who can start their own businesses and create jobs, it is essential to develop students who are Whole Brain® thinkers and have the meta-cognitive abilities to think and not merely plug into formulae (Lumsdaine and Lumsdaine, 1995). These authors also reported that they were able to increase D-quadrant thinking of students from first year to final year through their creative problem-solving model. This model focuses on D-quadrant thinking and on being sensitive and supportive towards their 'creative' and 'different' students.

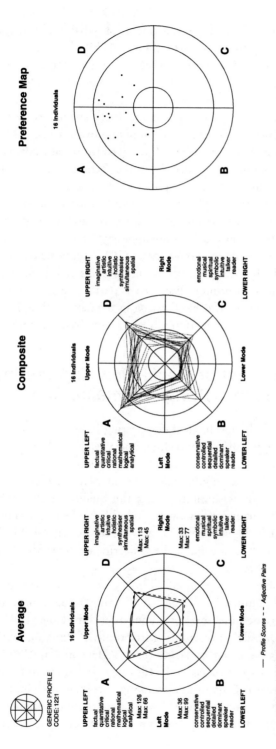

Figure 4.11 Profiles of lecturers from the Department of Civil Engineering at the University of Pretoria

At the same time that the Department of Civil and Biosystems Engineering opted to renew its curriculum in 1999, the Department of Electrical, Electronic and Computer Engineering introduced a compulsory module Technological Innovation for all its first-year students. This module focused on developing the innovative thinking of students. The lecturer who was responsible for this module had a strong preference for D-quadrant thinking and was passionate about innovation in engineering.

The results obtained and the feedback received from the students from both modules constituted the driving force behind introducing the compulsory module Innovation throughout the Engineering School of the Faculty of Engineering, the Built Environment and Information Technology. The purpose of the module was to address the soft and innovation skills needed by engineering students. A contemporary, extensive and objective research report by Liebenberg and Mathews (2012) supports the faculty's initiatives of applied Whole Brain® Thinking skills development. The compulsory module Innovation is discussed as part of the case study from the Department of Mechanical Engineering in the next section, followed by another Whole Brain® application model for creative problem-solving.

4.3.2 *Department of Mechanical Engineering (creative problem-solving and mentoring)*

The requirements in the mechanical engineering industry are for people who can function optimally in multi-disciplinary teams and communicate effectively, who are able to conceptualise ideas and express themselves, and adapt to the ever-changing environment. The challenge lies in addressing these needs without reducing the quality of the technical education, and without extending the period of formal education beyond the four years that is the international norm (Liebenberg and Mathews, 2012). The profiles of the mechanical engineering students are shown in Figure 4.12.

The generic profile of the group of 30 first-year students was found to be 1121 – a triple dominant profile for A-, B- and D-quadrant thinking. Similar results were obtained by Lumsdaine and Lumsdaine (1995). The composite group profile represents a distribution of thinking across all four quadrants as expected of larger groups (Herrmann, 1996). The group's preference map emphasises the tilt towards A-quadrant thinking and an avoidance of C-quadrant thinking. Only a few individuals preferred D-quadrant thinking and this data supports the statement by Lumsdaine and Lumsdaine – that 'a major broad-based effort is required

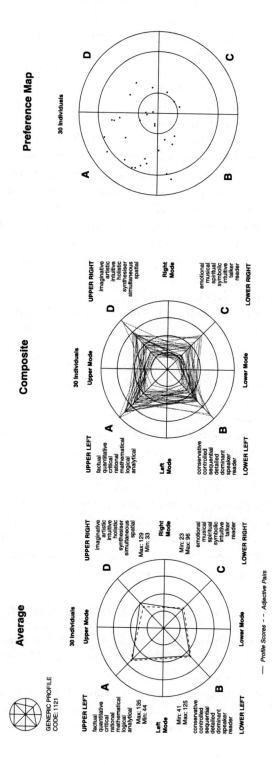

Figure 4.12 Profiles of students enrolled for a degree in mechanical engineering at the University of Pretoria

for change to start developing C- and D-quadrant thinking for mechanical engineering students' (1995, 195).

A solution that is also suggested by Liebenberg and Mathews (2012) is that C- and D-quadrant thinking should be included in the curriculum, although first-year students are initially uncomfortable in a course that accentuates C- and D-quadrant aspects.

Liebenberg and Mathews (2012) point out that right-brain skills and especially a C-quadrant preference are critical in modern engineering practices. Lumsdaine and Lumsdaine (1995) suggest that developing creative and interpersonal thinking skills should not merely be the responsibility of a first-year course. The best results will be obtained when this becomes an ongoing process. They suggest that this can be done during each term in every subject by every lecturer as an ongoing process. In this way students have the opportunity to practise and develop creative problem-solving skills, thereby reinforcing Whole Brain® Thinking activities during the initial course.

From 2002 onwards, all first-year students from all engineering disciplines at the University of Pretoria have been required to take a year-long module in innovation (MNV 100). The success of the single modules introduced by the Department of Civil and Biosystems Engineering and the Department of Electronic and Computer Engineering (documented in Section 4.3.1) was seen as the reason for promoting further exposure to skills development and using the innovation module and the Civil Engineering Practical Orientation module as exemplars for curriculum renewal. This module exposes students to theory and abstractions, but also implements a formal framework of creative problem-solving to address engineering design. This is because the most significant role of the engineer of the future is deemed to be innovation through the creation of new products, processes and services – a role that promotes systems integration (synthesis) above engineering sciences (analysis) and therefore renders the restructuring of the engineering curriculum crucial (Liebenberg and Mathews, 2012).

4.3.2.1 First semester: focus on theoretical aspects

The aim of the theoretical part of the module is to develop innovative knowledge and skills and gain confidence in creative problem-solving (Liebenberg and Mathews, 2012).

Every first-year student completes a Herrmann Brain Dominance Instrument® (HBDI®) and learns that thinking preference does not necessarily equate to competence. They are sensitised to start appreciating different thinking preferences, and to understand that people express themselves in different ways, using different vocabularies and solving problems differently. They also learn that their primary and secondary modes of thinking can be used more effectively through education, motivation and practice. In addition, the students are shown techniques to strengthen their least preferred thinking modes.

During the first semester of this module, the students learn a novel framework for creative problem-solving. This framework, based on the methodology of Lumsdaine, Lumsdaine and Shelnutt (1999), comprises six metaphorical mindsets associated with each of the four Whole Brain® Thinking quadrants identified by Herrmann (1996). For each of the six mindsets the students learn a selection of different techniques to carry out the particular problem-solving step (Liebenberg and Mathews, 2012). The techniques are well-documented in Lumsdaine and Binks (2003) and Lumsdaine, Lumsdaine and Shelnutt (1999). In Figure 4.13 the six mindsets of the creative problem-solving model are superimposed on the metaphoric Whole Brain® Model of Herrmann (Lumsdaine, Lumsdaine and Shelnutt, 1999).

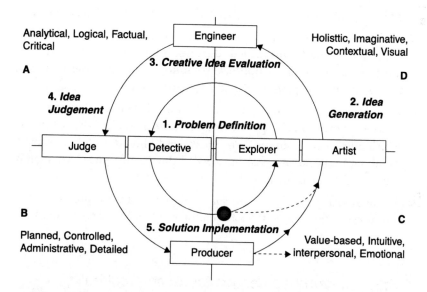

Figure 4.13 The metaphoric mindsets of the Creative Problem-Solving Model superimposed on the metaphoric Whole Brain® Model of Herrmann

Source: Lumsdaine, Lumsdaine and Shelnutt (1999, 80)

The model explains the thinking requirements of each step in the process by means of a corresponding metaphorical mindset. The *'explorer'* and *'detective'* discover and investigate the root cause of the problem and its context, and then define the problem clearly. The *'artist'* brainstorms many ideas, while the *'engineer'* synthesises better ideas. The *'judge'* determines the best solution and the *'producer'* puts everything into an action plan. The process iteratively cycles through all four thinking quadrants (Lumsdaine, Lumsdaine and Shelnutt, 1999, 80). Lumsdaine and Binks (2003) outline the cycles as follows:

- In *defining the problem*, the holistic mindset of a typical *'explorer'* needs to dominate the thinking by primarily using the D-quadrant. The focus is on the big picture or context of the problem, on discovering its opportunity and future-orientated aspects that use primarily D- and C-quadrant thinking. For finding the root cause of a problem, the dominant thinking needed is that of the *'detective'* looking for clues and asking questions, in other words using A- and B-quadrant thinking.

- The second phase is *idea generation*. Students are encouraged and assisted to brainstorm creative ideas based on the problem defined. To do this, the mindset of the *'artist'* is required. This implies being imaginative and using intuitive thinking associated with the C- and D-quadrants.

- With *idea evaluation* or *idea synthesis*, students are motivated to play around with the brainstormed ideas and finally to obtain fewer but more practical ideas for optimised solutions. This mindset is that of the *'engineer'* engaging in D- and A-quadrant thinking.

- *Evaluation* is the critical phase in the model. During this phase the mindset of the *'judge'* is prominent. Students determine the criteria on which ideas and solutions are based and should be implemented. Thinking requirements that are needed during this phase are mainly the A- and B-quadrants.

- The final phase of *solution implementation* requires the mindset of the *'producer'*. The focus is on B-quadrant (planning) and C-quadrant (communicating).

4.3.2.2 Second semester: focus on practical implementation

This semester focuses on practical implementation and multi-disciplinary teams. Where possible, a diversity of disciplines, race, gender and thinking preferences are used to select heterogeneous teams of four members who will work together for the entire semester. Lumsdaine and Lumsdaine (1995) state that when the University of Toledo's engineering curriculum was restructured, the formation of Whole Brain® student design teams resulted in optimal problem-solving.

Through these multi-disciplinary teams students experience at first hand the advantages (and challenges) of performing problem-solving tasks in heterogeneous teams. Support is provided in conflict management, developing interpersonal skills and appreciating the value of what other team members with different thinking preferences bring to the team. Teams are expected to work on their projects during the scheduled two-hour laboratory period per week, but a considerable amount of out-of-class time is usually required for successful completion of projects.

Students are assisted through a mentoring programme to develop all these skills. Senior postgraduate engineering students are selected, trained by psychologists of the University of Pretoria, and allocated to a team. Because of the high intensity of the mentoring, no more than four teams are allocated to one mentor. Mentors meet their team(s) weekly, and provide feedback to the lecturers on progress, also weekly (Liebenberg and Mathews, 2012).

Each year a different set of problems is given to engineering students to research. Lecturers assist the students in selecting appropriate project topics and then students are given the freedom to execute the project, using the methodology learned during the first semester. Here they simulate what they as professionals will do once qualified. Each week of the second semester is linked to the execution of at least one major step in the problem-solving process. Students are required to keep 'inventors' logbooks of ideas, which are assessed twice during the second semester. On selecting their final concept, and after performing suitable analyses of the design concept, the manufacturing process takes place in the mechanical workshops, with the assistance of technical instructors (Liebenberg and Mathews, 2012). All teams also have to submit a mini business plan for introducing their products to the market.

Ownership of intellectual property resides with the University of Pretoria since students make use of significant resources of the University. Through the Innovation Hub (a separate entity of the University responsible for product marketing and patent protection), further assistance is provided to students if their best ideas need a further incubation period to mature, if products need to be protected with trade marks, or if possible patents that could emerge from these projects need to be protected, thus providing students with support – from idea generation to product marketing.

A comparison of the new and the old curriculum shows that the new approach lends itself to critical and creative problem-solving with exceptionally positive outcomes (Liebenberg and Mathews, 2012). When asked to rate the new approach, students indicated that the innovative components of the module that introduced the HBDI® profile and creative problem-solving was significantly better than the module of previous years. The hands-on nature of project design improved their understanding of learning material. Teams responded very positively to the usefulness of the HBDI® profile regarding the conceptual design phase, although team work had been received sceptically in the beginning. Students suggested that at first they experienced the diverse selection of project teams as being imposed on them, but they later came to acknowledge the importance of simulating real-world scenarios. What remained a problem even after the second semester was the continuous development of the C-quadrant. Students reported that it was difficult to communicate effectively with practising engineers who were of the 'old-school type'.

4.3.3 *Department of Mining Engineering (personal development and innovation)*

Taking cognisance of the results and accomplishments of the Department of Mechanical Engineering thanks to their curriculum renewal, lecturers from the Department of Mining Engineering at the University of Pretoria also became interested in the new approach. They embarked on a self-discovery journey and spent a day using the HBDI® Survey to understand their individual profiles, but also to understand other colleagues' through the team's profile. They spent time looking at the advantages and challenges of individual profiles in their teaching practices and how to also incorporate the demands made by industry.

The data in Figure 4.14 were obtained from full-time academic staff who participated in the project.

The 1122 generic profile of the ten full-time lecturers represents a good example of thinking preferences for mining engineers (confirmed in research by Herrmann, 1995). The group average indicates a double dominant preference for the left A- and B-quadrant thinking. The composite profile confirms a tilt towards A-quadrant thinking, but also thinking preferences for B- and C-quadrant thinking. Depending on the field of specialisation of the individual, the tilt can shift from A-quadrant to a stronger preference for B-quadrant thinking, and for a lecturing

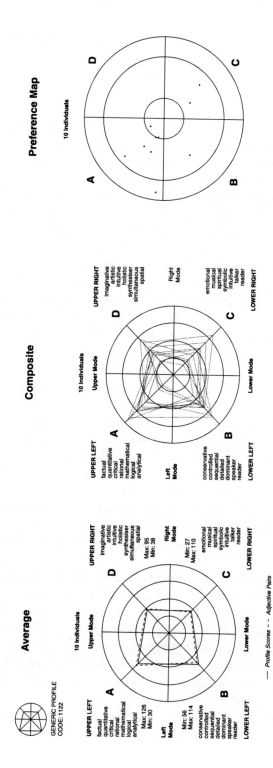

Average

GENERIC PROFILE
CODE: 1122

10 Individuals

Upper Mode

UPPER LEFT
A
factual
quantitative
critical
rational
mathematical
logical
analytical
Max: 126
Min: 30

UPPER RIGHT
D
imaginative
artistic
intuitive
holistic
synthesiser
simultaneous
spatial
Max: 95
Min: 38

Left
Mode

Right
Mode

Min: 56
Max: 110

Min: 27
Max: 114

LOWER LEFT
B
conservative
controlled
sequential
detailed
dominant
speaker
reader

LOWER RIGHT
C
emotional
musical
spiritual
symbolic
intuitive
talker
reader

Lower Mode

—— Profile Scores - - Adjective Pairs

Composite

10 Individuals

Upper Mode

UPPER LEFT
A
factual
quantitative
critical
rational
mathematical
logical
analytical

UPPER RIGHT
D
imaginative
artistic
intuitive
holistic
synthesiser
simultaneous
spatial

Left
Mode

Right
Mode

LOWER LEFT
B
conservative
controlled
sequential
detailed
dominant
speaker
reader

LOWER RIGHT
C
emotional
musical
spiritual
symbolic
intuitive
talker
reader

Lower Mode

Preference Map

10 Individuals

A   D

B   C

Figure 4.14   Profiles of lecturers from the Department of Mining Engineering at the University of Pretoria

position the tilt can even be towards C-quadrant thinking. The latter is a possible reason for opting for an academic career, where being involved with students is preferred to a career working in industry itself. From the preference map it seems that two lecturers have a strong preference for C-quadrant thinking.

Because of the value gained from insight in the diverse thinking style preference of lecturers and students, the part-time specialist lecturers also participated in a similar intervention (Figure 4.15). When their profiles were analysed, the tilt towards the A-quadrant became even more evident (again confirming research by Herrmann 1995). These part-time specialist lecturers teach students in their field of expertise and once the lecture is over they return to industry to continue their work as experts.

The generic average profile of the seven part-time specialist lecturers was 1122, indicating a double dominant preference for the A- and B-quadrant thinking modes. This profile is typical of people with occupations in technical fields such as engineering. Work considered most satisfactory would include accomplishing set objectives, analysing data, making things work, building things, establishing order and attending to detail. The composite profile was expected to have a stronger tilt towards A- and B-quadrant thinking preferences, while their preference map indicated a lowest preference for C- and D-quadrant thinking.

As a standalone, the compulsory innovation course for first-year students did not offer enough time for practice and engagement with students to develop C- and D-quadrant thinking adequately. The Department of Mining Engineering wanted to enhance these skills because of the demand from industry. The Department accommodated the identified gaps and, as part of ongoing support for the personal development of final-year students, added another module to their curriculum – Innovation in Mining Design – to further assist their students.

From 2009 onwards, all the final-year mining engineering students had to enrol for the module and therefore participated in our research project. The departing point of the project involved the completion of an HBDI® Survey and other assessment tools. The data of a total of 102 final-year mining engineering students were collected and its analysis confirmed similar findings reported on in the literature – a preferred generic profile of 1122, which indicates a strong preference for A- and B-quadrant thinking, as was expected (Figure 4.16).

The composite profile confirms these results and also shows that there are a number of profiles that embrace C-quadrant thinking (cf. the

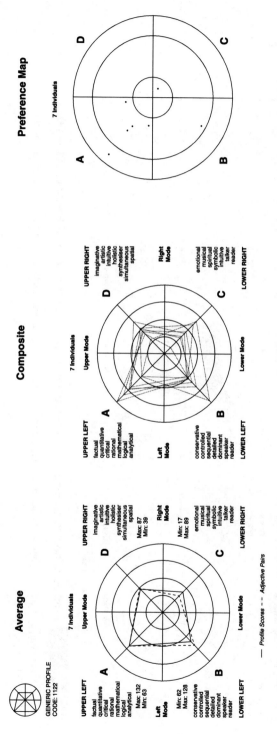

Average

Preference Map

Composite

Figure 4.15 Profiles of specialist part-time lecturers in the Department of Mining Engineering at the University of Pretoria

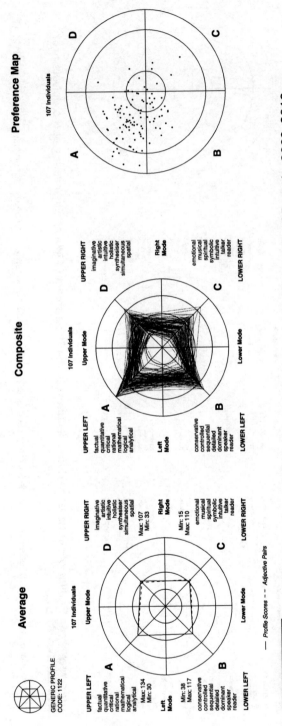

Figure 4.16 Profiles of final-year mining engineering students at the University of Pretoria, 2009–2012

preference map). It therefore seems necessary to pay special attention to the development of C-quadrant thinking. Through regular contact and feedback from the mining industry with regard to the progress of the students, the Department of Mining Engineering realised that, although they present industry with engineers with sound technical ability, they were failing in some respects. Feedback from their graduates confirmed the feedback from industry – that as graduates they lack skills in communication (presentation and report writing), how to work in and with teams, and how to influence and motivate others.

Mining engineers' output in industry is mainly measured according to the profit the company makes. Therefore, one of the questions they soon ask is: 'How do you motivate miners to produce more in order to increase profit?' An interest in 'people skills' soon becomes important to the newly appointed mining engineer, although it never seemed important while studying. This topic becomes even more relevant once the engineer starts moving up the leadership pipeline in an organisation. Drotter (2003) writes extensively about the thinking requirements of the different management positions within the leadership pipeline. The more flexible leaders become in adopting the thinking requirements of the new position, the more successfully they will handle promotions. The more strongly leaders hold on to the thinking requirements that got them promoted (if they remain the specialist), the more difficult it will be to make the mental shift, thus resulting in micro management and extended work hours. The higher the individual operates within the leadership pipeline, the more important the need to shift thinking from the A- and B-quadrants to also include thinking of the C- and D-quadrants (De Boer et al., 2012a).

Keeping this background knowledge in mind, the Department of Mining Engineering decided to address the gap between the hard technical nature of the existing curriculum and industry's demands and to incorporate a module that would enhance the softer skills as well, in line with the argument by Pulko and Parikh (2003). By incorporating the module entitled Innovation in Mining Design into the final-year curriculum, they are making a conscious effort to encourage C-quadrant thinking in students and to develop skills that would assist students to become more confident in expressing and using C-quadrant thinking.

Strong support for this project was given by the head of the Mining Engineering Department who appointed a part-time counsellor (a certified HBDI® practitioner) to co-facilitate this module with a senior professional mining engineering lecturer. The counsellor afforded students individual consultation time to support them throughout the semester on soft skills issues. Apart from individual counselling, coaching (when needed) formed part of the support process aimed at students' personal development.

The aim of the module Innovation in Mining Design was to supplement the hard skills of knowing and doing with much needed softer skills. In the past, the emphasis was on understanding the '*concepts*' (translated into engineering terms as hard skills), '*knowing*' (the core of what engineers have to know about the profession to be knowledgeable), '*doing*' (getting the job done) and '*being*' (focusing on who I am). In the new approach, '*knowing*' came to include an awareness of the self, one's strengths and development areas, while '*being*' was expanded to include an awareness of others as well, thereby enhancing collaborative learning.

Apart from completing the HBDI® Survey, students were also assessed with other assessment tools as part of enhancing the '*knowing self*'. Based on the information obtained through these questionnaires, students were selected and allocated to diverse work groups of between three and five students. In order to '*know*' others better, students were encouraged to discuss their own profiles with other members of their group during the duration of a learning opportunity. They had to compare similarities, look at differences, and also discuss possible implications of individuals' profiles and thinking preferences for the overall performance of the group (Knobbs, 2011). The module further stimulated independent learning through distributing relevant papers, articles and references to chapters in books via the university's learning management system, clickUP, thus creating an online teaching and collaborative platform for students to prepare in advance for the discussions and debate of the coming learning opportunities.

Encouraging collaborative learning and opening up to other students on a personal level was one of the biggest hurdles and challenges the lecturers had to overcome, because of these mining engineering students' preference for A- and B-quadrant thinking and doing. They wanted to learn about mining methods and not sit in a psychology class, as one student remarked during a formal feedback session early on in the module (Knobbs, 2011).

Shifting the focus away from individual learning to group learning and work was difficult at first and met with resistance, but through engagement and building trust relationships with the counsellor and lecturer, students actually expressed (towards the end of the module) how much they appreciated the new way of facilitating learning (see Figure 4.17).

Results by Lumsdaine and Lumsdaine (1995) confirm that faculties that start implementing collaborative learning strategies as part of their courses, create opportunities for students to become competent in creative problem-solving and apply the process in their lives are able to create

Figure 4.17 Mining engineering students at the University of Pretoria participating in group work

Source: Knobbs, 2011

'people friendly' learning environments. In this way students develop their C-quadrant thinking mode rather than lose it as they progress through the curriculum. Figure 4.17 shows how mining engineering students are engaging with one another, trying to solve a specific problem.

The profiles in Figure 4.13 are those of the specialist lecturer and the counsellor who co-facilitated the module Innovation in Mining Design offered to final-year mining engineering students.

The mining engineering lecturer responsible for the module is a senior lecturer with vast industry experience, holding degrees in commerce, leadership and psychology. However, the role of the lecturer in this module is that of a mentor. As mentor, the lecturer's role is to stimulate students to find alternative solutions to problems that turn up during class discussions. The lecturer's profile indicates a triple dominance (1112), with the stress profile (dotted line) stretching to accommodate D-quadrant thinking and to use a Whole Brain® Thinking approach with a quadruple dominant 1111. The advantage of having specialist lecturers with triple dominant preferences is that they are comfortable with the analytical, rational, quantitative processing of the A-quadrant, the structured, sequential and organised processes of the B-quadrant, and the interpersonal, intuitive skills of the C-quadrant – thus communicating easily with all students.

The counsellor's profile (Figure 4.18 on the right) shows a strong preference for D- and C-quadrant thinking, thus more dominant for right-brain thinking, with a 2211 preference code. Because the profile preference is for stimulating brainstorming sessions and looking at the big picture, and because this individual is most comfortable being

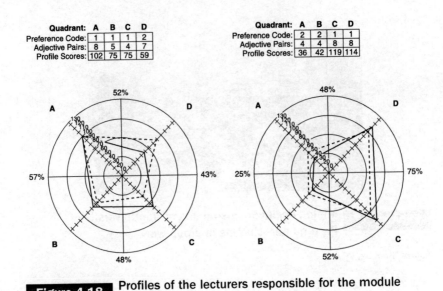

Quadrant:	A	B	C	D
Preference Code:	1	1	1	2
Adjective Pairs:	8	5	4	7
Profile Scores:	102	75	75	59

Quadrant:	A	B	C	D
Preference Code:	2	2	1	1
Adjective Pairs:	4	4	8	8
Profile Scores:	36	42	119	114

Figure 4.18 Profiles of the lecturers responsible for the module Innovation in Mining Design at the University of Pretoria

involved with others, the two lecturer profiles complement one another to the advantage of the students.

Finally, the Department of Mining Engineering endeavoured to develop more Whole Brain® learning material and to change the existing strong A-quadrant learning material by appointing a part-time instructional designer to assist the lecturing team in changing the learning material. The existing material was one-dimensional and only in text format. The instructional designer, together with the lecturing team, developed quality visual material and illustrations, created or searched for appropriate real-time videos and video clips, created animations to assist in explaining difficult concepts to the students, and thereby greatly promoted Whole Brain® facilitating of learning.

4.3.4 Graduate School of Technology Management (personal and team development)

The Graduate School of Management offers the professional engineer the choice of a Master's degree in engineering management or project management.

According to Benade (2006), the professional engineer in the knowledge-driven, technology-driven and service-orientated era of today needs to understand and manage complexity, and the process of innovation – all of which are aspects highlighted in this case study. The profiles in Figure 4.19 are a combination of the profiles of students enrolled for a Master's degree in engineering management and project management over the period 2002–2012.

The generic profile, 1122, again represents a double dominant profile with strong preferences for A- and B-quadrant thinking. The composite profile represents 661 thinking preference profiles of qualified engineers and indicates a diverse but balanced distribution of preferences across all four quadrants. The preference map indicates a stronger tilt towards A-quadrant thinking, and the lowest preference is for C-quadrant thinking. Similar results documented by Lumsdaine and Lumsdaine (1995) indicate that the majority of engineering students are still being 'cloned' in the A-dominant profile of the faculty. As previously highlighted, D-quadrant- and C-quadrant thinking tasks must be integrated into a curriculum to develop students' full potential and to constantly re-enforce Whole Brain® Thinking competencies.

In his book *Building Effective Project Teams* (2002), Wysocki lists the following essential characteristics of a project team to ensure successful delivery of projects: adaptable, analytical, strategic, creative, process-orientated and organised, and having strong personal, interpersonal and leadership skills. In order for a team to have these characteristics, individuals on the team should have some or part of these traits so as to create a balanced team and build strategy to mitigate risk. The traits are all embedded within the thinking preferences of the Whole Brain® Model and, if understood, can be developed for the successful delivery of projects.

The Team Building Institute in Pretoria was contracted by the Graduate School of Technology Management to complement the academic programme offered to students enrolled for Master's degrees in engineering management and project management during 2001. The programme, implemented in 2002, focused on personal development and comprised three phases. The methodology adopted by the Team Building Institute was adventure-related experiential learning, an interactive event-orientated process whereby a participant constructs knowledge, skills and values through guided reflection by participating in what results in an adventure experience (Heunis, 1997). The nature of adventure-related experiential learning brings participants physically closer to one another, stretching the more left-brain thinkers somewhat, and sensitising

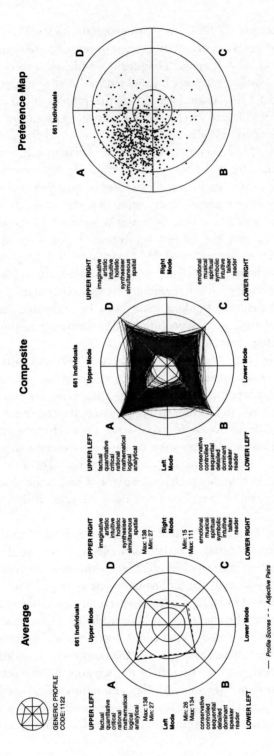

Figure 4.19 Profiles of students enrolled for a Master's degree in engineering management and project management at the University of Pretoria

participants to access more right-brain thinking (Heunis, 1997). Incorporating the HBDI® Survey as assessment tool and partnering Whole Brain® methodology with adventure-related experiential learning and its methodology constituted an ideal match and has been greatly beneficial to team growth during the past 15 years.

In the GSM@UP.news, the alumni newsletter of the Graduate School of Management, Benade (2006) outlines the three-phased programme. In Phase I, the adventure-related experiential learning programme focuses on mass recreational interventions. The entire group of students must be present, to get participants' buy-in for the team growth strategy and familiarise them with the Team Building Institute facilitators. During this intervention, the programme philosophy and scheduled interventions for smaller groups are introduced, and syndicates are finalised. In preparation for the second phase, participants complete the HBDI® Survey.

During Phase II the focus of the adventure-related experiential learning programme shifts to the individual. It starts with a journey of self-discovery and becoming aware of one's strengths and developmental areas. The HBDI® Survey completed during the first phase equips individuals with knowledge to understand themselves, while the adventure-related experiential learning methodology focuses on the individuals' growth in a team context. Each adventure-related experiential learning activity is also debriefed within a team context (Heunis, 1997) (Figure 4.20).

Phase III focuses on the formation and management of teams working in syndicate format. This phase requires of individuals to move away

Figure 4.20 Students at the University of Pretoria reflecting on experiential learning experience and participating in adventure-related experiential learning exercises

from self-awareness to an awareness of others. Participants are invited to share their HBDI® profiles with one another. During Phase III the challenge is to create opportunities to start understanding diverse thinking. Because a journey of personal growth is about developing thinking competencies in all four quadrants, the adventure-related experiential learning programme creates a safe environment that affords the opportunity for individuals to start moving outside their preferred modes, the so-called 'comfort zones', and to start stretching into lesser preferred modes of thinking in order to develop more balanced or Whole Brain® Thinking.

The programme is completed with each participant documenting their own personal journey of development through a personal development plan that is formally assessed along with the formal academic course component.

The positive response from the groups over the past years indicates that this programme makes them aware of the value of knowing their own and the diverse thinking of others. They also learn how the development and use of Whole Brain® Thinking can enhance project execution to achieve success, if applied in a team context.

The case studies for the Department of Information Science which are discussed in the next section highlight a different shift in curriculum development needs than that outlined in engineering case studies, and emphasise the need to develop stronger A- and D-quadrant thinking. These competencies need to be part of the curriculum from undergraduate to postgraduate levels if we want to empower our students with the innovative technical demands of the digital age.

4.4 Application of Whole Brain® principles in information science

The following case studies that are reported emanated from the initiatives of the Department of Information Science of the University of Pretoria. Building on the experiences of the past 15 years, they ensure that the curriculum offered to students remains relevant and aligned with what is needed in the industry:

- The first case study reveals the results obtained from the baseline data conducted in 1999 that involved 19 first-year students enrolled for a degree in information science (Section 4.4.1).

- Research findings of the thinking preferences of second-year students opting for a library position in cataloguing and classification are explained in Section 4.4.2.

- The insights that lecturers gained from understanding their own thinking preferences and their ability to move through the Whole Brain® Model with ease, because of their balanced preference code of 1111. This profile allowed them to embrace Whole Brain® facilitating for Whole Brain® learning (discussed in detail in Section 4.4.3 as a separate case study and focusing only on their thinking preferences).

- Based on the information obtained from case studies, feedback from students and professional staff in libraries, and the general lack of embracing the innovative technology available in the digital age, staff in the Department of Information Science wanted to ensure that this aspect gets serious attention. The opportunity was afforded to implement a Master's degree, 'Master in Information Technology', with the focus on enhancing the technological skills of students (Section 4.4.4).

- For libraries to remain leading resources of knowledge, it is paramount that each professional librarian is empowered to embrace the technological innovation offered by the 21st century and to operate effectively in the digital age. Library users (especially today's university students) are knowledgeable and use mobile devices, Google, Twitter and other social media platforms to get their information so professional library staff need to stay abreast of the latest technology. By incorporating the data and publications available on Whole Brain® application in facilitating learning, a library leadership development programme was implemented for middle and senior library managers and constitutes the case study described in Section 4.4.5.

Developing thinking preferences in areas of non-preference does not occur overnight or within an intensive two-week programme. It takes time and practice. The value of individual coaching sessions has been reported on in numerous studies. In concluding our case studies, we suggest a Whole Brain® Model or application tool specifically aimed at coaching leaders. The model takes into account individuals' preferred way of thinking and aligns it with the thinking requirements of the position they are promoted to. By structuring coaching sessions with a clear focus, the individual who excels within the organisation and aspires to higher levels of leadership roles is equipped with the necessary thinking skills required for the position.

4.4.1 *Results for first-year students*

As outlined in Chapter 2, the main aim of gathering the baseline data was to obtain data for developmental purposes, and to determine the direction that curriculum development needs to take for the Whole Brain® Model. Since no data were available on the thinking preferences of students enrolled for a degree in information science, 19 first-year students enrolled for such a degree participated in the baseline study to determine their preferred mode of thinking. The HBDI® Survey was the assessment tool used.

It should be noted that since it is a small group, the data obtained can be used merely as an indication of the thinking preference of students enrolled for the degree in information science.

In analysing the data, the average of the group proved to be a 2111 profile – a triple dominant profile with preferences for B-, C- and D-quadrant thinking (Figure 4.21). The composite profile indicates a distribution across all four quadrants, while the preference map indicates a tilt towards the B- and C-quadrants and a lower preference for A- and D-quadrant thinking processes. Only one individual in this group had a preference for A-quadrant thinking, while no individual preferred D-quadrant thinking (implications highlighted in Chapter 1).

It can therefore be concluded that the preferred thinking of the B- and C-quadrants will fit in well within the library profession. The job requires of students to follow processes and procedures, and to assist users.

4.4.2 *Results for second-year module on cataloguing and classification*

De Boer, Coetzee and Coetzee (2001) conducted research on the thinking preferences of 28 second-year students who studied the module on cataloguing and classification. Based on the results, they decided what thinking skills needed to be developed and incorporated into the information science curriculum.

The data revealed that the generic average profile of the group was 2111. This confirms the results obtained from the baseline data for first-year students (Figure 2.2). Although the composite profile reveals a triple dominant preference for B-, C- and D-quadrant thinking, a stronger inclination towards only B- and C-quadrant thinking was noted when the composite map and preference map profiles of the 28 students were analysed (Figure 4.22).

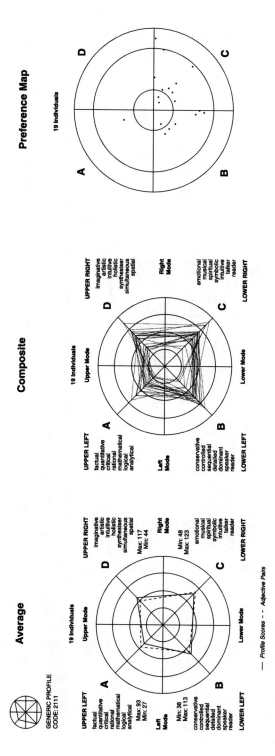

Figure 4.21 Profiles of first-year students enrolled for a degree in information science at the University of Pretoria

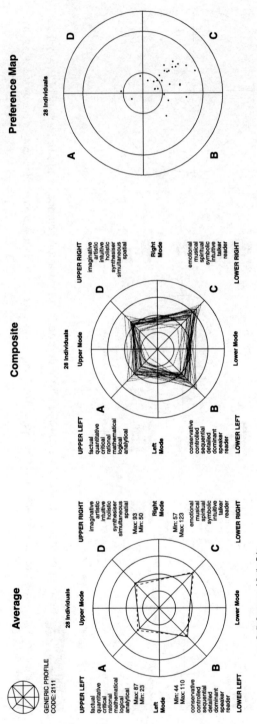

Figure 4.22 Profiles of students enrolled for a degree in library science (taking second-year cataloguing and classification) at the University of Pretoria

Looking at the job profile, the job requires of someone holding a position in cataloguing and classification to have strong B-quadrant preferences and competencies. It requires accurate and precise data capturing. Hence the preferred modes of thinking of undergraduate students are in alignment with the requirements of the profession they have chosen.

Although the data from both studies (a total of 47 students) represents a small group, the general assumption is that there is a lack of preference for A- and D-quadrant thinking among the students enrolled for the degree in information science. If not addressed within the curriculum at undergraduate level, this shortcoming will have adverse consequences for higher levels of the profession.

4.4.3 *Results for lecturers in the Department of Information Science*

With the information pertaining to the students known, lecturers in the Department of Information Science wanted to complete their HBDI® profiles as well. They wanted to understand their own thinking preferences and to develop their professional competence in facilitating learning so as to improve their teaching practices and be better equipped to offer their students opportunities to learn. The data illustrated in Figure 4.23 reveal the thinking preferences of 15 academic staff members in the Department.

The generic profile is 1111 – a quadruple dominant profile with preferences for A-, B-, C- and D-quadrant thinking. The characteristics of this multi-dominant profile reflect a balance and ease to understand and implement mental diversity due to the four primary quadrants. The composite profile indicates that the individual profiles of the 15 lecturers are in balance across all four quadrants. The preference map, however, tilts towards the A- and C-quadrants.

The Department, IT laboratories and School of Information Technology is responsible for offering information literacy modules to close to 8000 students annually. The data obtained from the baseline data (Figure 2.2) and from the case studies that reflect the research conducted in the Department enable them to be the front runner at the University for innovative curriculum change in the module Information Literacy.

The Department of Information Science was not only made aware of what it needs to do in order to facilitate Whole Brain® learning – it actually developed and implemented a Whole Brain® curriculum that fosters Whole Brain® facilitating of learning.

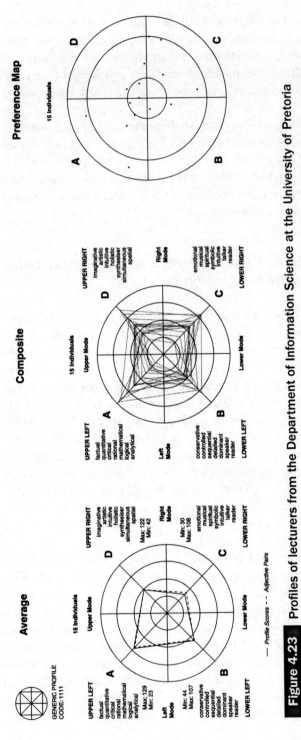

Figure 4.23 Profiles of lecturers from the Department of Information Science at the University of Pretoria

The four-quadrant graphic is a registered trademark of Herrmann Global and is reproduced under written contract for display in this text. © 2012. All rights reserved

The module Information Literacy offered to all first-year students embraces Whole Brain® facilitating of learning and is discussed in detail in.

4.4.4 *Results for Master's degree students*

Keeping the baseline study's data as point of departure for curriculum design, a supportive grant from the Carnegie Corporation of New York has enabled the Department to develop and introduce a Master's degree in information technology. The aim of the programme is to develop students' Whole Brain® Thinking skills, and it focuses especially on the development of A-and D-quadrant thinking skills that are not only needed but actually demanded from library users operating in the digital age.

The emphasis of the programme is on Web 2 technology:

- understanding and using information technologies (A-quadrant)
- understanding the role of social media and Web 2.0 technologies in libraries and using these technologies in their libraries (A-quadrant)
- understanding the 'bigger picture' of globalised networking on information services and the implications thereof for their libraries (D-quadrant)
- planning for technology innovation in their libraries (D-quadrant).

The data collected were from two intakes over a two-year period and information obtained from 42 postgraduate students.

The generic profile of students selected to take part in a Master's degree in information technology was 1112. This triple dominant profile indicates a preference for A-, B- and C-quadrant thinking. The composite profile of the 42 students indicates preferences for all four quadrants. However, looking at the preference map, the tilt towards the B- and C-quadrant thinking modes is evident. A few students showed a preference for the A-quadrant, though not very strong, and only one student had a slight preference for D-quadrant thinking. The information confirmed what we have seen in the undergraduate studies – that these students prefer B- and C-quadrant thinking (Figure 4.24).

The content of a Master's degree in information technology focuses mainly on A- and D-quadrant thinking. In order to develop and ultimately embrace the innovation that technology brings for libraries, graduates need to develop innovative technological skills so as to apply these

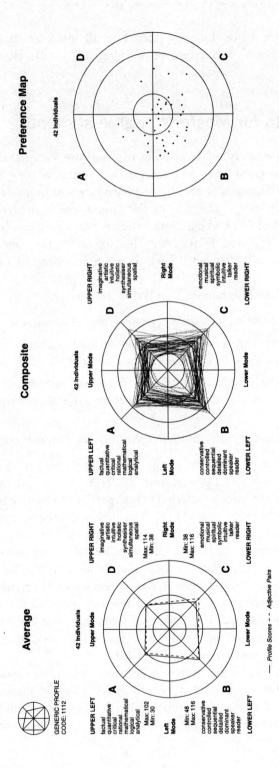

Figure 4.24 Profiles of students enrolled for a Master's degree in information technology at the University of Pretoria

innovations in their libraries. Our experience from both groups is that the majority of the graduates find it very difficult to stretch outside their comfort zones of thinking preference – some even showed an aversion to stretching into the A- and D-quadrants.

The focus of the academic programme was not only on developing A-quadrant thinking (technology) but also on facilitating D-quadrant thinking. The programme afforded these students the opportunity of global exposure. By visiting other institutions, they were provided an opportunity to observe, engage and learn how others in their libraries are doing things – including other cultures on different continents. At the same time, more C-quadrant thinking was stimulated as they were expected to interact and engage more with one another in group work and with subject specialists.

4.4.5 *Library leadership*

Learning is a life-long journey, and in order to take the professional development of librarians to the next level, the focus was placed on developing leadership skills – a necessity in any industry.

Once again funded by the Carnegie Corporation of New York, a two-week intensive library leadership programme was presented in association with the University's formal structure for continued education, CE@UP. The Department of Information Science was the academic custodian of the programme and the Centre for Library Leadership at the Department of Library Services, the managing and administrative partner. Academic professionals invited as specialists in their field also participated as presenters on the programme.

The following data were collected from 120 middle and senior library managers from diverse library service backgrounds who had been selected to attend one of the six library leadership programmes offered during a three-year period.

The data in Figure 4.25 show a generic group profile of 2112. This triple dominant profile with two primary preferences, B- and C-quadrant thinking, was documented from the baseline data with undergraduate students. The composite profile is balanced, as expected, with a distribution across all four quadrants, but the preference map indicates a stronger tilt towards the B- and C-quadrants and a lower preference for A- and D-quadrant thinking.

This not only confirms the evidence collected from our case studies, but also indicates that unless attention is given to the development of

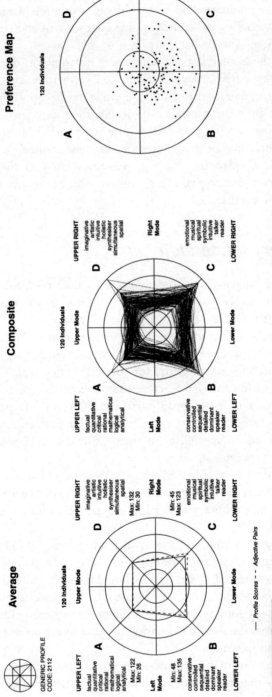

Figure 4.25 Profiles of professional staff attending a course in library leadership at the University of Pretoria

The four-quadrant graphic is a registered trademark of Herrmann Global and is reproduced under written contract for display in this text. © 2012. All rights reserved

specific thinking preferences, individuals will not necessarily develop them by themselves. The lack of a strong preference for A- and D-quadrant thinking is clearly evident from the 120 professional staff members working in the various libraries.

Management is about organising the functions that need to be done, while leadership is about empowering, inspiring and mentoring. We associated the following core competencies applicable to library leadership and documented by researchers Ammons-Stephens et al. (2009) with Herrmann's Whole Brain® Model (1996):

- *Cognitive ability* and *higher-order thinking skills* include creative thinking, critical and analytical thinking, data manipulation, synthesis and decision making (Ammons-Stephens et al., 2009). According to Herrmann's Whole Brain® Model (1996), this requires A- and D-quadrant thinking.

- *Vision* includes the ability to think globally and creatively and to foster innovation, and the ability to be forward-thinkers. According to Herrmann's Whole Brain® Model (1996), this requires mainly D-quadrant thinking.

- *Interpersonal effectiveness* creates a positive atmosphere centred on respect, responsibility and motivation. According to Herrmann's Whole Brain® Model (1996), this requires mainly C-quadrant thinking.

- *Managerial effectiveness* includes managing change and resources, planning for the future, collaborating with others and being flexible. According to Herrmann's Whole Brain® Model (1996), this requires mainly C- and D-quadrant thinking.

Based on a comparison of data, Hopper (2005) highlights that the most mentioned trait from a total of 96 traits in library leadership was *being a visionary* (D-quadrant). The challenge for library leaders is to become skilled in *seeing* and *reading* the future of libraries. For this they need to embrace the innovative technology available. The ability to be visionary, embrace change and anticipate the future with regard to information technologies requires strong A- and D-quadrant thinking.

The second most mentioned trait (Hopper, 2005, 12) reported on is to 'inspire people with the shared vision to ensure that the institution moves ahead in the right direction'. According to Herrmann's Whole Brain® Model (1996), this requires strong C-quadrant thinking. The focus for leadership is therefore no longer focusing as much on the B-quadrant thinking and on embracing A-, D- and C-quadrant thinking instead. Such leadership determines whether philosophy and vision are articulated and to what extent they are implemented.

Taking cognisance of the information gathered over the past few years and the need for library leaders to acquire A- and D-quadrant thinking skills, a programme was designed to develop these skills. The programme focused on developing Whole Brain® thinkers. Apart from the theoretical focus of the programme (A- and to some extent B-quadrant thinking), the programme facilitated a paradigm shift in thinking so as to also address future library needs. The programme included:

- how to accommodate the needs of next-generation library users (D- and A-quadrant thinking) and challenge the digital age enforced with the advent of the Internet, search engines and social media

- opportunities to meet colleagues and engage with senior professional staff from diverse backgrounds and geographical regions (C-quadrant thinking)

- using leadership development instruments such as the Campbell Leadership Descriptor (Center for Creative Leadership, 2012) and the HBDI® Survey to become aware of the need to stretch out of one's comfort zone and start developing thinking in lesser preferred modes

- mentoring by senior academic staff members from a number of participating universities, assigned to each student's research project to guide and coach the research, but also to assist them with professional and personal development (A- and C-quadrants) (De Boer, Bothma and Olwagen, 2012).

Many curriculum changes have been made since the onset of this research project in the Department of Information Science. Looking back on the case studies reported and the fact that the profession in general embraces the preferred B- and C-quadrants, we acknowledge that for leadership the overarching need is for A-, D- and C-quadrant thinking. The question is: How do we develop such leadership talent and skills?

Developing thinking skills in least preferred quadrants is not easy, nor does it happen overnight. It is necessary to ensure that the newly exposed thinking skills are embedded within the individual's time and practice. This can only be achieved through effective coaching. The HBDI® profile has proven to be invaluable in assisting the future library leader coach with a tool that will add value to the coaching sessions, not only as an assessment tool to determine thinking preference, but also to focus on the thinking skills that need to be developed.

4.5 Application of Whole Brain® principles in the coaching of leadership talent

According to Drotter (2003), one of the major problems experienced by newly promoted managers within an organisation is that they find it difficult to let go of habits that were responsible for getting them promoted. They often cling to thinking patterns, behaviours, attitudes and skills that made them successful in the past. Drotter (2003) argues that managers accept a promotion to a higher level in an organisation without also accepting the thinking requirements, behaviour attitudes and skills of the new position. Too often a manager gets promoted based only on high technical ability. An important aspect that is often overlooked is the specific thinking requirements needed by the individual to excel at the level of the promotion (Charan, Drotter and Noel, 2001). If the necessary adjustment in thinking does not happen, the leadership pipeline gets clogged, and the whole organisation gets pushed down, operating on levels lower than it should.

In an article that reports on innovation options for designing training programmes for library leaders and for building competencies in the digital age, De Boer, Bothma and Olwagen (2012) discuss the value of Whole Brain® coaching as a tool for developing thinking competencies required for the specific leadership positions.

Reconceptualising the leadership pipeline (Charan, Drotter and Noel, 2001) through the lens of Herrmann's Whole Brain® Model (Herrmann, 1996) is a valuable tool for coaching individuals and developing their thinking competencies in lesser preferred quadrants. Only through individual coaching someone can develop the thinking competencies that are necessary to make a success of the leadership position to which they are promoted.

Drotter's concept of a leadership pipeline (Figure 4.26) comprises a basic level of ability and self-knowledge (managing self) that is followed by six higher levels of leadership functions. Each level requires new responsibilities, competencies and thinking requirements.

4.5.1 Managing self

The basic level, *managing self*, implies that young graduates enter the workplace (the library) as specialists. Drotter (2003) remarks that in order to manage yourself, you need to move from being told what to do, to manage yourself and contribute through engagement of your brain.

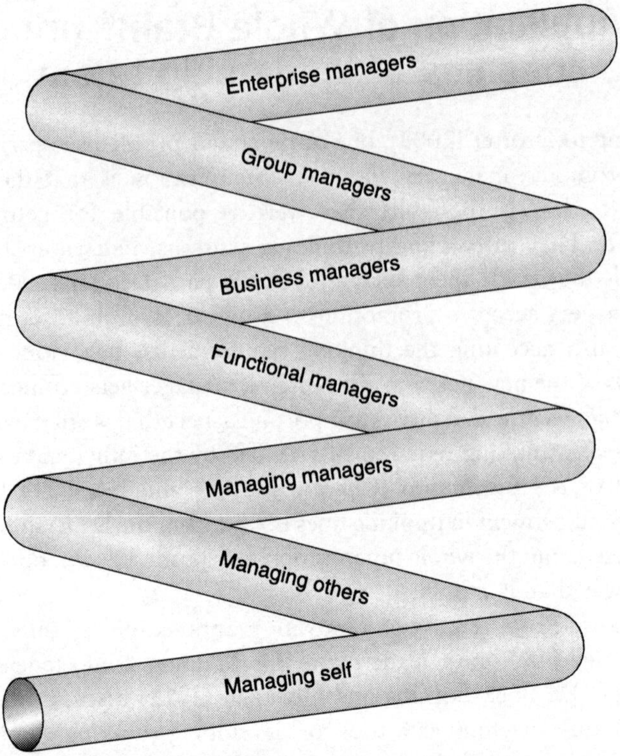
Enterprise managers
Group managers
Business managers
Functional managers
Managing managers
Managing others
Managing self

Figure 4.26 Drotter's Leadership Pipeline Model showing the management levels

Source: Charan, Drotter and Noel (2001, 29)

The main focus for first entrance professionals according to Drotter (2003) is adopting professional standards; deliver on the tasks given to them by their managers. Part of excellent delivery on tasks for individuals includes effective collaboration with others.

According to Herrmann's Whole Brain® Model, the thinking requirements of this position are mainly associated with the B-quadrant (we have allocated five stars for this quadrant, because of the planning, accurate, process-driven nature of the position) and to some extent the C-quadrant (three stars) but of course also require a minimum degree of focus in the other quadrants. High performing individuals are also goal-directed and purpose-driven, therefore the A-quadrant in Figure 4.27 was allocated four stars. Managing self does not require the individual to operate on a strategic level, but because this quadrant is used by the individual to think about their

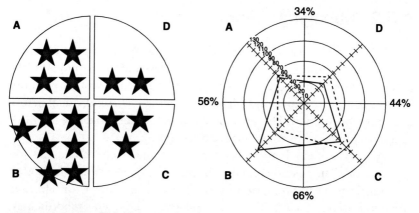

Figure 4.27 Thinking requirements for managing self (left); an HBDI® profile (right)

personal future development, only two stars are allocated to the D-quadrant.

On the right in Figure 4.27 is an HBDI® profile of an individual working in the library as a professional. The profile represents the majority of profiles collected from our baseline data for the library profession. This individual has strong preferences for B- and C-quadrant thinking, and prefers to *do* things. The individual needs to have clear guidelines on what is expected and how the work must be done, and prefers to operate in an environment where the details are covered, daily tasks are well-planned and structured, and goals are implemented. Getting things right the first time is a critical factor for success. The preference is also to work with other people like themselves.

Individuals with this type of profile typically deliver results.

The problem that occurs most often, especially if these individuals have a very strong multi-dominant A- and B-quadrant preference or a single dominant A- or B-quadrant preference, is that they are unable to let go of *doing* and *delivering* tasks (Charan, Drotter and Noel, 2001). They often start working longer hours to get the workload done. This is often a reason why the pipeline gets clogged, especially when this individual has to manage others, and allow others to deliver on this level.

Given the growth aspirations of the individual, the focus in coaching should be on developing competencies aligned with the requirements of the next leadership level, discussed in the next section.

4.5.2 *Managing others*

The library level is associated with first line managers. In promoting the individual the position requires *managing others* and the position is often accepted without also accepting the thinking requirements of the position. Very little if any training and support is offered to the individual before accepting the position. This position requires a shift from doing the work to ensuring others are doing this (Drotter, 2003).

Managers can no longer spend most of their time *doing* the job (B-quadrant). The position requires the manager to assist and coach other individuals to perform. Therefore the main focus now is on effective communication, facilitating open dialogue between subordinates, assisting and coaching others to perform. Motivating others and building trusting relationships now becomes the core function of the position. In addition, setting departmental goals, and monitoring and measuring individuals' performance remain subsidiary functions.

Without training and support in managing others, newly appointed managers find this position very difficult, because they have to give up tasks and responsibilities that they like, and that earned them the title of manager (Drotter, 2003). The thinking skills of this position therefore require a definite shift away from wanting to deliver on everything (B-quadrant), to step back and allow other competent individuals to perform the work assigned to them.

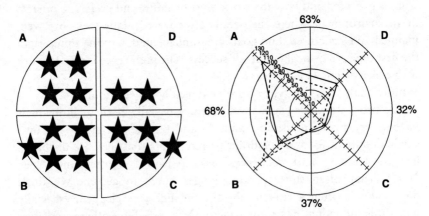

Figure 4.28 Thinking requirements for managing others (left); a coachee's HBDI® profile (right)

Often an individual's thinking profile does not match the required thinking of the promotion position. Looking at the thinking requirements of this position that are graphically displayed in Figure 4.28, there is a balance between the stars allocated to the B- and C-quadrants, while the A- and D-quadrants remain the same as in the previous position. The individual who is being coached displays a strong A-quadrant preference and under stress the B-quadrant thinking (Figure 4.28, right) also becomes dominant. The coaching sessions for this individual should focus on a shift towards developing C-quadrant competencies.

The individual as a specialist in the library is empowered with knowledge and experience on executing tasks quicker and more accurately, and a track record with very little comeback on work delivered. The individual is more of an independent employee than a team player who prefers to deliver on set goals and makes things happen, rather than motivate others to do the assigned work.

The shift in thinking to develop stronger C-quadrant competencies will therefore not be easy, and without coaching interventions individuals are not likely to achieve it on their own. An awareness of how to engage with workers, provide more support through coaching and provide guidelines for subordinates on how, what and when to deliver will dominate the sessions.

From our experience the most difficult part of the position of *managing others* for a single dominant A- or B-quadrant individual will be how to motivate others, taking the time to get consensus of subordinates, and coaching others to do the tasks as they think best (De Boer, Bothma and Olwagen, 2012).

An interesting point made by Charan, Drotter and Noel is that 'although the newly appointed manager recognises intellectually the shift in thinking that needs to take place [he or she] psychologically rejects it' (2001, 18), and the individual should be made aware of this during the coaching sessions.

4.5.3 Managing managers

The next level on the pipeline is *managing managers*. In the library this is a senior management position. The requirements on this level are totally different. Drotter (2003) states that people selected for these positions will eventually become organisational leaders. They get results by getting managers to manage. The biggest challenge for managers on this level is to think beyond the function they previously fulfilled. They are no longer specialists of one area, and now have to divest themselves from individual tasks and be concerned with strategic issues that will support the overall business (Drotter, 2003). The role of the manager who manages other managers is to assist others to remain focused on the critical issues, execute their responsibilities, and assist them in achieving their departmental goals. Coaching others to execute high-level analytical work and focus on strategic issues becomes the main focus of the position (Drotter, 2003).

This requires the individual to display conceptual, innovative thinking and have an open mind to new ideas of others, preferences associated with D-quadrant thinking. Maintaining and building relationships, improving efficiency and teamwork, and coaching other managers now become crucial factors for a successful manager operating on this level.

This leadership level requires a definite shift in thinking, away from the technical expertise of the specialist librarian. Figure 4.29 (left) indicates the marked shift from the B-quadrant to the C-quadrant (six stars) and an increase in D-quadrant thinking of the position (three stars). The only thinking requirement that remains unchanged from the onset of the pipeline is for A-quadrant thinking (four stars) (De Boer, Bothma and Olwagen, 2012).

In the example provided in Figure 4.29, the possible clogging of the pipeline becomes even more deeply entrenched if individuals are not made aware that their thinking preference is actually inappropriate

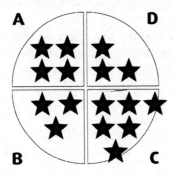 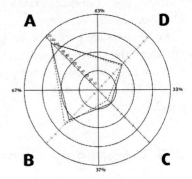

Figure 4.29 Thinking requirements for managing managers (left); a coachee's HBDI® profile (right)

for this level. The position requires stronger C- and D-quadrant thinking.

In this example the manager who is being coached (right profile in Figure 4.29) has a strong preference for A-quadrant thinking and the profile does not alter under pressure. The coaching sessions should focus on the fact that the position no longer requires a specialist mindset but building relationships with the managers reporting to the position. Give direction, support enthusiasm of others, and assist them to achieve their department's goals and targets. A concerted effort must be made to alert the newly promoted manager to treat building networks and creating trusting relationships with other managers as top priority.

4.5.4 *Managing the function*

The next level of the leadership pipeline is *managing the function*. In the library, this could be at the level of assistant or deputy directors. This level according to Drotter (2003) is totally focused on productivity of the team, even if they are involved in strategy. Often individuals need to manage outside their expertise, but leaders on this level need to push the envelope to find sustainable competitive advantage rather than immediate success. This level requires A-quadrant thinking, as indicated in Figure 4.30, but a complete shift from B-quadrant thinking. The requirements are towards the C- and D-quadrants (De Boer, Bothma

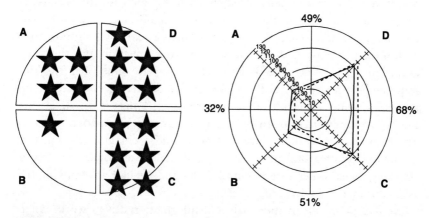

Figure 4.30 Thinking requirements for managing the function (left); a coachee's HBDI® profile (right)

and Olwagen, 2012). The stars allocated in Figure 4.30 (left) remains four for the A-quadrant, while there is a shift away from the B-quadrant, with only one star allocated in this quadrant. The increase in stars is in the C-quadrant, having increased to six and for the D-quadrant increased to five.

The thinking requirement is mainly associated with long-term strategy. Functional strategy is combined with the overall business strategy of the organisation, keeping the focus on the vision of where the library wants to be in five years' time, while at the same time integrating global trends. Communication needs to penetrate through several layers of the library, and could even extend geographically, horizontally and vertically.

The profile of the coachee in Figure 4.30 reveals a strong C- and D-quadrant preference, but in accordance with the thinking requirements of the position, the focus of the coaching sessions will have to be on also developing communication skills and competencies in the A- and B-quadrants. Looking at the left circle, the stars allocated to the D-quadrant have increased, while the stars allocated to the B-quadrant decreased for this position.

4.5.5 *Managing the business*

Managing the business equates to director level for library leadership. Drotter (2003) highlights that this is the hardest job of all in the pipeline, and in many ways the most satisfying. On this level functions must be integrated, but the position offers also significant autonomy and leadership freedom. There is always a balancing act between future goals and present needs, and the most important function for this level according to Drotter (2003) is to create time to think. The thinking requirements for this level therefore involve delivering on the business strategies, considering scenarios and thinking longer term. It is very important to pay attention to environmental challenges and opportunities and their impact on the library (business), and decide how the business would or could respond and set the overall goals that should be achieved. A strong focus is therefore required on D- and A-quadrant thinking (De Boer, Bothma and Olwagen, 2012).

We live in an information-rich and information-driven world where access to information is key:

> the digital consumer is now King, and communication and delivery channels that have opened up are the King's Horses but you would

hardly know this from the responses of many information professionals (Nicholas et al., 2008).

Considering the strong user orientation of libraries, the leadership position should not only give direction, but also be the front runner in being aware of these needs and ensuring that the library remains a value-added service for users. In our digital age the focus on innovative technology must be embraced.

The profile example in Figure 4.31 (right) reflects the profile of a library director (business head) and shows a strong thinking preference for the A- and B-quadrants. Looking at the thinking requirements of the position, on the left, the stars allocated in the D-quadrant have increased to six, and decreased to five in the C-quadrant. This reflects a strong tilt towards D- and C-quadrant thinking.

The focus of the coaching sessions needs to be on supporting this individual to consider different scenarios and to think proactively about 'what-if' contingencies (D-quadrant thinking). Tapping into strong A-quadrant thinking will help the individual to analyse different scenarios. But the overall focus of the coaching session for this individual is definitely on developing C-quadrant competencies to ensure greater cross-functional cooperation within the different sectors of the library. Coaching will also be needed to develop D-quadrant competencies in positioning the library in the digital age.

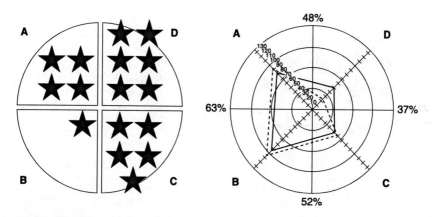

Figure 4.31 Thinking requirements for managing the business (left); a coachee's HBDI® profile (right)

4.5.6 *Managing the group*

Managing the group falls beyond the scope of our case study; yet we would like to refer briefly to the thinking requirements of the position and the coaching focus of an individual with a very strong preference for the B-quadrant, which becomes even more dominant under stress. This level requires the leader to think holistically.

Being the CEO, the final responsibility lies with the group manager to ensure that business managers deliver on the goals set for them (A-quadrant thinking). The thinking requirements of the position at this level involve sustainable competitiveness (A- and D-quadrants), while having a compelling value proposition and a clear distinctive focus on each of the businesses are of paramount importance. Balancing strong stakeholder engagement (C-quadrant) and managing the image of the group in the market place (C- and D-quadrants) are considered important thinking requirements. The stars allocated on the left side of Figure 4.32 remains 6 for the D-quadrant and an increase to five for the A-quadrant. The C-quadrant shows a decrease of stars to four while the B-quadrant remains unchanged with only one star allocated to the position.

For an individual with a strong thinking preference for A- and B-quadrants as shown in Figure 4.32 (right), the coaching session will focus on creating a shared desired outcome for the entire organisation and keeping the businesses committed to the shared vision. To assist the coachee to engage with stakeholders and create synergy to unlock the value of all

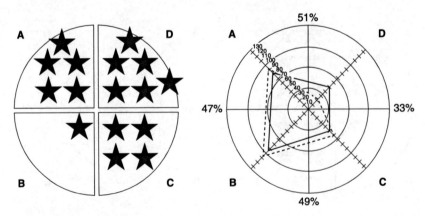

| Figure 4.32 | Thinking requirements for managing the group (left); a coachee's HBDI® profile (right) |

the businesses within the group, all while delivering against goals. The focus will be on developing stronger C- and D-quadrant competencies.

4.5.7 *Managing the enterprise*

Managing the enterprise is the highest leadership position in the organisation, and leaders need to be visionaries (Drotter 2003). According to Herrmann's Whole Brain® Model, all four quadrants of thinking are essential, with a stronger emphasis on A-, D- and C-quadrant thinking (De Boer, Bothma and Olwagen, 2012). In Figure 4.33 five stars were allocated to the A-quadrant, seven stars to the D-quadrant, three stars in the C-quadrant, and one star to the B-quadrant.

In short, the executive coaching should be aimed at assisting the individual to seek opportunities to expand globally (D-quadrant) and to build relationships at high levels, persuading and influencing multiple stakeholders (C-quadrant) (De Boer, Bothma and Olwagen, 2012). The main focus of the job is to inspire the entire organisation with the vision to achieve the desired goals (A-quadrant).

In conclusion, reconceptualising Drotter's Leadership Pipeline Model and re-imaging it by using Herrmann's Whole Brain® Model and the HBDI® profile provide a framework that can assess individuals, leadership teams and coach managers in any position, to the benefit of the organisation.

Leadership programmes offered through the formal channel of continued education by CE@UP over the past ten years use the Pipeline

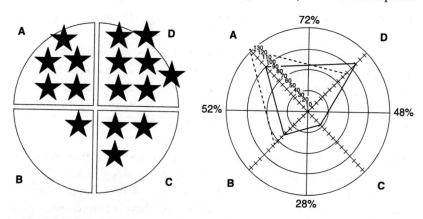

Figure 4.33 Thinking requirements for managing the enterprise (left); a coachee's HBDI® profile (right)

and the HBDI® profile as their unifying mental model to develop individuals and groups of leaders. The aim of coaching sessions is to create an awareness of different thinking requirements on the hierarchical levels of the leadership pipeline model, an understanding of the thinking preferences required on each level, and an awareness that a Whole Brain® Thinking approach is not only advantageous, but also essential to the prevention of clogging of the pipeline.

Research emphasises that certain quadrants are more dominant during certain stages. According to Herrmann (1996, 102) it is often one's own preference that leads to the clogging, as one would naturally tend to revert to one's comfort zone and emphasise one's own preferences. His Whole Brain® Model and the HBDI® profile can serve as a coaching model and tool to develop thinking skills required for the specific roles to which individuals are assigned. This will allow individuals to ascend through the pipeline and not become a prisoner of their own thinking style preferences. Leaders' willingness to stretch and develop their thinking skills in all four quadrants will ultimately determine whether the leadership pipeline can be successfully unblocked. By expanding their thinking skills and flexibility, leaders will be empowered and equipped with the necessary thinking tools that will enable them to make a smooth transition to every next level.

4.6 Further applications of Whole Brain® principles

4.6.1 *The School of Dentistry: tooth morphology*

The School of Dentistry resides within the Faculty of Health Sciences at the University of Pretoria. The innovation reported in this section and the application of Whole Brain® learning in the Department of Family Medicine (see Section 4.6.3) are the first steps in implementing meaningful strategies for accommodating and developing students' thinking preferences in the faculty.

Awareness of the diverse Thinking Styles™ of the students assisted the lecturer responsible for the subject tooth morphology in tailoring his strategies of facilitating learning to incorporate Whole Brain® teaching techniques that will accommodate and develop thinking preferences in all four quadrants.

He achieved this by introducing group work activities in the classroom and embracing co-operative learning. The feedback he subsequently received from peers endorsed the findings reported by Lumsdaine and Lumsdaine:

It is becoming clear that creativity and teamwork act synergistically – both have to be developed systematically and simultaneously for students to achieve improved learning and problem-solving outcomes (1995, 199).

4.6.1.1 Profiles of dentistry lecturers

Before illustrating the results of the dentistry students, we want to demonstrate the thinking preferences of 42 dentistry lecturers who completed the HBDI® Survey as part of our baseline study.

The generic profile of the lecturers in the School of Dentistry is 1122. This implies a double dominance for the upper left A- and lower left B-quadrant thinking. All lecturers are specialists in their field and that may be the reason why the tilt was so strong towards left-brain thinking. When we look at the composite profile, at least one lecturer showed strong preference for D-quadrant thinking. The preference map confirms the stronger tilt towards A- and B-quadrant thinking and a lower preference for C- and D-quadrant thinking modes (Figure 4.34).

4.6.1.2 Students' profiles

The data shown in Figure 4.35 were obtained from the students in the School of Dentistry at the University of Pretoria who participated in the baseline study.

Looking at third-year students enrolled for a degree in dentistry, the generic profile is a multi-dominant (quadruple) 1111 profile. This can be interpreted as having equal representation of preference in all four quadrants (Herrmann, 1996). The composite map represents 45 profiles and clearly shows a diverse but balanced distribution of thinking preferences across all four quadrants. The preference map highlights the well-balanced distribution and sufficiently strong preferences in all four of the quadrants.

Comparing the profiles of the lecturers with those of the students, a mismatch is noticed. Lecturers, who are specialists, prefer to facilitate learning through formal lectures, to supervise students with clear instructions, and to have students who practise their newly acquired skills under their supervision. They prefer a strong left-brain orientated approach to facilitating learning. The students, on the other hand (those who are multiple-dominant), can function within the A- and B-quadrants with ease, but the lecturers' styles of facilitating learning did not meet

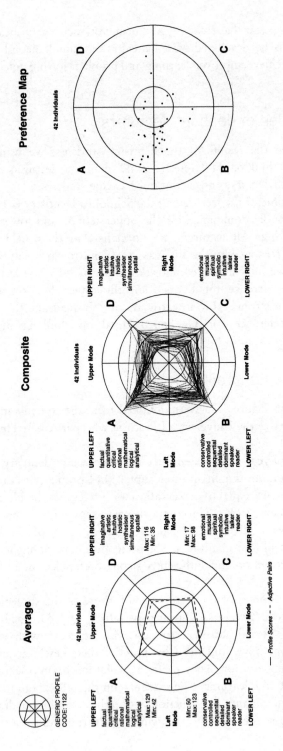

Figure 4.34 Profiles of lecturers from the School of Dentistry at the University of Pretoria

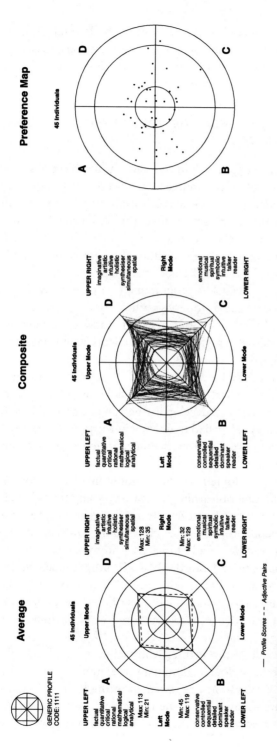

Figure 4.35 Profiles of students in the School of Dentistry at the University of Pretoria

their need for more right-brained activities of the D- and C-quadrants. Activities such as lecture room discussions, sharing experiences, engaging with others, being allowed to learn through experimenting and discovery of alternatives have not been used.

4.6.1.3 A changed teaching style in the Department of Tooth Morphology

The lecturer responsible for tooth morphology as a subject observed and reported to the curriculum committee of the School of Dentistry on the perception that students have a low motivation for participating during formal class. This has an impact on their performance when questions are asked during a formal class. The general average of the class had been 62 per cent for the past few years, although these students had been selected based on the high school grades they had obtained.

Having attended the PGCHE programme (see case study 4.2.1), the specific lecturer responsible for presenting tooth morphology was sensitised to Whole Brain® facilitating of learning and to the consequences that ignoring the thinking preferences of students could have on their academic performance.

As part of the formal and final assessment of the PGCHE programme, lecturers had to design and implement Whole Brain® facilitating of learning to accommodate and develop learners in using the Whole Brain® Thinking methodology. They had to document the process they followed and the effect it had on themselves for their professional development, and the effect it had on their students.

The new approach adopted by this lecturer involved incorporating Whole Brain® facilitating of learning for learners using the Whole Brain® Thinking methodology, and to create a learning environment that would promote class attendance, enhance classroom involvement through discussions and interactions, and ultimately lead to higher performance. Through experience gained from the PGCHE programme, the lecturer realised that these ideals would be achieved only if methods of facilitating learning were to appeal to all four quadrants of thinking preferences and were supported by knowledge of the preferred ways of thinking within the group.

The preference code of the lecturer who facilitated tooth morphology is 2112 and reflects a double dominant preference – with the two primaries, B- and C-quadrants, represented in the lower left and lower right modes (Figure 4.36). The profile is characterised by a very strong preference for conservative thinking and controlled behaviour, with a

Quadrant:	A	B	C	D
Preference Code:	2	1	1	2
Adjective Pairs:	4	7	9	4
Profile Scores:	50	104	101	59

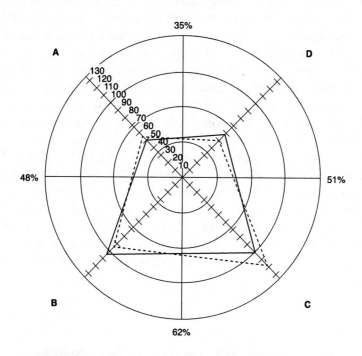

Figure 4.36 Profile of the tooth morphology lecturer at the University of Pretoria

desire for organisation and structure as well as detail and accuracy – all associated with the B-quadrant (Herrmann International, 2009). All of these thinking requirements were necessary for facilitating learning in an exact science subject such as tooth morphology. The lecturer's strong preference for the interpersonal skills of the C-quadrant was the reason for offering this module in a totally different way so as to enhance students' engagement and create a co-operative learning environment.

Transformation of the learning environment

The intent was to start transforming the learning environment (laboratory) by stimulating creativity and, through transforming the learning environment, to ensure the next steps: an increased interest in the module, students starting to work together as teams, and students ultimately obtaining higher grades in the module.

The ideal place to start transforming the learning environment was the tooth morphology laboratory. Not only did students spend most of their time in the laboratory, trying to master and practise the requirements of the module, but the laboratory also afforded an opportunity to encourage interaction through class discussions and group work, thus allowing students with a strong C-quadrant the opportunity to engage and share their perspectives. In Figure 4.37 the workstations are shown, displaying the Whole Brain® problem-solving toolbox. In Figure 4.38 the contents of the Whole Brain® problem-solving toolbox are displayed.

The toolbox was a replica of the colours of the HBDI® profile: blue represents the A-quadrant, green represents the B-quadrant, red represents the C-quadrant and yellow represents the D-quadrant (Herrmann, 1996). Initially the colours did not mean anything to the students other than creating a colourful environment. However, the lecturer took them by surprise with the creative content of the toolbox, something new and colourful in a tooth morphology laboratory. The Whole Brain® toolbox

Figure 4.37 Workstations in a laboratory displaying the Whole Brain® problem-solving toolbox

Figure 4.38 The Whole Brain® problem-solving toolbox

contained problems that students needed to solve during that specific learning opportunity. Each problem was written on different white cards and placed inside the toolbox. As the HBDI® profile of the lecturer indicates a strong preference for detail, clear goals and instructions were written on the cards (A- and B-quadrant preference), while relevant referencing and time frames ensured that the B-quadrant thinkers would have a sufficient degree of structure. In the four corners of the toolbox were placed replicas of exact molar models in tooth morphology, made by the lecturer, and this too represented all four quadrants, further stimulating the interest.

The rest of the learning environment catered for A- and B-quadrant preferences. In order to assist students in solving the problems outlined in the toolbox, the lecturer collected library books (Figure 4.39) and selected relevant up-to-date journals on the topics for the specific session. These were scattered around the laboratory and were available to all students at all times, ensuring that no time would be wasted in finding the appropriate books and journals, and that A- and B-quadrant needs were met.

In order to start stimulating D-quadrant thinking, the lecturer not only displayed the creative Whole Brain® toolbox at each work station, but also gave the students a creative assignment that would stimulate their C- and D-quadrants. The final assessment of the module would be to present the subject content in a Whole Brain® way at the end of the semester. They could choose to work in groups, or as individuals. The choice was theirs.

Throughout the design and development phase of the Whole Brain® facilitating of learning, the lecturer kept C-quadrant thinking as the focus point of the interventions. The emphasis was placed on collaboration – collaborative teaching (peer to peer), collaborative participation (group work and interaction with the lecturer) and collaborative learning (engaging and sharing) (see Figure 4.40). The lecturer was very successful in creating a learning environment where collaborative learning formed the core.

The ripple effect of collaborative learning started to create enthusiasm among the students for the subject and project. They began sharing their project ideas with one another, to participate more in class and to engage with the lecturer. The students actually enjoyed the new way of facilitating learning (Figures 4.41 and 4.42), and expressed this on numerous occasions.

Figure 4.39 Text books and journals on tooth morphology

Figure 4.40 Students working collaboratively in groups

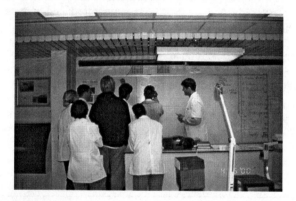

Figure 4.41 Collaborative teaching

Figure 4.42 Collaborative learning

Table 4.2 documents the activities used within the tooth morphology module to address the different quadrants (Oosthuizen, 2001).

The statistical analysis that was made of questionnaires regarding this module revealed that the students experienced more meaningful learning through the application of the Whole Brain® Model than through

Table 4.2	Student classroom activities used within the tooth morphology module to address the different quadrants

A-quadrant	D-quadrant
Various textbooks Clinically orientated journal articles Real-life case studies Short informal lectures to introduce, orientate or summarise content Facilitator taking on the role of expert	Students introduced themselves by means of a metaphor Fun experienced during role-plays and scenarios Colourful innovative learning material Drawings and illustrations to illustrate learning material A variety of movie clips or newspaper cartoons based on tooth morphology used as icebreakers or during a learning opportunity Futuristic design activities future-orientated discussions

B-quadrant	C-quadrant
Providing a study manual with clear outcomes and time frames Learning opportunity on Whole Brain® Thinking concept Organising each learning opportunity on whiteboard with time frames Summary of each learning opportunity, and relating it to the learning outcomes Students keeping record of their own learning (action learning) Information on how and when assessment would take place Lecturer taking on the role of co-manager, co-organiser and co-administrator	Working in groups of three Playing music during certain sessions Allowing personal stories of experience in practice Physical activities, e.g. walking around to collect data, short drama, role play Walking around and speaking to other students Display of mutual respect and appreciation Warm and friendly mood in class Facilitator acting as mentor, motivator and friend

Summarised from Oosthuzen (2001)

any of the previous ways in which they had been taught. The word 'taught' is used here on purpose, as the previous model did not provide for Whole Brain® facilitating of learning, but involved one-way communication, which reflected the preferred way of communicating by the lecturer.

Stronger emphasis on Whole Brain® assessment

Assessment during the tooth morphology course included both formative and summative assessment. Formative assessment included tests performed during learning opportunity, self-assessment and peer assessment. The facts and details expected in the tests that students had to complete during learning opportunities required A- and B-quadrant thinking. Students also had to synthesise their knowledge into answers that indicated the relevance of tooth morphology in the clinical setting, which required D-quadrant thinking (Oosthuizen, 2001).

Summative assessment included a project and a final test at the end of the series of learning opportunities. The project required students to produce, manufacture or create something that would show what they had learned about tooth morphology in a Whole Brain® Thinking manner. They were free to do it in any way they chose. The freedom of choice, and the requirement to create an artefact to illustrate their knowledge, addressed D-quadrant thinking preferences. The content of these artefacts – the facts and application of these facts – required students to use A-quadrant abilities. The details of the content required B-quadrant competencies, while the physical activities necessary to complete the assignment involved C-quadrant skills.

The students created extremely creative artefacts that illustrated their mastery of the subject and ability to construct new knowledge in a meaningful way. The different products were evidence of the students' diversity, commitment and willingness to be different. The artefacts they produced included games (Figures 4.43 and 4.44), an in-flight magazine (Figure 4.45), a clinical jacket (Figure 4.46) and a family album (Figure 4.47) (Oosthuizen, 2001).

The dialogue between the lecturer and students and among students improved considerably. Discussions were now taking place throughout the sessions and from the results of their projects it is clear that the students were highly motivated.

While the students were completing their projects, it was interesting to note that some preferred starting with the big picture first, and then breaking it down to detail. Others started with the detail and then

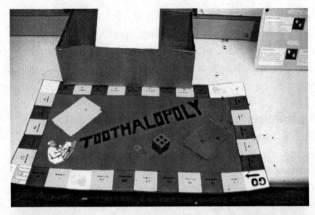

Figure 4.43 Games: Toothalopoly (top); Dental Pursuit (bottom)

constructed the big picture. Similar findings from student projects are documented by Lumsdaine and Lumsdaine (1995).

It was a positive experience for the students to become involved in their own learning process. When they were assessed and the final marks for the module compiled (including their projects), the students on averaged performed 30 per cent better in the module than during previous years, for an average grade of 92 per cent vs 62 per cent. Their experience of the Whole Brain® Thinking nature of the curriculum, the friendly and supportive learning environment and the option of creative Whole Brain® assessment were all features that motivated students and led to exceptional individual academic achievements.

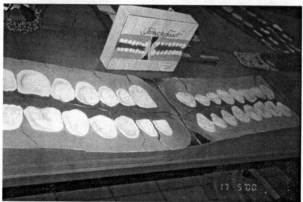

Figure 4.44 Games: Odontaquiz (top); tooth morphology puzzle (bottom)

Figure 4.45 In-flight magazine prepared by a tooth morphology student

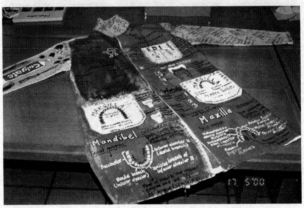

Figure 4.46 Clinical jacket designed by tooth morphology students, back and front

4.6.2 *The Department of Taxation*

(We would like to acknowledge the assistance of Marius van Oordt and Theresa Hills from the Department of Taxation for the permission granted to use the data included in this case study.)

The Head of the University of Pretoria Department of Taxation took the initiative to have her academic members of staff introduced to the construct of Whole Brain® learning and related learning theories. I ran informal workshops for them in which Whole Brain® learning was addressed. During the workshops I mentioned the value of action research. This became the focus of another workshop. The workshop on Whole Brain® learning was extended by inviting lecturers in the field of taxation from other higher education institutions across South Africa.

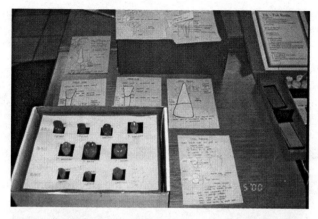

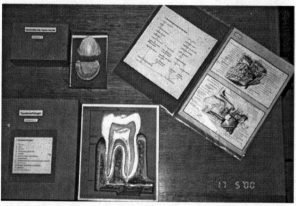

Figure 4.47 Representations: tooth morphology in wax (top) and family album (bottom)

A group of young lecturers from the Department who are creative picked up some ideas and verified that what they were doing fits the idea of Whole Brain® learning. From their own action research studies on their practices they could gather adequate quantitative and qualitative evidence for publishing articles in journals and presenting papers at conferences. This is evidence of taking responsiblity for one's own professional development.

For example, these lecturers challenged their students to design and print a booklet on taxation for novices or to design posters or games on taxation. Figure 4.48 shows the lecturers proudly showing evidence of the outcome of their projects. The winning artefact was a booklet on taxation in layman's terms, which was to be published by an accounting firm at the time. At the time of documenting my case study, the outcome of the publication was not finalised.

Figure 4.48 Examples of innovation in the Department of Taxation

I was proud of the young and innovative lecturers and eagerly reported on their progress in a presentation at the University of Macquarie in Australia during 2011. I took some artefacts to show the audience what they were capable of. In this way I could contribute to the lecturers' professional development and their professional confidence – including my own, as I observe daily how the principles of different learning theories are applied in practice by my colleagues.

The audience was amazed by the professional products the students had come up with. They realised that professionalism is a core value of their profession and therefore agreed that if quality learning is at stake, their students' work should be of the highest quality.

Figure 4.48 shows the proud lecturers in the Department of Taxation and the products their students created.

It is important to me that students who participate and make innovation a reality should be acknowledged. Figure 4.49 shows the winners of the competition – an event that served as a celebration of the outcome of the initiative.

Two of the lecturers (one male and one female) who became fully engaged in the construct of Whole Brain® Thinking started a collaborative project called 'Two teachers are better than one: collaborative teaching as an approach to promote Whole Brain® learning'. They recently presented their findings at a conference (Hills and Van Oordt, 2012). The reason for the choice of the title of their presentation is that their profiles are opposites, and combined they form a Whole Brain® profile. The collaborative effort is evidence of peer mentoring. I also act as peer mentor, but the professional learning is reciprocal.

Figure 4.50 shows a representation of the combination of the two lecturers' profiles. The male lecturer takes responsibility for the part of the

Figure 4.49 Students celebrating creativity

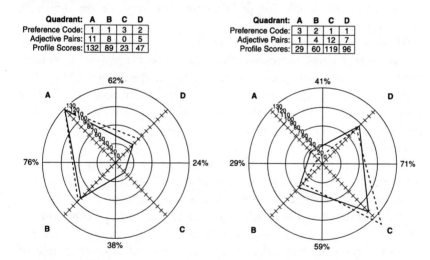

Figure 4.50 Profiles of two lecturers' in the Department of Taxation

lecture that requires fact-based learning and the female lecturer focuses on the part of the lecture that requires a more people-orientated style.

4.6.3 *The Department of Family Medicine*

(We would like to acknowledge the assistance of Professor Jannie Hugo, Head of the Department of Family Medicine, for the permission granted to use the data included in this case study.)

Only recently an action research project was commenced by the Department of Family Medicine. A colleague who also specialises in higher education and I offered several workshops (I prefer the construct 'learning shops') aimed at promoting professional learning in the Department. All the learning theories discussed in our book are continuously addressed in these 'learning shops'. The Department consists of a small group of lecturers and the programme offered focuses on being practice-based and patient-centred. With that comes the responsibility of the lecturers to accommodate all Thinking Styles™ and we expect students to take note of such an approach to facilitating learning. The baseline for this action research project is the knowledge about Whole Brain® Thinking that the students acquire and the baseline data gathered for the group of lecturers. The profiles of the Department's lecturers are shown in Figure 4.51.

Although there is only a very small group of ten lecturers in the Department of Family Medicine, their generic profile represents a multi-dominant profile with presentation in all four quadrants (1111). The composite profile also represents thinking preferences in all four quadrants and a balanced distribution within the four quadrants. The preference map reveals the least preferred thinking preference to be for A-quadrant thinking.

At the beginning of each year, the cohort of first-year students is introduced to the concept of Whole Brain® learning as the entire programme is based on its principles. A learning opportunity for this purpose is offered and feedback requested on the students' experience of the application of the principles of Whole Brain® learning during the contact session. The qualitative feedback received from a sample of 32 students is presented verbatim in Table 4.3. It is divided into two sections: Section A, students' responses to the lecturer teaching Whole Brain® principles and related learning theories; and Section B, students' experience of Whole Brain® learning and related learning theories, and their contribution to making the learning opportunity worthwhile for themselves and others.

It is clear from the feedback above that the students are not clear about the notion of learning-centredness. They are not used to reflecting on themselves and their learning, as most of the feedback still focuses on the lecturer and not on their own contribution. It is my intention to design a questionnaire that would fit this notion. The questionnaire needs extensive work to ensure it is valid. What is reported here is merely part of a pilot project to get an idea of how to refine it.

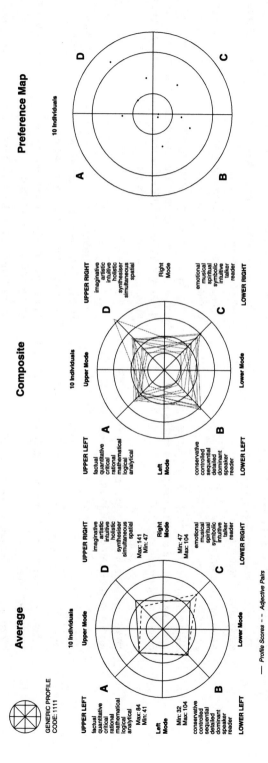

Figure 4.51 Composite profiles of the lecturers from the Department of Family Medicine at the University of Pretoria

Table 4.3 Qualitative feedback from 32 first-year students in the Department of Family Medicine at the University of Pretoria on the application of principles of Whole Brain® learning during contact session at beginning of year

Respondent number	Section A Response to lecturer's facilitating of learning	Section B Response to student's contribution
1	'He was allowing everyone to feel free and talk free and he also provide learning opportunities'	'In this class I have understand myself better than ever before and to know my brain function'
2	'The presentation was lively, well structured and overall applicable to students'	'Enjoyed and learnt from the session. Thank you Dr Pieter du Toit and well done'
3	'Gave an excellent lecture'	'I've learnt a lot on discovering more opportunities . . . doing things'
4	'Well he teaches us to adapt to other sorts of learning because we are all different but there can be a way of communication amongst us'	'The class was very good and even the lecture was very well organised and allow us to express our self and to share our thinking/mind and to think out of the box by this draw 3 lines to form a seven (7) [practical exercise to be executed]'
5	'Made the best of a very "bad" classroom setting' [Group work had to be carried out in an auditorium style venue]	
6		'The visualisation was not enough and also not that much relative to the learners and their way of thinking. So we cannot contribute in much of the lessons'
7	'It was a good session the lecture was flexible helping us to know ourselves'	'It helped me a lot, helped me to understand myself and that I have to understand others'
8	'This is the best experience I ever gained'	'It made me realise that I don't realise that I can figure out how I think and that's great'

9	'World class lecturer ☺'	'Very Good Learning Opportunity For Introduction And Understanding Oneself And Learning On How To Increase One's Potential In Every Aspect Of Life And How To Deal And Engage With Others Without Any Problems Towards Every Situation The Is Presented To One Or In A Group'
10	'Very Clear Presentations Done By Dr, To Allows Students To Participate In All Aspects'	'More than 2 hours was needed. Group discussions helped lot as I learned to work with other people and to understand their way of thinking and doing things'
11	'Probably didn't tell us about the solution in the collision . . . anyway so flexible and would love to teach us again'	'Just realise that I am not yet responsible'
12	'The lecture encouraged us not to only think of ourselves but also for the other people since we will be in the clinical practice'	'I as a student gained knowledge of working with different people of different minds. And I got a chance to discover myself and know how my brain works'
13	'Was very Insightful Since I Learnt About The Way People View Different Situations As Well As Their Everyday Lives'	'I still have to develop an enquiring mind and learn or get used to expressing myself even in front of the class. Though, I am willing to learn more'
14	'I enjoyed this session and learnt a lot about myself, things that I didn't know will benefit me in the future'	
15		'As a student I'm also responsible for the energy I use during a lecture, I'm responsible for how much information I take up'
16	'I like that he went to find out the opinion of each student. That way we were all able and free to express ourselves and not just blend in and agree with others' opinions'	'The exercise made me aware of my weaknesses, which in turn gives me room to improve. I also learned about how others think and how to accommodate them and work with them productively'

(Continued overleaf)

Table 4.3   Continued

Respondent number	Section A Response to lecturer's facilitating of learning	Section B Response to student's contribution
17	'It was an excellent session, I learned a lot about myself as well as about others. The lecturer gave me ample opportunity by his way of teaching to pick up and grasp information for my benefit easily'	'I may grasp stuff at a different pace, but I always try to learn as well as contribute to others'
18	'Clearly explained and creative'	'I discovered that I try to base a lot of my learning on structure as opposed to emotions'
19		'Think this is a fun and active way of getting to know yourself and others'
20		'The participation in group work made a learning opportunity to see the importance of working and learning in different ways and not acording [sic] to my own prefered [sic] mode'
21	'What a wonderful lecture, thought more as in the self – creativity dimension'	'I learn a lot course some of the things I wasn't aware of. Now I know what's the benefit of putting all things together'
22		'The lecture has been useful to me'
23	'I enjoyed the way the lecture was accommodating all the different aspects of learning and the way he explained whole-mind learning'	'The lecture thought [sic] me more about myself, he made me realise that there is a way of learning differently through the whole mind learning'
24	'I gained a lot knowing my brain profile but mostly about knowing that we have different brain profiles but we can form a good team'	

25 'The lecture was good and made me to understand more easy and clear'

26 'He was very insightfull and forthcoming with his lecture and his slides were very educating'

27 'Pretty good to change your perception a learner and build up a good character'

28 'Fun filled session and learning quite a lot at the same time ☺'

29 'The lecture today was fun; touchy; factsful; straight forward because the lecture was able to lecture in our different comfort zones'

30 'Learned from the lecture'

31 'This session was very insightfull because a bit more about myself and many other people that exist out there'
    'Ambitious to learn and adopt good qualities of life especially for saving lives and giving hope'
    'Inspired me to change and be flexible in terms of communicating with others. Realised that people think differently and I should explain to patients in their way of thinking'
    'I now realise that I should be more open to other ways of thinking. I should make this a opportunity for my own personal development. To be more flexible'

32 'Very good introduction to WBL [Whole Brain® learning]. Wish one could be more detailed for one-selves Preferance!'
    'Very good introduction to WBL. Wish one could be more detailed for one selves Personal Preference!'

4.6.4 *University of Antwerp*

(We would like to acknowledge the assistance and contribution of Professor Peter van Petegem, who was the supervisor for the larger project financed by the Flemish government.)

Innovation in higher education has become a focal point in our practice. Tabled differences between the old and new paradigms in education in general (Brandes and Ginnis, 1996; Van der Horst and McDonald, 1997) are evidence that we had to make a radical shift in this regard. The prospective teacher or lecturer and the current students in our higher education context need to master competencies necessary for adding value to their future teaching practices. Learning how to think creatively and critically, and gaining insight in the entire work (school) context, at a technical and social level, would enable teachers to gain value-adding attributes.

Such teachers would be able to make use of mastered thinking strategies and methods and competencies needed for problem-solving. Coupled to this, they would have the willingness to learn continuously, demonstrating the essence of life-long learning (Olivier, 1998). For the sake of encompassing all of these attributes and many more not mentioned, we would term this type of learning deep learning (Biggs, 1999; Ramsden, 1999; Entwistle, McCune and Walker, 2001).

Deep learning, then, in the context of teacher education should be a reflection of the realities of the world of work (school context) and society at large. Students and prospective teachers need to take responsibility for their own professional development and the value of life-long professional learning. This does not happen by a process of osmosis. It is our responsibility as practitioners in higher education, specifically in teacher education, to intentionally provide opportunities for developing related competencies.

Visionary thinking on the implementation of our vision has as imperative the establishing of a learning environment that is conducive to deep learning at grassroots level for our students. Such an environment would, *inter alia*, create opportunities for self- and peer assessment and learning with others. The focus is placed on the *process* in tandem with the end *product*. In the world of work most of the work and learning processes (planning) are executed (facilitating learning) in collaboration with others – to a varied extent. Learning with others has become an essential life skill. Making mistakes in the process and critically reflecting on them is an integral part of professional learning for which we have to make provision.

The previous paragraphs are not at all meant to be all inclusive of our vision on innovating our practices. They only set the scene for reporting part of our research outcome in this section and for rethinking our practices in teacher education. If this is true for all professional learning and all prospective teachers, there is only one option for teacher education – *demonstrating the implementation of the principles of deep learning in our practices*. Indeed it asks for cultivating self-regulated teachers who are in the position to cultivate self-regulated learners in the school context. The process that would ensure this is putting student teachers through authentic learning experiences, as these student teachers ought to do with their learners.

This section reports an investigation into a group of student teachers at the University of Antwerp who had been put through a process of mastering the competence of self-regulated learning. The same theoretical underpinning of the module they enrolled for forms the core of the conceptual framework for this study. Among others, the work of Kolb (1984) is used to offer them the opportunity of engaging in a process of experiential learning. This is supported by the work of Vermunt (1995) on learning styles in higher education, and learning style flexibility as adapted from the learning styles model of Herrmann (1995).

4.6.4.1 Research problem

Self-regulated learning and complementing meta-cognition (Biggs, 1985; 1999; Ramsden, 1999) are useful for promoting deep learning. It is common to find these theories part of the curricula of teacher education programmes worldwide. The unilateral inclusion of the theory in a curriculum and presenting the essence during lectures is not our challenge. The challenge facing us as practitioners is offering our students the opportunity of hands-on experiences of what self-regulated learning entails in an authentic context.

This case study reports on a small case involving only four lecturers offering a module that challenged a group of students to develop competence in executing small-scale action research projects. The group consisted of a sample of 32 education students. Three full-time lecturers were permanent staff members at the time and responsible for the module. I participated as visiting lecturer during a postdoctoral study.

Apart from an array of learning opportunities offered by the permanent lecturers, I facilitated learning during a learning opportunity on Whole Brain® learning. The students were familiar with the construct learning styles as learning styles were addressed as part of the module.

Unfortunately the HBDI® Survey could not be used, as funding was not available and students were expected to complete Vermunt's learning style questionnaire.

The learning opportunity I offered was designed in such a way that it was a practical demonstration to the students of how to apply the principles of Whole Brain® learning in their classes and how such an event can be made more authentic. As my profile reflects a preference for the C-quadrant (see Figure 4.1), I walked around in the class between the students so as to narrow the distance between them and me – an interpersonal approach. The class environment was typical of university lecture halls where a cinema style (rows) is evident, which did not allow for group work. I demonstrated that irrespective of circumstances one can change the situation. I expected students to work in groups for some of the tasks. This is aligned with my people-orientated style of facilitating learning.

As part of my planning (B-quadrant, for which I have a low preference) I started well in advance. This included packing my artefacts – the different hats I mentioned in the case study on the induction programme, which is evidence of a fun aspect of teaching, typical of the D-quadrant. I also planned for taking my own markers and other educational material, such as PowerPoint slides and a DVD that would have been necessary. This was done as I realised that it would make my teaching life abroad easier.

When addressing fact-based learning (A-quadrant, which I usually attempt to avoid), I asked students to reflect on a video and challenged them to reflect on the contents, and to share the most important new facts that they had learned about Whole Brain® learning with the student next to them and the larger class (typical of the C-quadrant). In this way I promoted A-quadrant learning. It should be noted that with this exercise it was not only the A-quadrant that was activated but also the C-quadrant as the students had to explain the new knowledge gained to others. This demonstrated attributes of interpersonal competence and accommodated D-quadrant thinking as the video was visual and offered some 'fun'.

When dealing with process and step-by-step procedures I had to plan for the learning opportunity to begin and end on time (B-quadrant), and to have everything run smoothly by ensuring that the laptop and data projector were activated, and so on.

My preference for the C-quadrant made me interested in knowing what the students thought as part of self-assessment – an intrapersonal attribute. Linked to that, I was eager to know what the project leader would observe and give feedback on. The latter was informally discussed several times.

As part of the final stage of the session (the 'end' phase of the B-quadrant), the group of students completed a feedback questionnaire, which served a scholarly and didactic purpose, and generated data for my investigation. At the same time students had an example of self-assessment, and how to assess another practitioner – something that is extremely valuable for deep learning. I completed a matching self-assessment questionnaire. The questionnaire consists of 20 statements to which the respondents had to respond. A five-point scale was used (1 = negative and 5 = positive). By this means quantitative feedback was generated. An open question 'General Comments' was added to generate qualitative feedback that would substantiate the quantitative feedback.

In summary, the group of learners responded quantitatively in the following way. According to the data recorded, the respondents were satisfied about most of the items they had to respond to, with a mean score of 69.5. For item 2 (Finds ways to help students answer their questions), though, only 47 per cent of the respondents indicated that they were satisfied (4 and 5 on scale collapsed), and 47 per cent that they were neutral (3 on scale). The same was found with item 16 (Provides a user-friendly study guide) for which 47 per cent indicated neutrality and 47 per cent satisfaction. This low rating might be because the students did not use the time before the session to read the applicable section in the document.

For all of the following items a significant percentage of above 80 was indicated as positive responses:

- *Item 3*: encourages students to express themselves freely and openly (88 per cent).
- *Item 4*: shows enthusiasm about the subject matter (93 per cent).
- *Item 6*: speaks with expressiveness and variety in tone and voice (81 per cent).
- *Item 7*: demonstrates the importance and significance of the subject matter (86 per cent).
- *Item 8*: provides learning opportunities and presentations that are lively and encouraging (84 per cent).
- *Item 15*: creates a climate conducive to learning (84 per cent).

Qualitative feedback on my learning opportunity was obtained by means of an open-ended section completed by a sample of students (n = 11) (Table 4.4).

The outcome of this case study is satisfactory as I could experience how implementing the principles of Whole Brain® learning enriched my

Table 4.4	Qualitative feedback by respondents (n = 11) on learning opportunity to develop competence in executing small-scale action research projects

Respondent	Response
1	'A lesson that I'll remember! I enjoyed the video, group discussions, group tasks, visual aspect with the different hats. A very colourful session, straight to heart and mind!'
2	'I really enjoyed this "lesson"! Your enthusiasm and examples were inspiring'
3	'The focus was on yellow and red, is this to compensate the regular blue/green combo?' [This remark demonstrates that this respondent has a clear understanding of the application of the Herrmann theory]
4	'I really enjoyed the way you teach. It was very creative and easy to follow!'
5	'The introduction was well timed, I was just falling asleep when there was a sudden change in teaching method' [The introductory part was deliberately presented in a boring academic tone, as an ice-breaker]
6	'Very nice and learning college'
7	'Very good lesson, learned a lot. You really know how to keep your students interested'
8	'This was a refreshing experience! Enlightening and tasty! Thanks so much!'
9	'It would have been even more outstanding when it was presented in Zuidafrikaans!'
10	'A nice change! Different as other classes; the different tasks could be explained more clearly'
11	'OK'

facilitating of learning. For me it especially meant that my Whole Brain® practice is viable, but also at an international level.

4.6.5 *University of Eduardo Mondlane, Mozambique*

(I would like to acknowledge the assistance of my PhD student, Jorge Fringe, from the University of Eduardo Mondlane, who did a study on

Whole Brain® peer mentoring which informs this case study. I would also like to thank the Swedish International Development Agency who sponsored the study.)

Peer mentoring of academic staff in the context of higher education has recently become a specific gap (unit of analysis) that needs to be investigated. The formal agreement between the University of Pretoria and the University of Eduardo Mondlane in Mozambique opened up several opportunities for academic staff to engage in peer mentoring interventions. The present case study highlights this as a point of departure for continuous mentoring initiatives within the University. Initially a peer mentoring leader rolled out a peer mentoring intervention, which in a reciprocal way – typical of peer mentoring – had a beneficial effect on the professional development of all participating academic staff in one way or another.

At the next level, the leader who initiated the intervention took responsibility for initiating peer mentoring at his own institution – the University of Eduardo Mondlane. This level of action is seen as quality peer mentoring. The focus was not on peer mentoring itself, but on facilitating the process in such a way that the entire focus on peer mentoring from a traditional point of view is re-constructed as new meaning that contributes to the current body of knowledge – through the use of Whole Brain® learning. Referring to this actually means that the current body of knowledge is outdated. Little is written specifically on peer mentoring in the context of higher education and new views relating it to current and applicable learning theories for adults. The focus brings clarity to this notion and helps to fill the gap that exists.

Peer mentoring is multi-dimensional and therefore an array of learning and educational theories needs to be merged. This multi-dimensional nature of peer mentoring, specifically in the context of higher education, implies that any researcher focusing on this phenomenon should use a multiple lens and this is what the initiator of the intervention did. He managed not only to stay focused, but at the same time also to have a holistic view of the context especially in developing countries, such as in Mozambique. Therefore the focus of the case study was on promoting Whole Brain® scholarly reflection for academic professional development in higher education. The combination and integration of theories as a whole includes constructs, of which the following are included in the work of Du Toit (2012):

- a Whole Brain® approach to facilitative mentoring
- a Whole Brain® approach to action research-driven mentoring

- a Whole Brain® approach to mentoring
- a Whole Brain® approach to self-regulated mentoring
- a Whole Brain® approach to constructivist mentoring
- a scholarship of a Whole Brain® approach to mentoring
- a Whole Brain® approach to reflexive mentoring.

The case study aimed at looking into quality mentoring that includes a holistic approach, as indicated above, using relevant recent learning theories for adults. Since reflection is an important part of action learning and research, it is highlighted and deepened as a scholarly act. The new construct 'scholarly reflection' (Du Toit, 2012) brings a different focus to the topic. In addition, it is linked to the theory on Whole Brain® learning and by doing so the focus of the case study is also widened and deepened.

In the context of the case study, scholarly reflection has to do with enquiring about one's own practice. The focus indicates that the practices within the case study were transformative in the sense that they constructed new understanding of peer mentoring. Instead of the construct 'critical reflection', to which most scholars of reflective practice refer, 'scholarly reflection' was preferred during the intervention as the scholarship of teaching has become an integral part of the professional development of academic staff. In the same way promoting the scholarship of a Whole Brain® approach to mentoring was one of the goals of the case study. It is considered not adequate to only reflect on one's practice in a critical way, but one should in a scholarly way allow and challenge oneself to make the outcome of such reflection public. Those who are involved in any professional development intervention should be offered the opportunity to write journal and conference papers. More often than not, peer mentors who are involved in their own professional development in a self-regulated fashion have never been challenged by these options.

As professional development and scholarly reflection are actions that are an integral part of intrapersonal quality assurance, the case study looked into the notion of considering oneself as co-learner who, in collaboration with colleagues (learning community or community of practice), contributes to building a learning organisation. For this purpose and for the purpose of professional development of all participants, the peer mentor leader proposed an action learning or research approach, which was appropriate. As a proponent of action research for professional development he uses himself as example when reflecting on one's practice.

This focus on the phenomenon in question is not static but 'alive' and offered the participating peer mentors the opportunity to construct their own living theory as McNiff (2002) proposes. This is the line of argumentation followed in Section 3.4, which substantiates the claim that a Whole Brain® approach to scholarly peer mentoring (Du Toit, 2012) serves as the epistemological underpinning of peer mentoring as a practice .

My student and I argue that apart from the expectations any university might have regarding educational change (including professional development), it is the responsibility of each lecturer to ensure quality at micro-level (own class). It is expected that lecturers become flexible and adaptable (as underpinned by the notion of a Whole Brain® approach to scholarly reflection) and take responsibility for their own professional learning and professional development. With this aim in mind, the peer mentoring intervention highlighted the fact that participating lecturers embarked on a journey of becoming independent, scholarly and reflective practitioners. They enacted constructivist professional learning in a Whole Brain® Thinking way – as they would expect of their students. A Whole Brain® approach to scholarly reflection has become an important aspect of professional development and deep professional learning. It is therefore important that a Whole Brain® approach to scholarly reflection be promoted in professional development interventions, such as the one under investigation in this case study. At the same time, any specialist involved in a professional development intervention, such as the peer mentor leader who is an academic at the University of Eduardo Mondlane, had to act as role model in this regard. The peer mentor as leader demonstrated that he practises what he preaches – he reported his scholarly reflection by means of several conference papers and drafted a concept journal paper reflecting on his own practice as peer mentor and facilitator of the professional development of colleagues.

This case study clearly demonstrates that professional learning for lecturers complements student learning and follows a synchronous model. As constructivist learning is desired for students, it is desired for lecturers; as action learning is appropriate for students, action research is appropriate for peer mentors, lecturers, supervisors, and so on.

The theoretical framework for this case study is to be found in the array of theories included in our book, and in the research design for the case study – action research. Within the context of a Whole Brain® approach to professional development, the peer mentoring leader referred to the construct of a Whole Brain® approach to action research. It should be kept in mind that action research serves a dual purpose: it constitutes the research design but also serves as an integral part of the theoretical framework as it is an appropriate process (theory) when it comes to professional development and is linked to all the theories discussed in our book, especially a Whole Brain® approach to constructivist professional learning, which forms an integral part of the epistemology of this case study.

A whole constructivist approach was used to contribute to the existing body of knowledge. The peer mentor leader studied literature that was closely related to the concept of professional learning (which he had to adapt), such as literature on learning styles and multiple intelligences, constructivism and professional co-operative learning to enable him to construct his own meaning. However, his constructing of meaning did not occur as a theoretically abstract process, as practical value was tested and used to inform theory. Our understanding of the theoretical basis of the constructs under investigation was practically enriched. The peer mentor leader aptly gave proof of what McNiff and Whitehead (2006) regard as the purpose of action research – to integrate theory and practice and to see the process as living theory. Therefore, in the context of this case study, it is not critical to outline a theoretical framework based on current literature, but rather to construct new theory based on experience, consulting scholarly work and scholarly discourse (by the peer mentor and the participating peers and lecturers regarding their own practices).

The action research design that was followed clearly indicates the leading peer mentor's understanding of the action research design and its execution as a complex and multi-dimensional process. He indicated his experience of action research-driven professional development not only as a spiral consisting of several cycles, but for all the participating peers – each with their own spirals and cycles. The study executed indicated that the intervention that was designed, developed and executed for the specific model of peer mentoring investigated was creative and visionary.

He employed different data collection techniques, such as questionnaires (including the HBDI® Survey), interviews, visuals (including photo evidence) and other artefacts such as ideas written on flip-chart paper. The Statistical Support Services of the University of Pretoria substantiated the case study in a quantitative way. In this way the mixed-methods approach that complements action research was appropriately executed.

The innovation of the case study lies in the alternative focus on scholarly reflection – a Whole Brain® approach to scholarly reflection.

The case study brings a holistic view to peer mentoring at the level of creating professional development interventions among colleagues and self-assessment of professional learning. It also refers to the fact that quality peer mentoring – as embedded in Whole Brain® scholarly reflection – contributes to converting a university into a learning organisation that offers professional and high-quality learning opportunities for its students.

The case study is innovative as it included professional development of all lecturers (practitioner-researchers) involved, and introduced action research as a new construct and practice to the participating peer mentors. Furthermore, it shows the possibility of synchronising lecturers' action research and students' action learning.

Since our book extensively reports on the visual profile of the HBDI® Survey specifically, this case study documents the results of the HBDI® Survey for the initiator of the peer mentoring intervention and other aspects, and the HBDIs® profiles of eight participating lecturers in narrative format. By narrating the 'Whole Brain® Thinking context' of the case study, I deliberately refer to the peer mentoring group as a community of thinkers using a Whole Brain® Thinking approach as the practical aspects of transforming one's practice and so on are not addressed. In some cases I also extrapolate the general outcome of the HBDI® Survey to the peer mentoring context, using only a few examples.

According to the HBDI® profile data summary, the preference code of the peer mentor who took a leadership position is 1112, which means triple dominance with primary preferences for the A-, B- and C-quadrants and a secondary preference for the D-quadrant. The HBDI® profile data summary indicates that the thinking style he most prefers is the B-quadrant (with 83 points), followed by the C-quadrant (77) and the A-quadrant (71). His descriptors in the B-quadrant are *Controlled* and *Dominant*, with *Conservative* being his key descriptor – the one most descriptive of his mentoring style. He took control of the intervention. He initiated and monitored it by applying the principles of action research in such a way that he could report it in a scholarly fashion. In the C-quadrant his descriptors are *Emotional* and *Intuitive* (his emotive thinking side fits the context of peer mentoring where it is about people), while in the A-quadrant the descriptors are *Critical, Quantitative* and *Factual* – typical of the research on mentoring in which he became involved. His least preferred quadrant is D, with a value of 59. In this quadrant *Intuitive* is his characteristic. These descriptors represent a general overview of his preferences in day-to-day life that may influence his peer mentoring style.

According to the HBDI® profile data summary, the work elements that peer mentors strongly relate to include *Planning* and *Implementation* (B-quadrant), *Writing* and *Expressing* (C-quadrant) and *Technical* and *Financial* (A-quadrant). These elements reflect the mental preferences at work, including his peer mentoring practice, and may align completely with general preferences. They may also stem from situations unique to his working environment, which include peer mentoring. When planning the peer mentoring intervention, he especially took care to make the intervention reach its goals. Implementing the plan fits the steps to be taken within an action research process. Writing and expressing was evident in his reporting on the outcome of the intervention. The technical and financial elements could be observed in the accuracy with which he handled all aspects of the peer mentoring process and report writing.

His communication style (essential in mentoring) includes well-articulated ideas presented in a logical format, step-by-step unfolding of the topic, explanation in writing and empathy for the listener. Visuals, an overview and long-term objectives may be overlooked, however. When problem-solving he focuses on value analysis, gathering data, following a step-by-step process, time lines, team processes and asking for others' input, while mediation, new ideas and sketching may not form part of it. When he might have struggled with questions such as: Do I have all the facts? How will others be affected? Will I be in control? Yet he kept the 'big picture' and aspects such as unusual possibilities in mind.

One of the participating peers (Respondent 1) reflects the following attributes to thinking that a contribution was made to the community of peer mentors. His profile is triple dominant with a preference code of 1112. His descriptors are *Sequential, Speaker, Controlled* and *Dominant* (B); *Talker* and *Emotional* (C); and *Critical* and *Mathematical*, with *Rational* representing his key descriptor (A). According to the HBDI® profile summary, work elements to which this respondent strongly relates include *Administration* (B-quadrant), *Teaching, Writing, Expressing* and *Interpersonal* (C-quadrant); and *Financial* (A-quadrant). Key descriptors and work elements represent his mental preferences at work and may be aligned completely with general preferences, or they may stem from situations unique to one's working environment, including where one is involved in peer mentoring interventions.

The following attributes and avoidances (Herrmann International, 2009) can be adapted to this respondent's participation in the peer mentoring intervention. His participation is divided into three categories – communication, problem-solving strategies and decision making. Communicating within a peer mentoring context, the communication style of Respondent 1 may include brief, clear and precise information, well-articulated ideas presented in a logical format, step-by-step unfolding of the topic, explanation in writing, empathy for the listener. Avoidances when communicating in peer mentoring and other contexts may be visuals, an overview, long-term objectives. The respondent's most natural problem-solving strategies include factual analysis, research, logic, re-engineering, step-by-step processes, time lines and team processes. What may be overlooked are mediation, new ideas and sketching. To take a decision, he may ask: Do I have all the facts? How will others be affected? Will I be in control? He might overlook the 'big picture' and unusual possibilities. Since these attributes of communication, problem-solving and taking decisions are aligned with those of peer mentors, it is assumed that they got along well, as little or no conflict would have been part of their peer mentoring.

Respondent 2 has a triple dominant profile coded as 2111. His descriptors are *Conservative, Detailed, Controlled* and *Reader* (B-quadrant), *Emotional* (C-quadrant) and *Imaginative* (D-quadrant), with *Logical* and *Critical* representing his key descriptor (A-quadrant). The work elements that he strongly relates to are *Organisation, Planning* and *Administrative; Teaching* and *Expressing; Integrating; Conceptualising* and *Innovating.* These elements reflect his mental preferences at work, which included peer mentoring. Work preferences may align completely with general preferences, or they may stem from situations unique to one's working environment, such as peer mentoring.

According to the HBDI® profile data summary, Respondent 2 preferred processing modes such as *Creative, Holistic, Interpersonal, Feeling, Planning* and *Organising.* Although the A-quadrant is least preferred, he is typically still fairly functional in the use of the logical and analytical aspects of this quadrant. His most comfortable communication approaches include written communication beforehand, providing an overview, idea chunks, involving others, personal touch and being sensitive to others, which are in contrast with the communication styles of the two peers above. He might overlook written schedule and plan and staying on track. It is clear that when communicating in a community of peer mentoring, his most natural problem-solving strategies include visualisation, brainstorming, intuition, building on the ideas of other team members, and implementation aspects. Again, these are not aligned with the problem-solving styles of the peers above. What may not be considered are observing strict procedures and all details. To take a decision, he may ask: Do I see all the hidden possibilities? Can I form a plan to make this work? How will others be affected? He may also fail to keep the details and a proper sequence in mind during the mentoring process.

The profile of Respondent 3 is multi-dominant with two primaries in the left mode and the third primary in the upper right. Her profile is characterised by its multi-dominance, yet, in a relative sense, it lacks a level of 'personal touch' that would be present if the lower right

C-quadrant was also a primary. According to the HBDI® profile data summary, her preference code is 1121.

Descriptors that are characteristic of Respondent 3 are *Artistic, Intuitive* and *Imaginative* (most descriptive of her D-quadrant), *Logical, Critical, Rational* and *Factual* (A-quadrant), and *Controlled* (B-quadrant). These descriptors represent a general overview of her mental preferences in day-to-day life. The work elements, including peer mentoring, to which she strongly relates include *Conceptualising, Creative, Analytical, Organisation* and *Planning*. Descriptors include organising, administrative preferences, conservative, safe-keeping preference, conceptual, holistic, creative and risk-orientated.

Her most comfortable communication approaches involve brief, clear and precise information, well-articulated ideas presented in a logical format, step-by-step unfolding of the topic, providing an overview, and using visuals, although she might overlook eye-to-eye contact, the personal touch and informality. Some of these attributes might have been a challenge to the other peer mentors. Her most natural problem-solving strategies are factual analysis, research, step-by-step processes, time lines, incubation and modelling. Her problem-solving style would be aligned with that of the peer mentors discussed above. It might not include team processes and feelings. To take a decision, she may ask: Do I have all the facts? What's the 'big picture'? Will I be in control? What may be excluded is asking about others' opinions and the impact of her decision on others. Again, some of the questions, such as the one about having the facts and being in control, are similar to the decision-making styles of the two styles explained above.

The profile of Respondent 4 is triple dominant with two primaries in the right mode and a third in the lower left. Her preference code is 2111. Key descriptors are *Emotional, Spiritual* and *Intuitive*. The other descriptors include *Imaginative, Conservative, Controlled, Logical* and *Rational*. The work elements she strongly relates to, and which will inform her peer-mentoring style, include *Teaching, Writing, Interpersonal, Conceptualising, Creativity, Organisation* and *Implementation*.

Her most comfortable communication approaches may include written communication beforehand, providing an overview, idea chunks, involving others and personal touch and sensitivity to others. What may be overlooked are data and facts. The most natural problem-solving strategies may include visualisation, brainstorming, intuition, building on ideas of other team members, and implementation aspects. Research, logic and problem definition may be overlooked. When she has to make decisions she might like the following questions answered: Are there hidden possibilities? Can I form a plan to make this work? How does my decision affect others? (without focusing on numbers, gathering facts and focusing on detail). When the attributes of her communication style, approach to problem-solving and decision-making are compared with the three examples above, it is clear how Respondent 4 with her different profile may have contributed to the peer mentoring process.

According to the HBDI® profile data summary, the preference code of Respondent 5 is 2112. He selected the following descriptors: *Talker, Emotional, Conservative, Spiritual, Intuitive, Critical, Reader*, with *Musical* his key descriptor. The work elements, which include involvement in peer mentoring and to which he strongly relates, include *Teaching, Writing, Expressing, Interpersonal, Integrating, Conceptualising, Creative* and *Innovating*.

The most comfortable communication approaches this respondent may have followed during the peer mentoring process may have included step-by-step unfolding of the topic, which is aligned with some of the mentors' communication styles explained above, such as step-by-step unfolding of the topic. His communication style would have included practical answers to 'who', 'what', 'when', 'where' and 'how', understanding how others react, personal touch and being sensitive to others. Data and facts, technical accuracy, visuals and an overview may be overlooked. The most natural problem-solving strategies may include a step-by-step method and time line principles (again both aligned with some of the respondents' approaches explained above), intuitive feelings and team processes. Defining the problem, critical analysis, visualisation and incubation might not form part of the communication strategy. To take a decision, this respondent is likely to ask (because of his profile): What is the appropriate sequence? How does my decision affect others? He might not include risk-taking and gathering facts.

According to Herrmann International (2009) the profile of Respondent 6 is the most common of all profiles, with a code of 2111. Descriptors selected are *Conservative, Detailed, Controlled, Critical, Rational, Imaginative*, and *Musical*, with *Emotional* his key descriptor. He is involved in peer mentoring, and his work elements include *Integrating, Creative, Innovating, Teaching, Expressing* and *Interpersonal* from the A-, C- and D-quadrants.

His comfortable communication approaches may include written communication beforehand, providing an overview, idea chunks, involving others, and personal touch and being sensitive to others, but may overlook data and facts and technical accuracy. From these attributes it can be deduced that Respondent 6 differs markedly from the others.

The same applies to problem-solving and decision-making. The most natural problem-solving strategies which may have been included are visualisation, brainstorming, intuition, building on the ideas of other team members, and implementation aspects. Research, logic and problem definition most probably will be secondary. When making decisions, it might be worth asking questions such as: Have I seen all the hidden possibilities? Can I form a plan to make this work? How will others be affected?

The emotive thinking and people-orientated attributes of the C-quadrant are evident and it is clear that these are the main aspects lacking in the other profiles. Since peer mentoring is in essence about people, all peer mentors had to use their strengths in this regard, and others were challenged to 'get out of their boxes' and develop the appropriate people skills.

In the same way as above, the communication style, problem-solving style and way of decision-making of Respondent 7 with a preference code of 1221 can be compared with all the other peer mentors. As the profile of Respondent 8 reflects the same code – 1221 – it corresponds with some of the scores and attributes above and is therefore not also analysed.

Suffice it to conclude that within this Whole Brain® approach to peer mentoring intervention, different ways of thinking and doing based on all participants' profiles enriched the mentoring process. The contribution of this case study to the current body of knowledge is constructing new meaning for peer mentoring by indicating the richness that a Whole Brain® approach to peer mentoring brings to the scholarship of mentoring.

4.7 Collaboration in higher education: applying the Whole Brain® principles

This section uses the Whole Brain® Walk-Around™ to explain different aspects of a multi-disciplinary collaboration project. The discussion starts in the A-quadrant highlighting the purpose of the project and then moves to the C-quadrant to share the Whole Brain® principles for multi-disciplinary collaboration between participants. This is followed by the details on the processes that were followed and implemented for effective management of the project (B-quadrant). Finally the reader will discover how the wealth contained within the Whole Brain® Model may enrich the design and development of learning tasks and material (D-quadrant).

4.7.1 *Purpose of the project*

The Department of Information Science in the Faculty of Engineering, Built Environment and Information Technology at the University of Pretoria is responsible for offering an annual semester module, information literacy, to approximately 8000 first-year students across all faculties.

The aim of the module is to empower students with the necessary information skills needed for successful undergraduate and postgraduate studies. Approximately 16 assistant lecturers present classes in computer laboratories to groups of 40 students, resulting in the assistant lecturers having to repeat the same lecture a number of times each day, up to five days a week. The assistant lecturers are postgraduate students who are busy with their own studies in a variety of disciplines across the University. They often do not have any background in facilitating of learning.

The textbook written by academics of the department, *Navigating Information Literacy* (Bothma et al., 2011) (Figure 4.52), is supplemented with PowerPoint slides and examples to show students step-by-step how to access databases. The module covers these topics:

- information sources and resources
- portals, gateways and library websites
- constructing a search query
- Internet searching
- searching databases and online journals
- organising and retrieving information on your computer
- ethical and fair use of information
- referencing and referencing techniques
- evaluating information and information sources
- writing assignments and research reports
- communication in the twenty-first century.

Although the module has an acceptable pass rate, the scholarly application of the applicable skills linked to the subject content and learning outcomes is limited and in some cases lacking in subsequent academic years of study (De Boer, Bothma and Olwagen, 2012). In this article it is reported that the traditional approach of education design and delivery of a 'one-size-fits-all' approach in mega classes could fall short of desired results because the lecturer is dealing with a composite group

Figure 4.52 The cover of Navigating Information Literacy, a prescribed textbook

of students with a preference distribution across all four quadrants of the Whole Brain® Model.

It can be accepted that in mega classes there is a composite array of thinking preferences distributed across the Whole Brain® Model. A second important fact, which is often overlooked, is that there is also an equal distribution of learning avoidances (non-preference thinking modes) across the four quadrants. Taking into account that 'learning avoidance turns students off – and a turned-off learner is a waste of educational time and effort' (Herrmann, 1996, 152), and considering the data generated in the baseline data (Figure 2.2) and 25 years of personal experience in higher education in the field of academic development of students and academic staff (De Boer, Steyn and Du Toit, 2001), a move away from a teaching methodology of 'one size fits all' was desired.

A multi-disciplinary team was put together by four project leaders to start a collaborative multi-disciplinary research project entitled:

'Facilitating Whole Brain® information literacy: an inter-disciplinary research project'. The collaboration for this research project involved groups and individuals from different disciplines at one university – information science specialists, educational consultants, instructional designers, librarians, staff development professionals, specialists in the field of higher education and a graphic designer (referred to as the project team in later discussions).

These are the research questions formulated for the project:

- What is the current status of the information literacy programme offered at the University of Pretoria in terms of promoting Whole Brain® learning?
- How can the Whole Brain® Thinking theory be utilised to improve effective learning?
- How can the principles of Whole Brain® learning be used to innovate the Information Literacy Programme?
- How can action research be implemented to ensure the continuous innovation of the Information Literacy Programme by individual lecturers?
- What additional learning material needs to be developed to facilitate Whole Brain® learning?

The different aspects of this project are illustrated in Figure 4.53 and discussed throughout our book:

- baseline study (generating different sets of data) (see Section 2.2.2)
- professional development of academic staff regarding their teaching practices and an induction programme for newly appointed academic staff (see Section 4.2.2)
- learning material design (see Section 5.4).

Every member understood their own profile and the value of the project team lay in the members' diverse thinking preferences, especially during brainstorming sessions.

The first action step for the team was to analyse the existing learning material (Figure 4.54) offered to the students by using Herrmann's Whole Brain® Model. The general conclusion was what they had expected – that not only the learning material but also the classroom activities primarily address the A- and B-quadrant preferences. Students who preferred Thinking Styles™ inherent to the C- and D-quadrants were not taken into account at all.

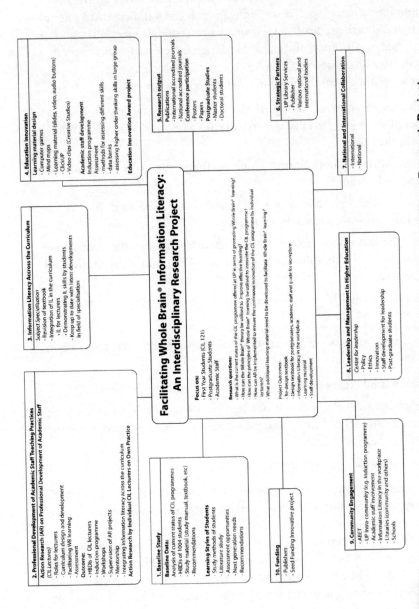

Figure 4.53 Facilitating Whole Brain® Information Literacy: An Interdisciplinary Research Project

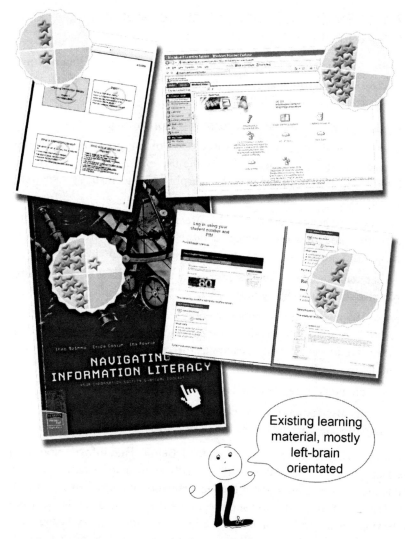

Figure 4.54 Analysis of prescribed textbook, Microsoft PowerPoint slides and database steps as outlined in Herrmann's Whole Brain® Model

The Department of Information Science also wanted to get feedback from the students on the course content and course presentation before starting to design supporting learning activities. They wanted to determine what the students viewed as shortcomings in the presentation of the module.

4.7.1.1 Feedback from students regarding the course content and presentation

Students' feedback was evaluated through semi-structured focus group interviews and questionnaires. The following information was obtained from the 2675 students who participated:

- 75 per cent reported that the course was worthwhile.
- Students reported that their expectations of the presentation of the course material were met as far as the use of PowerPoint slides, the Internet, the white board and the learning management system were concerned.
- However, 50 per cent stated that lecturers did not use diverse classroom activities, and that they expected more use of the textbook, videos, games and multimedia in the presentation of the content.
- 55 per cent stated that they would make use of a CD with exercises to practise skills on their own at home.
- Some chapters of the textbook were rated as important because they created an overall impression of the module; others were identified as difficult to present (by the assistant lecturers) and difficult to understand and learn (by the students).
- Some chapters were identified as just being boring.
- Students also remarked that classes could be offered in fewer periods as the allocated periods were not used fully by lecturers.

Taking into account the results from the baseline data, information from the Department's case studies, and the feedback from information literacy students, the academic staff of the Department committed themselves to the design of a toolkit for assistant lecturers that would address the needs of learners using the Whole Brain® Thinking methodology and ensure the same quality of facilitating of learning across all the classes.

The team decided to start off by identifying the most difficult chapter or chapters that most of the students struggled with, and to design additional learning material covering the Whole Brain® Model. Once this had been accomplished the next step would be to tackle the textbook chapter by chapter. The process to follow would be to analyse the content of Herrmann's Whole Brain® Model, to design activities that cover the whole spectrum of thinking preferences and to reflect on the activities, always ensuring that the toolkit includes a balanced array of Whole Brain® Thinking activities. A description of some of these activities is provided in Chapter 5.

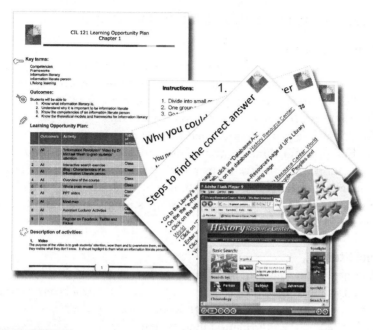

Figure 4.55 A lecturer's toolkit and a few learning tasks

Results obtained after the implementation of the toolkit and the Whole Brain® learning material and tasks (Figure 4.55) were very positive. Assistant lecturers and students increased their class attendance. Students stated that they frequently (45 per cent) or almost always (39 per cent) experienced variety or change in their classes, developed a greater sense of their own responsibility (88.6 per cent), developed self-confidence (81 per cent), reconsidered many of their values and attitudes (72 per cent) and developed learning style flexibility in order to learn in different ways (67.6 per cent).

4.7.2 People contributing to the project: multi-disciplinary collaboration

This section focuses on how the application of Whole Brain® principles improves multi-disciplinary collaboration. Collaboration, communication and the ability to work effectively in a team are essential to the success of any project.

4.7.2.1 Profiles of the collaborative team

Research leaders

The project was initiated by four research leaders. The 2211 generic profile of this team of four implies a double dominant primary for the D- and C-modes and typically represents characteristics that include the ability to be *creative* and *holistic*, and to *synthesise*.

The composite profile reveals that there is a strong preference for A-, D- and C-quadrant thinking and a lesser preference for the B-quadrant thinking mode. The preference map indicates a strong preference by one individual for A- and D-quadrant thinking, while the rest of the team prefers D-quadrant thinking and also some strong C-quadrant thinking (Figure 4.56).

Project team

The project team consisted of 15 individuals. The HBDI® profiles of each person participating in the project were used to compile a group average, group composite map and group preference map for the team members who worked on the information literacy design project.

The composite map (Figure 4.57) showed strong representation in each of the four quadrants. It culminated in a stronger tilt towards the C- and D-quadrants, with more individuals who preferred C- and D-quadrant thinking. There were only a few individuals in the group who preferred A- and B-quadrant thinking, which would be useful for addressing the A- and B-quadrant requirements of the project. From the map, the following challenges for the team were identified: lack of B-quadrant preferences for project implementation and the following possible causes of conflict:

- Individuals with strong A-quadrant preferences might hinder the brainstorming sessions if they start to analyse and evaluate the ideas too quickly, resulting in less creative solutions.

- Individuals with strong B-quadrant preferences might likewise hinder the creative process by insisting on organisation, execution and control of activities too early in the course of the project.

- Individuals with strong C-quadrant preferences might be offended by the 'matter-of-fact' way of A- and B-quadrant thinkers and want more time to process and discuss.

- Excessive sharing and discussions by C-quadrant thinkers could offend A- and B-quadrant thinkers who are more focused on executing the task.

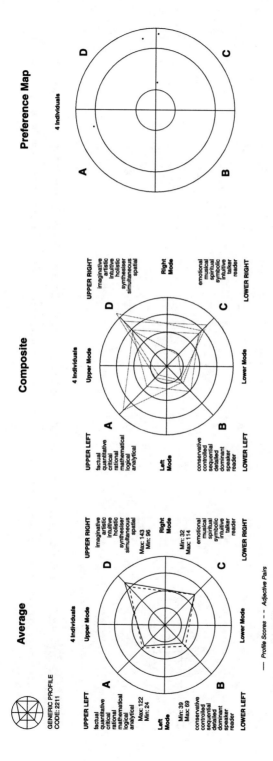

Figure 4.56 Profiles of the research team contributing to the project Facilitating Whole Brain® Information Literacy

The four-quadrant graphic is a registered trademark of Herrmann Global and is reproduced under written contract for display in this text. © 2012. All rights reserved

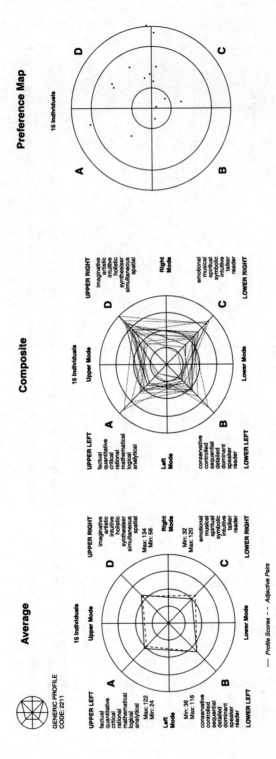

Figure 4.57 Profiles of the project team contributing to the project Facilitating Whole Brain® Information Literacy

The four-quadrant graphic is a registered trademark of Herrmann Global and is reproduced under written contract for display in this text. © 2012. All rights reserved

- Individuals with D-quadrant preferences who keep on generating new ideas, even in the later stages of the project, and should be cautioned to cease their idea generation to ensure that products are delivered on time, which would irritate them.

The project team preference map (Figure 4.58), where an individual's preference is represented by a single data point on the graph, confirmed that the strongest preferences of the team were for C- and D-quadrant thinking, so the individuals concerned already preferred working in the personalising and strategising quadrants. Preference maps also served to identify blind spots in a team. In the project team, this blind spot was for B-quadrant thinking preferences and the team would be challenged to deliver on the organisational aspect of the project.

Learning design team

The preferences of the learning design team (instructional designers, education consultant and graphic designer) were analysed as a subset of the project team. This group of eight individuals was responsible for participating in idea generation for the project. As a group on their own, they were also responsible for implementing these ideas by designing and developing the learning tasks and material. It was essential to understand the thinking preferences of this subgroup in order to ensure proper management of their activities.

When the composite and preference maps (Figure 4.58) of the learning design team were analysed, it became clear that synergy was for D-quadrant thinking. It is important to understand that similar Thinking Styles™ will gravitate towards one another and therefore important viewpoints and problem-solving strategies of other quadrants may be missed if these are not represented in the team's dominant thinking profile. It is also important that the learning design team had just one person with strong B-quadrant preferences (for organising and sequencing activities), which implied that this person would be the appropriate candidate to do the project management in this subgroup.

Before the outset of the project, all members of the collaborative team participated in professional development opportunities that were available to develop their knowledge and understanding of Whole Brain® principles to be able to make meaningful contributions to the project (see Section 4.2.3).

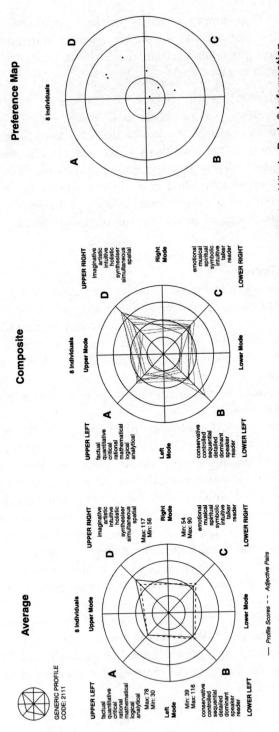

Figure 4.58 Profiles of the learning design team contributing to the project Facilitating Whole Brain® Information Literacy

4.7.2.2 Collaboration

Experiences gained during the collaboration to design and develop learning material (consequently referred to as the information literacy design project) are used to illustrate how this application of Whole Brain® principles enriches every aspect of the collaborative process.

The *Oxford Dictionary* (2012) defines multi-disciplinary as 'combining or involving several separate academic disciplines' and collaboration as 'united labour, co-operation; esp. in literary, artistic, or scientific work'. Collaboration has been used in various fields of study, such as social work, education, medicine, communication, history, environmental science and organisational behaviour. The unique interpretation given to collaboration by each of these disciplines has led to different understandings and descriptions of collaboration. For example, in medicine and education, collaboration is described as a process. Anthropologists and researchers of organisational behaviour management describe collaboration as a structure, while researchers in communication and sociology see collaboration as something that may be both structure and process (Petri, 2010; Bedwell et al., 2012). Henneman, Lee and Cohen (1995) argue that collaboration has been used in inappropriate ways in research and practice, in effect hindering its usefulness.

In response to the above claim, Bedwell et al. (2012) explored the constructs that explain collaboration to clarify the concepts and practical implications of collaboration. They propose the use of the following definition for collaboration: 'an evolving process whereby two or more social entities actively and reciprocally engage in joint activities aimed at achieving at least one shared goal' (2012, 130). Collaboration is described as 'an evolving process' as it is a dynamic process that can improve and develop as relationships grow over time. The 'social entities' denote 'individuals, teams, units, departments, functional areas, organizations' (2012, 130). Teamwork is only one subset of collaboration, as different combinations of individuals, teams and functional areas may work together in a collaborative project. Reciprocity is another key element of collaboration, as each of the parties should be engaged to work interdependently and contribute sufficiently (although not necessarily equally) towards the achievement of goal(s). The social entities need to commit to reach at least one shared goal to make collaboration possible. The goal(s) of the collaboration should be focused on some sort of joint activity, where social entities from various fields and domains join knowledge, resources and decision-making to solve a problem or to execute certain tasks.

Taking advantage of diverse thinking preferences

Multi-disciplinary collaboration implies that diverse individuals will join forces to achieve a specific goal. Diversity may manifest in various aspects such as age, race, language, interpersonal skills, thinking preferences, and definitely academic disciplines and experience. This diversity may benefit or hinder the collaboration (Van Knippenberg and Schippers, 2007). A team's success depends on its ability to leverage the characteristics of all of the team members to create a balanced team (Wysocki, 2002). A common understanding of Whole Brain® principles and thinking preferences within a collaborative group might support the collaboration positively on various levels.

The different qualities and characteristics that are inherent in each individual will have a direct influence on the collective unit (Bedwell et al., 2012). In a successful multi-disciplinary group, each member who participates is valued and appreciated for their disciplinary knowledge and skills. If individual preferences are understood, the individual's contributions are appreciated and valued not only as the artefacts of their knowledge base, but also as a creative contribution borne from a particular thinking preference. This leads to accepting ideas on a topic from an individual who might not be the 'specialist' in the field. However, acceptance of the ideas put forward by team members will have various spin-offs; for example, the idea of the 'novice' contributing on an equal level might stimulate the specialists' higher-order thinking and further stimulate their creative processes. Furthermore, the acceptance of each individual's contribution will most probably lead to building trust, which again has a positive impact on the collaboration as the collaborator continues to contribute more openly and eagerly. This stimulates free and open sharing of ideas and may result in higher levels of creativity within the group with a view to solving problems. For example, during the information literacy design project, one of the instructional designers with a strong C-quadrant preference illustrated with a short cartoon story how the use of storytelling (C-quadrant preference) could be used to demonstrate the value of particular learning material to the students. Although this person is not a specialist in information literacy but in learning design, the information specialists (lecturers) accepted the idea and started writing a series of cartoon stories that was implemented for each chapter of the textbook (see Section 5.4).

Enhancing team work

In a multi-disciplinary collaboration effort, the individuals who participate in the collaboration typically fulfil a specific role based on their preferences and specialist competencies. This might not necessarily lead to successful collaboration, as the collaboration in itself also needs certain functions to be fulfilled, such as leadership, organising and coordinating. It is therefore necessary to ensure that the right people perform these additional roles to ensure the success of the collaboration. Deploying and allocating the right individual to fulfil the correct function within the collaboration will lead to greater productivity within the team.

An additional advantage of understanding thinking preferences is selecting the right person in the group to perform the tasks of a specific role. This might lead to more effective task execution, as the person who has a preference for a specific task is allocated that task and can therefore function optimally. For example, specialists on the team may be responsible for a specific role or area arising from their expertise. If their thinking preference reveals other strengths that are needed for the success of the project, they may be allocated an extra role within the team. In the information literacy design project, one of the instructional designers was particularly strong in the B-quadrant, which indicated that she had stronger organising capabilities than the rest of the group. This led to the decision in the group to appoint her in the role of project manager, in addition to her (specialist) role as instructional designer. The success of the project depended on her willingness to use her natural ability to organise the activities, ensure that deadlines were met and make sure the project was completed on time.

According to Wysocki (2002), effective communication is key to the success of any collaboration. An advantage of the Whole Brain® Model is that it can be used for effective communication as part of a collaborative initiative (Herrmann, 1996). Right from the launch of a project, and throughout the collaboration, each of the four quadrants' communication preferences need to be incorporated when communicating. It is important that individuals with A-quadrant thinking preferences are informed about the 'what', for example the rationale, facts, cost and analysis of data. People with B-quadrant thinking preferences will want answers on 'how' things are going to be done and how the risks will be addressed. Individuals with C-quadrant thinking preferences would more often than not be satisfied with 'who' is involved, for example that all parties affected are engaged, values are considered and interpersonal relationships are taken into account. Individuals with D-quadrant thinking preferences will be concerned with answering the question 'why' – they want to be informed about the big picture or about the future impact that the collaboration will have, and be allowed the freedom to contribute. An example of how this was accomplished in the information literacy design project is the way buy-in was obtained from all collaborators during the initial stages of the project.

The Whole Brain® Model does not only provide guidelines on the content of what should be addressed during communication, but also suggests the manner in which the message should be conveyed in a collaborative context. In the compilation of end-products, e.g. report writing, the Whole Brain® principles should be applied. The ways in which team members would like to receive messages according to their preferred style of communication can be summarised as:

- A-quadrant: quantified, short and to the point (short, clear messages containing, for example, figures in spreadsheets)
- B-quadrant: details in sequential order with an appropriate format
- C-quadrant: examples to illustrate a point
- D-quadrant: metaphors, visual or colourful displays (Herrmann, 1996).

Managing potential conflict

The Whole Brain® Model also contributes to managing potential conflict within a collaborative group as it provides a way of understanding and managing the differences of opinion that typically occur in a diverse group of collaborators. Conflict may well arise between individuals with opposing thinking quadrants or modes, since their preferences typically clash. It can also be difficult for single dominant persons to understand the viewpoints of individuals who represent other thinking quadrants, and this may lead to conflict that could be difficult to defuse.

Successful project teams should be mindful of individuals' preferences that are least preferred or even avoided. Without going into excessive detail about effective communication between the quadrants, we would like to highlight a few typical examples. The single dominant A-quadrant's possible avoidance of expressing emotions and considering team members' feelings while pushing for attaining a goal, as opposed to engaging with others during a stressful situation, might lead to conflict. The inability of single dominant C-quadrant persons to minimise interpersonal relationships and to express their own ideas, and their avoidance to get straight to the point during discussions, may also lead to conflict. Individuals with single dominant B-quadrant preferences often demonstrate an inability to let go or to allow for flexibility and risk, and this can frustrate a creative team. The single dominant D-quadrant's avoidance of structure, processes, staying focused on one aspect and rigid time management will in turn infuriate other quadrants.

During the information literacy research project the collaborators endeavoured to find a balance that would address the preferences of all four quadrants. The first step was to reach an understanding among all collaborators of what the Whole Brain® principles mean for collaboration. The group attended a workshop to introduce the model, and each received their individual profile and information pack, which assisted them to understand themselves better. Time was allocated for sharing their profiles with one another, and that led to an appreciation of diverse thinking preferences and avoidances.

4.7.3 Process followed: focus on project management

In any project management process, one should acknowledge that thinking style diversity will be evident throughout the different phases of the project. Understanding the mental diversity of each team member will not only improve team effectiveness, but ultimately promote the quality of the end-result. Wysocki (2002) ascribes the failure of projects to inadequate communication, ineffective use of the project team and inappropriate project management processes. He published an extensive work on the application of Whole Brain® principles within project teams and in project management, in which he concluded that 'no other assessment tool in the market has the breadth of application to project management as the HBDI® [Survey]' (Wysocki, 2002, 88).

Wysocki (2002) recommends that the Whole Brain® principles be used to:

- establish the profile of the project itself
- establish the profile of the project team
- develop and deploy the project team.

4.7.3.1 The profile of a project

Every project typically contains characteristics that correspond with all four of the Whole Brain® Thinking quadrants. In extreme cases a project may have dominance in only one of the quadrants. Projects that require a high incidence of logical processing, formulae and data analysis (probably associated with problem-solving, diagnosing, explaining how things work and clarifying issues) fall in the A-quadrant (Herrmann, 1996; Wysocki, 2002; Scheepers et al., 2011). Projects that require high organisation, where planning and an ordered and controlled environment are necessary, fall in the B-quadrant. Such projects typically follow proven processes and procedures and have repetitive elements. Projects with C-quadrant characteristics are most probably dependent on a high degree of interaction between individuals or groups of people and agreement on matters by all parties. Such projects typically require a good communication plan and significant interaction between the project manager, team members and client(s) to create a shared vision and collaboration between all parties. D-quadrant characteristics of a project include the requirements to experiment, find or create innovative solutions, take risks and effect change. Typical of such projects is that they involve the establishment of a new product or new ways of doing things (Herrmann, 1996; Wysocki, 2002).

The information literacy design project had characteristics of all four Whole Brain® Thinking quadrants. The Whole Brain® creative process (described later in this chapter) was adapted to meet the needs of the project. The highest requirements were for the C- and D-quadrants, as the success of the multi-disciplinary collaboration required a high level of interaction between different groups of people (C-quadrant) and new learning material and tasks had to be designed and developed (D-quadrant). For example, the D-quadrant requirements of the project included new and creative ideas and the design of new learning material and tasks to present information literacy in a Whole Brain® Thinking manner. The information literacy design project also had A-quadrant requirements, as the analysis of the learning material and student feedback at the beginning of the project were all associated with A-quadrant thinking. Since the project had to be delivered on time, it was necessary to employ B-quadrant characteristics to ensure everyone knew who had to do what, at what stage (the when and the how).

4.7.3.2 Profile of the project team

The profiles of the project team members shed light on the overall inclination of the team for specific thinking preferences. It is essential that the correct 'fit' be obtained between the project requirements and thinking preferences within the project team, to ensure the success of the project. A Whole Brain® Thinking team consisting of people with different strengths can obtain optimum problem-solving results (Lumsdaine and Lumsdaine, 1995). According to Herrmann (1996) and Wysocki (2002), the way people think relates to what they prefer to do. As people are more inclined to do what they prefer to do, it will be beneficial in a project to get the 'right' person allocated to the correct function so that the team would perform better and have high motivation to carry out the tasks required.

This 'correct fit' principle was applied in the information literacy design project. The individuals who participated in the project were all invited based on the expertise they have in a specific discipline. The team consisted of information science specialists, librarians, instructional designers, educational consultants, staff development professionals, specialists in the field of higher education and a graphic designer. Each group within this multi-disciplinary collaboration context had to be convinced of the necessity of the project, the importance of using the Whole Brain® Model and the products that were needed to ensure the success of the project. All the members of the group were introduced to and understood the Whole Brain® Model, and they were alerted to their individual preferences and potential avoidances and the effect these preferences could have on the project. They were also made aware that they would have to lead at times and would be required sometimes to stretch outside their mental comfort zones to address the expectations and needs of the project.

The group average map for the whole project team (Figure 4.57) revealed that the team profile was a perfect fit with the project requirements for strong C- and D-quadrant thinking preferences.

As proper coordination and organisation of the project were essential to its success and timely delivery, the early recognition of the B-quadrant as a possible avoidance area of the team was essential. It was necessary to identify at least one individual in the team who had the best thinking preference (and ability) to organise the activities of the team, perform the administrative tasks, and document the decisions taken at meetings. Reflecting on the project, the acknowledgment of this important aspect at the beginning of the project was an important contributory factor to its overall success.

4.7.3.3 The creative process

During the life cycle of a project, different quadrants may be involved in the different phases of a project. In the design project for instance, a clear cycle developed. This cycle closely linked up with the Whole Brain® Creative Process (Figure 4.59) and required that diverse thinking preferences and associated abilities be applied during the cycle. An understanding of these requirements within the project ensured that the person with the most appropriate thinking preference could be assigned to take the lead during the different phases of the project.

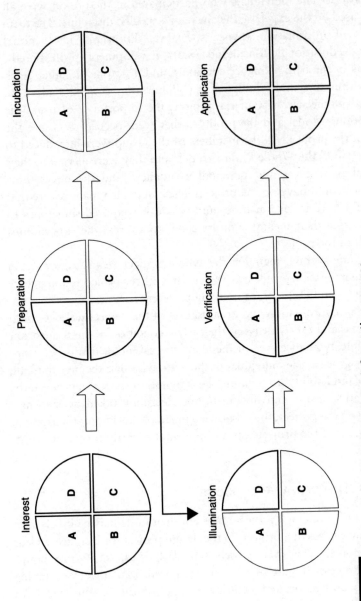

Figure 4.59 The six steps of the Whole Brain® creative process

Source: Herrmann (1996, 217)

The Whole Brain® creative process (Herrmann, 1996) proved helpful during collaboration within the information literacy design project to create learning material and tasks (Scheepers et al., 2011). The process consists of six steps: interest, preparation, incubation, illumination, verification and application, as depicted in Figure 4.59 (Herrmann, 1996, 217).

At the start of the collaborative information literacy design project, it was necessary to obtain buy-in from all the different stakeholders and ensure their motivation to collaborate fully. Motivation of the team members was enhanced by getting each team member's attention and demonstrating the relevance of the project as highlighted by Keller (1987). Since every member has different thinking preferences, different aspects of the project can be expected to capture their attention or seem relevant to them. This is where the first step of the Whole Brain® creative process plays an important role. In order to create interest among a group of people, it is necessary to address all four quadrants during the very first session or meeting. Once all members of the team are interested, they may be more motivated to participate and to engage in the process by contributing to the best of their ability.

During the first work session of the information literacy design project, interest was raised and motivation created through various factors that addressed the different quadrants. Facts and a quantitative analysis of the students' feedback on the module, which indicated the need for change, sparked the interest of those individuals with a preference for the A-quadrant. The interest of individuals with B-quadrant thinking preferences was ignited by the detail of the students' feedback, the structure of the envisioned project, and the organisation of learning tasks into the different quadrants of the Whole Brain® Model for learning and facilitating learning. The fact that the project would contribute to learning fuelled the interest of those collaborators with C-quadrant thinking preferences, while the opportunity to influence the future of the module and to create new learning material and tasks fuelled the interest of the D-quadrant thinkers.

Once all parties shared their interest to participate, the information literacy design project entered the preparation phase. The collaborators used their A- and B-quadrant thinking abilities to work through the detail and analyse the chapters of the prescribed textbook starting with those that were identified as most problematic by the students and assistant lecturers.

Each individual then entered the incubation phase, during which they had to use the C- and D-quadrants to reflect on and think of possible

Whole Brain® learning material and tasks for each chapter. The illumination phase, during which the D-quadrant was actively used, consisted of brainstorming work sessions that were conducted for each chapter. The whole project team brainstormed potential Whole Brain® learning material and tasks to enhance the existing learning material. The end result of these work sessions was a list of ideas for each chapter.

From the outset of the information literacy design project, the collaborators agreed to hold regular brainstorming work sessions during which members would be allowed to come up with and share ideas, with a view to enhancing each chapter with Whole Brain® learning material and tasks. These sessions typically favoured C- and D-quadrant preferences, because ideas were discussed and reconceptualised over and over. It was sensed that some individuals with strong A- and B-quadrants at times experienced these sessions as frustrating, as they did not always appreciate the vagueness or lack of structure and closure that are typical of a brainstorming process. Their attempts to derail the creative process by analysing ideas and allocating tasks too soon in the brainstorming session were seen as counteractive by the strong D-dominants in the group. These attempts were politely nipped in the bud to ensure stimulation of as many ideas as possible during the brainstorming work sessions. Collaborators with D-quadrant preferences enjoyed these work sessions, as they allowed freedom to explore new ideas and generate as many solutions as possible to enhance learning. Collaborators with C-quadrant preferences enjoyed the sessions because of the collegial atmosphere, which allowed for sharing and discussions. Once everyone understood that one starts with the end in mind (the future), and that generating ideas was only a first step, the next step that needed attention was to analyse the different ideas.

This subsequent step was achieved by means of follow-up meetings between the subject specialists and instructional designers focusing on A- and B-quadrant thinking. During these meetings the brainstormed ideas were analysed and evaluated to determine which ideas would be most suitable and practical to implement. At this point, individuals were assigned tasks, timelines were set and a learning opportunity plan was formulated for each chapter. Often six or more people were involved during these meetings. Individuals with D-quadrant preferences were gently reprimanded every time they deviated from the process and attempted to generate more ideas, so as to ensure that productivity was not affected by their tendency to generate more possibilities. Because all members of the group understood the Whole Brain® principles, they appreciated the corrective actions that were taken at different stages in the execution of the project to ensure creativity, but at the same time to stay on track to deliver the products on time.

Another work session was scheduled for each of the chapters to determine which of the tasks on the list of ideas would be developed and implemented. This constituted the verification phase and required analysis and evaluation of the ideas to determine the suitability and practical implications of each idea.

In addition to leaders who took on the role of managing the different stages of the information literacy design project in a Whole Brain® Thinking manner, individuals also had separate discussions with one another to try and understand the internal conflict that either occurred because of their diverse thinking during work sessions or that they experienced during meetings. After a few of these discussions, the group understood the core areas of conflict. This led to self-reflection and self-management by each individual regarding their experienced internal conflict, as they now understood the thinking preferences of the others and how they harmonise or clash with one another.

During the application phase, the new Whole Brain® learning material and tasks were developed. These were demonstrated during a work session and at the same time evaluated by the whole team to determine – before implementation – if the learning material and tasks addressed all four Whole Brain® Thinking quadrants in a balanced way. This process served as a feedback loop and the ideas generated for a chapter served as inspiration for the team to develop new and better learning tasks for the next chapter. Many of the group members were so inspired by this process that team members who had described themselves as 'not creative' ventured into new territory (less preferred quadrants). They stretched outside their comfort zones to create learning material and tasks that they would not normally have done. This confirmed Herrmann's statement that 'creativity can be unleashed with greater efficiency and success with an individual or a group that has been trained in the creative process' (Herrmann, 1996, 221) and that individuals have access to their lesser preferred modes should they choose to access them.

4.7.4 Product development: Whole Brain® learning material

All four quadrants should be included in teaching and learning tasks. Cognitive functions are accommodated when teaching tasks are constructed to comply with a student's preferred way of thinking (Steyn,

1998). Structuring educational tasks to incorporate the expectations of students in all four quadrants enhances the full development of student potential. This will accommodate students' thinking preferences and areas of lower preference, while areas of avoidance are activated (De Boer, Steyn and Du Toit, 2001). For example, if the learning content contains fact-based data and research results, a student with a strong thinking preference for the A-quadrant will feel comfortable if the content is presented in a straightforward, lecturing type of instruction. For a student with a thinking preference for the C-quadrant, fact-based data and research results should be constructed to include group discussion and personal involvement.

The focus of the project was therefore on developing C- and D-quadrant tasks, but through reflection also to ensure that there is a balance of learning activities across the Whole Brain® Thinking spectrum.

Examples of the information literacy Whole Brain® learning tasks and material that were developed by the multi-disciplinary team by using the Whole Brain® creative process are presented and discussed in Section 4.7.3.3.

4.8 Conclusion

Students must be taught flexible thinking, creative problem-solving and teamwork skills so they can cope successfully with a constantly changing environment. Lumsdaine and Binks (2003) postulate that if C- and D-quadrant skills had been integrated into programmes from the onset, curriculum direction would have been far more innovative. Unless a comprehensive facilitating of learning model that embraces Whole Brain® principles is adopted, curriculum change remains difficult to implement. Often Engineering Faculty members who are involved in and responsible for curriculum restructuring meet considerable resistance to change from their peers. Getting faculty members to buy-in and actually adopt the necessary broad-based changes in engineering education that will embrace C- and D-quadrant thinking is difficult. On the other hand, resistance to change also comes from the students themselves. Their thinking preference is for A- and B-quadrant thinking and they consider a new approach to facilitate learning as a threat.

Understanding the Whole Brain® Model and individual thinking preferences is an essential requisite for multi-disciplinary collaboration. It supports the collaborative process through allowing personal growth, improving creativity and cultivating relationships. As collaborators start to understand and appreciate their own and each other's thinking preferences in different contexts, the communication between members and conflict management skills are enhanced within the group. Understanding one another leads to greater respect and appreciation for, and trust in, each other's contributions. The Whole Brain® Model also serves to help identify the correct individual or group to fulfil extra roles that invariably exist within any collaboration. When mental models are understood and shared with one another, they enhance communication and team work, accelerate knowledge creation and innovation, and improve learning and information management (Lumsdaine and Lumsdaine, 1995, 49).

Project management is greatly enhanced when the principles of the Whole Brain® Model are implemented. This model may be used to determine the profile of a project so as to ensure that the correct team is assembled to address the requirements of the project. The project team profiles provide strong instruments to indicate upfront where the strengths and possible blind spots or weaknesses within a project team might exist. These blind spots or weaknesses can then be proactively addressed to ensure that the project does not suffer. The team members' thinking preferences should preferably be aligned with the specific tasks and phases within the project to ensure maximum productivity and success. The additional implementation of the Whole Brain® creative process serves as a powerful tool to enhance creativity in projects that require creative thinking.

5

Learning material that makes a difference

Abstract: This chapter focuses on the design and development of Whole Brain® learning material and tasks, and describes how instructional design processes and products may be enhanced with the use of the Whole Brain® Model. We describe exemplars from an information literacy module and provide an analysis of these examples to illustrate how each example addresses Whole Brain® learning, facilitating of learning and assessment.

Keywords: Whole Brain® learning material, Whole Brain® learning tasks, motivation, instructional design, assessment.

5.1 Introduction

Learning material has been used for centuries to illustrate theoretical facts in a more concrete way and to allow students not only to learn more and better, but also to apply basic knowledge to life and work. The growth in technology through the ages has contributed to the plethora of learning material that is available today. The learning material each lecturer creates personally can easily be augmented with material from textbooks, photos, illustrations, podcasts, videos, films, information from the World Wide Web, open educational resources, e-books, and so on.

Responsible selection of the best learning material for a particular learning opportunity is a skill that requires a lecturer to take various aspects into consideration. The design of learning material requires a thoughtful exploration of the context in which learning and facilitating learning will occur. In the first place, these learning contexts consist of:

- lecturers as facilitators of learning and their teaching philosophy (philosophy of facilitating learning), thinking preferences and avoidances
- students with their pre-knowledge, thinking preferences and avoidances
- the nature of the field of specialisation
- the curriculum of a specific module, which includes:
    - learning outcomes that need to be addressed and achieved
    - learning material and learning opportunities that are designed and structured to challenge students to attain competencies at a higher level
    - assessment strategies and opportunities that must provide evidence that students have achieved the particular learning outcomes

- the larger institutional system (Biggs, 1996).

Second, the lecturer also needs to consider the inherent characteristics of specific learning material. The coding possibilities for different learning material are not the same, e.g. movement will best be illustrated through the use of video, while the pronunciation of a new word in the students' vocabulary is better addressed through audio recordings. Third, in order to avoid overload, a lecturer has to take note of the time a student will need to read text, watch a video or listen to audio, process the material and understand the message.

Finally, the lecturer has to think about how particular learning material or a task will engage the student. Edgar Dale (1969) developed a 'cone of experience', which provides a guide to lecturers in selecting learning tasks. The cone illustrates how various educational experiences relate to reality. The tasks or activities at the base of the cone represent reality or the closest aspects to real, everyday life, e.g. an apprenticeship or internship. As one progresses through each level above the base of the cone, the student moves further away from real-life experience, and the abstractness of the experience increases. The use of verbal symbols or text provides the most abstract experience. The cone also incorporates the student's use of various senses (sight, smell, hearing, touching, movement) with most senses being involved at the bottom, and fewer senses being used as one moves up each level. The larger the number of sensory channels that are involved while working with a particular resource, the better the chance that more students can learn from it.

All of the above components therefore need to be addressed when Whole Brain® learning and facilitating of learning are brought into a module or programme.

5.2 Instructional design

The design of learning material and tasks forms part of a process known as instructional design or instructional systems design. According to Reiser, the field of instructional design

> encompasses the analysis of learning and performance problems, and the design, development, implementation, evaluation and management of instructional and noninstructional processes and resources intended to improve learning and performance in a variety of settings, particularly educational institutions and the workplace (2001, 53).

The instructional systems design field, which had its origin during World War II, developed through the subsequent decades, influenced by the learning theories and educational research that prevailed in each period.

Instructional designers follow a systematic approach that involves developing new learning programmes or material that can be condensed into the colloquial term ADDIE (analysis, design, development, implementation and evaluation) (Molenda, 2003). Although various models exist to describe the instructional design process, only the ADDIE process is discussed for simplicity's sake. The analysis phase requires an investigation of students' needs and characteristics and the learning objectives or outcomes of the learning module or programme. During the design phase, the results from the analysis phase are used to:

- create learning objectives and outcomes
- write the assessment criteria
- design learning material and tasks that will enable students to meet the stated objectives and outcomes.

During the design of any learning material, the lecturer or instructional designer should strive to achieve constructive alignment. Constructive alignment, a term coined by Biggs (1996), has had a great impact on higher education and combines the ideas of constructivism and instructional alignment.

Constructivism (as described in Chapter 3) requires students to create their own meaning during a module, and this necessitates a student-centred approach to learning. Students have actively to interpret and construct their own new knowledge representation during individual and collective tasks (Biggs, 1996; O'Connor, 2009; Slabbert, De Kock and Hattingh, 2009).

Instructional alignment as introduced by Cohen (1987) addresses the tasks of the lecturer or instructional designer to ensure that the curriculum, methods of facilitating learning and assessment are aligned with one another. Biggs (1996) argues that constructivism should form the framework that guides decision making throughout the stages of instructional design. This integration of constructivism and instructional alignment should be achieved at three key points:

- setting of clear learning outcomes that describe the level of performance of students with regard to the specific knowledge and skills they should achieve, as well as attitude, values and virtues that the student should develop

- designing methods of facilitating learning and a learning environment that will place students in the appropriate contexts to elicit the applicable learning outcomes

- setting assessment tasks that will provide the necessary evidence to prove that students have achieved the learning outcomes.

The designed learning material and tasks are then created during the development phase. Once the students and lecturer start using the learning material and tasks, the implementation phase is reached. Evaluation is a central theme throughout the application of the ADDIE model (Figure 5.1). Formative evaluation is used continuously and iteratively during the first four phases to make revisions where necessary. During the analysis phase, the instructional designer will for example evaluate whether the set outcomes apply to the specific group of students studying a module, then during the design phase determine whether the designed learning tasks for a particular outcome will address that outcome or ensure that students will be able to meet the assessment criteria. During the development phase the prescribed design specifications will be evaluated to determine their practicality. Summative evaluation of the material and tasks is carried out during or at the end of the implementation phase to gather data that will be used to modify or augment the module or programme.

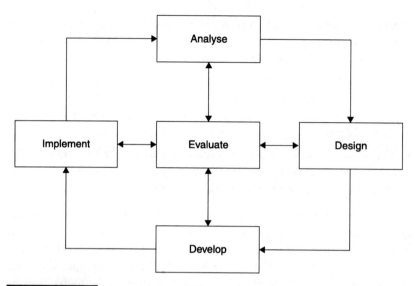

Figure 5.1 The ADDIE process of instructional design

The Whole Brain® Model enhances the products and process of instructional design. All instructional designers who design learning material (or every lecturer who designs learning tasks) have their own set of thinking preferences, which might influence them to design and develop in favour of elements that support their personal thinking preferences. The Whole Brain® Model provides an invaluable guide, which can direct the designer to enrich different ADDIE phases or any other instructional design models. These are some of the ways in which the analysis phase may be augmented:

- The analysis of the students can be enriched by the understanding that, although there might be a slight shift towards certain quadrants within very specialised groups, every group of students will constitute a 'Whole Brain® Thinking group'.

- Analysis of the learning outcomes that need to be addressed within a particular module can provide a clear indication of which of the four quadrants will have to be emphasised to achieve a particular learning outcome. For example, the requirement that a visual art student should be able to provide a particular product within a scheduled time will require the student to display strong visual and conceptual competencies that are typical of the D-quadrant, combined with planning and organising abilities that are described in the B-quadrant. The learning material and tasks should therefore make provision for the development of visual, conceptional, planning and organising skills to ensure the student achieves the learning outcomes.

- Existing learning material could be evaluated against the Whole Brain® Model for Learning and Facilitating of Learning to determine the extent to which the material addresses each quadrant of the Whole Brain® Model.

- The same could be done with existing learning tasks to determine the extent to which Whole Brain® learning and Whole Brain® facilitating of learning are addressed for each quadrant.

Whole Brain® learning principles and principles of facilitating learning also enhance the design phase by providing an instrument that might augment the design of learning material and interventions. Combining a variety of learning material and ways of facilitating learning from the different quadrants of the model ensures that all thinking preferences of students will be addressed and that less preferred but equally necessary preferences are also attended to. The Whole Brain® Model for Learning and Facilitating of Learning can be used in exactly the same way to make a formative and summative evaluation of the newly developed learning material and interventions.

Instructional design should also include approaches to enhance students' motivation to learn. It is important to pay attention to the motivational aspects of learning material, as motivation is the critical factor that inspires and sustains learning behaviour (Berliner and Gage, 1998). Motivational design provides a 'process of arranging resources and procedures to bring about changes in motivation' (Keller, 2006, para. 2). The goal is to increase students' intrinsic motivation to learn by creating learning material and interventions that grab the attention and support learning outcomes without being purely entertaining (Keller, 2006). However, in the context of Whole Brain® learning as proposed in our book, the constructivist approach as discussed in the section on learning theories for adults has 'deep learning' as a goal.

Keller's (1987) model describes four conditions for motivation – attention, relevance, confidence and satisfaction – the ARCS Model. Attention is essential for learning. Getting someone's attention might be easy, but sustaining it may prove to be a challenge. One of the strategies that support getting and sustaining attention involves adding variability to and ensuring participation in the classroom. The Whole Brain® Model provides an instrument for quality learning and quality of facilitating learning whereby lecturers can address the requirement for variability to sustain attention. Choosing and integrating learning material and tasks from each of the four quadrants of the model will have a positive impact on the attention levels of students, as will be illustrated later in this chapter.

The second requirement, relevance, may be achieved through supporting students to associate their previous learning experience with the new learning material and to use real-life tasks that present the importance of competencies that will be needed in future. Keller (1987) describes various strategies that may be used to enhance students' experience of learning material as relevant to them:

- Relate new information to the experience of students.
- Demonstrate the intrinsic worth of specific knowledge.
- Highlight the future usefulness of a specific topic.
- Satisfy the needs of students for affiliation and achievement.
- Model relevance through own enthusiasm or enthusiastic guest lecturers.
- Provide choice to students with regard to alternative methods and personal choices.

The Whole Brain® Model provides an instrument by means of which the last-mentioned strategy, providing choice to students, can be attained easily.

Confidence levels can also be enhanced through the use of the Whole Brain® Model, especially where particular thinking skills are required within a field of specialisation. A lecturer will or should purposefully include learning material and tasks that require students to use the particular Whole Brain® Thinking quadrant(s) to practise the necessary thinking skills. As students are required to work through tasks or learning material that might be situated in a quadrant that is naturally avoided by them, practice in the use of the lesser preferred quadrants might develop their confidence as they become more proficient. For example, students who usually avoid A-quadrant analytical thinking might grow more confident and hence be more motivated to complete a specific module when they have been forced to develop analytical skills by means of the learning tasks provided by the lecturer.

A lecturer can contribute to the satisfaction that students experience by allowing ample opportunity for them to practise and use their newly acquired skills and constructed knowledge. It is also important to ensure that timely feedback is provided in a constructive and inspiring way. Keller (1987) advises that negative influences such as threats and surveillance should be avoided. Inclusion of timely feedback and clear directions on what needs to be done will prevent the A-quadrant thinkers' struggle with vagueness. Allowing time to develop new skills and knowledge may alleviate the loathing of excessive strictness experienced by students with a preference for the D-quadrant. Students with B-quadrant preferences will most probably be accommodated through skills practice, while the personal attention provided with feedback will most probably fulfil the need for interaction of students with a C-quadrant preference.

5.3 Blended learning environments

The introduction of the Internet has irrevocably changed learning and the higher education arena. In the late 1990s futurists predicted that e-learning or web-based learning would result in changes and trends ranging from the incremental adoption to the radical conquest of e-learning and a gradual demise of traditional environments within higher education (Drucker, 1997).

Early experiences with online learning have confirmed that new learning and collaboration technologies such as learning management systems and online discussions are beneficial as far as convenience, quality, increased effectiveness and lower cost of learning opportunities are concerned. However, scholars also revealed that students who used these fully online courses need more choices, engagement, social contact, relevance and context to learn successfully (Singh and Reed, 2001). The lessons learned have resulted in a new movement in teaching and learning that is characterised by combinations of traditional and new learning technologies.

As early as 2002, Graham B. Spanier, President of Penn State University, suggested that the convergence of classroom and online education was 'the single greatest unrecognized trend in higher education today' (Young, 2002, A33). This new trend became known as blended learning, hybrid learning or mixed learning. Eight years later, Chew and Jones confirmed Spanier's statement and pronounced that of all 'instructional methods in the modern day, the term "blended learning" is pervasive among higher educational institutions' (2010, 71).

In 2005, the participants of the Sloan C workshop on blended learning approved the definition of blended learning as 'courses/programmes that integrate online with traditional face-to-face class tasks in a planned, pedagogically valuable manner, where a portion (institutionally defined) of face-to-face time is replaced by online activity' (Picciano, 2006, 97).

Blended learning therefore provides flexibility and allows the lecturer to take advantage of the benefits of different learning environments and technologies (Table 5.1) that focus on optimising the achievement of learning outcomes. Other benefits of a blended model include reduced

Table 5.1	Advantages and challenges of the contact and e-learning environments	
	Advantages	Challenges
Contact environment	Fast-paced, spontaneous verbal communication	Communication is temporary in nature
	Intensive interpersonal communication	Very expensive
	Opportunity to build social relations	Large class sizes may impede social interaction
	Opportunity to practise practical skills	Communication and understanding might be hampered by noise, or the language proficiency of lecturers and students
Online environment	Provides a convenient and flexible environment for students	Students need guidance on how to learn online
	Expands student access to resources within an institution's educational offerings	Design of effective online learning environments to support students
	Emphasises written communication that encourages reflection and precision of expression	Students with dyslexia and students communicating in a second or third language might experience the environment as very challenging
	Allows students to collaborate and work together at different times (asynchronous) although they are at different locations	Students must take greater responsibility for their own learning
	Provides resource rich environments for students needing additional support	Students from disadvantaged backgrounds may be further deprived by the use of technologies
	Reduces class time	Some lecturers and students have a poor level of computer and information technology literacy

contact time, while it also allows for educational diversity, improved learning, higher retention rates and lower costs to the students and institution (Bleed, 2006; Dalsgaard and Godsk, 2007). The advantages and challenges of the contact and e-learning environments are shown in Table 5.1, adapted from Garrison and Kanuka (2004) and Hughes (2007).

Blended learning does not mean that online learning material or tasks are just added on to or duplicate face-to-face sessions. It requires a fundamental reconceptualisation of learning and strategies for facilitating learning to strike a harmonious balance between the face-to-face and online environments, resulting in a good blend that represents 'a quantum shift . . . in terms of the nature and quality of the educational experience' (Garrison and Kanuka, 2004, 97). This blend differs from module to module (programme to programme), as the learning outcomes, student characteristics, resources and educational philosophy of the lecturer vary. Troha (2002, para. 10) proposes the development of a 'Content/Learning Activities Outline' to enhance the design of blended learning. This outline is a table in which the learning outcomes of a module are listed next to each learning task that would best promote the achievement of each learning outcome in the face-to-face environment. Other learning tasks that could augment the attainment of each learning outcome in the online environment are listed in a third column. A choice is then made on which environment would best address each learning outcome. By applying this process, a blended model is developed, with the focus on effective learning. Lotriet, Jorissen and Nagel (2008) expand on this idea by adding administrative, support and assessment components to the learning material and learning tasks so as to ensure that all components of facilitating learning are included when blended learning is designed. They emphasise that the context in which the module is presented should form the basis for designing the blended learning. The context includes the field of specialisation, the lecturer's educational philosophy, the profile of the students (age, year of study, preparedness and disabilities) and the contextual challenges within the module and the environment in which it is presented, e.g. class size and geographical distribution of students.

Singh (2003) reports on an increasing number of studies that indicate that blended learning proves to be more effective than any single learning mode. A meta-analysis of experimental and quasi-experimental studies of online and blended programmes that made significant use of the web for facilitating learning further proved the effectiveness of blended learning as documented in a report by the Department of Education of the USA

(US Department of Education, 2009). This report indicates that blended learning is more effective than face-to-face learning on its own, not because of the mode through which the learning is facilitated, but because of the differences in learning material and related learning outcomes to be achieved through the different modes, pedagogy employed and learning time available to students. Although the programmes reported in the different studies (US Department of Education, 2009) used the online component in different variations, the only two variables that had a positive impact on learning outcomes were the use of blended learning rather than fully online programmes, and increased time on task for online students. The report (US Department of Education, 2009) also indicates that the best results are obtained in the online environment if the pedagogical approach follows a 'facilitator'-directed expository or collaborative interaction with other students. Programmes in which students had to learn independently in the online environment through the manipulation of digital artefacts did not show a significantly positive impact (US Department of Education, 2009). It is therefore clear that careful attention should be paid to how students use the online environment as part of a blended learning model to ensure the greatest learning value for students.

Blended learning caters very well for different thinking style preferences. The contact environment provides opportunities to address the needs of students with different thinking preferences. Fact-based lectures, research in laboratories and solving case studies most probably address A-quadrant preferences, while the interpersonal communication between the lecturer and students and among students themselves most probably addresses the needs of students with C-quadrant preferences. Students with B-quadrant thinking preferences should benefit from practising practical skills in the contact environment, while the use of explorative tasks, illustrations, pictures and photos most probably activates D-quadrant thinking.

Similarly, the online environment may activate students' thinking in each Whole Brain® Thinking quadrant. The flexibility of studying or collaborating whenever or wherever they have access to the Internet particularly appeals to students with D-quadrant preferences, as they struggle with the inflexibility and excessive strictness that often form part of face-to-face environments. Students with strong B-quadrant preferences also value self-paced learning opportunities. The thinking preferences of A-quadrant students are addressed by the facts available on websites and wikis, and in online research articles. The selection of appropriate sources requires analytical and critical thinking, which are also key descriptors within the A-quadrant. Students with D-quadrant preferences may enjoy the many visual elements (illustrations, pictures, photos, simulations, virtual reality environments) that are available online, and the freedom to discover new information and synthesise the different sources into one product.

Although the face-to-face environment affords instantaneous and rich opportunities to interact (which is so necessary for the C-quadrant thinkers), the online environment strengthens this capacity for students with other thinking preferences who have to think carefully before they formulate messages. New Web 2.0 technologies such as wikis, blogs, Facebook and Twitter bring further enhancement to the previous Web 1.0 technology where the user was a consumer, not a participator. Through engaging with these programmes, students learn to collaborate and interact with one another in constructing new meaning.

While it is possible to address all the Whole Brain® Thinking quadrants through blended learning, it is essential also to pay attention to those aspects of Whole Brain® Thinking with which students with different thinking preferences might struggle if learning material and tasks are chosen to address mainly a particular quadrant. For example, giving students the opportunity to explore the Internet to find resources on a particular topic might cause problems for some students based on their thinking preferences. While the rich World Wide Web resources that are available may address the need of A-quadrant thinkers, this same environment might cause students with C-quadrant thinking preferences to struggle with too much data and analysis. Students with B-quadrant preferences may be inclined to become frustrated if there are not clear instructions provided on what to look for. It is therefore essential that a lecturer provides guidance and scaffolding as part of an array of methods of facilitating learning. More examples of how the different environments can be combined to facilitate Whole Brain® learning are discussed in the next section.

5.4 Whole Brain® learning material

A research project that focused on the implementation of Whole Brain® Thinking principles in an information literacy module for first-year students provides examples of how Whole Brain® learning material impacted on student learning (see Section 4.7.1).

In an effort to enhance learning through Whole Brain® facilitating of learning, a 'learning material toolkit' was developed for the information literacy module to ensure that the 16 assistant lecturers maintain the same quality of facilitating learning throughout the module. This toolkit consists of a variety of learning tasks for each chapter of the textbook, makes provision for Whole Brain® learning and facilitating of learning, and offers students the opportunity to explore, conceptualise and share learning environments inside and outside the classroom. The learning tasks are presented in a blended format, with some performed during class time, while others are available on the learning management system to do whenever or whereever a student wants. Because of the nature of the subject, many online tasks are conducted during class time. A learning opportunity plan that contains instructions on how to employ the tasks was developed to guide lecturers towards optimal use of the learning tasks.

The first learning opportunity was identified as critical to get students interested in this compulsory module. The ARCS motivation model (Keller, 1987) suggests that students' motivation to attend the module would be enhanced if their interest could be captured. To achieve this, the following learning tasks were designed or selected to supplement the textbook and Microsoft PowerPoint class notes.

The learning opportunity starts with a YouTube video that was selected to illustrate to the students the information explosion and the importance of being competent at finding one's own way through the sea of information that exists. This task grabbed students' attention as it causes perceptual arousal (Keller, 1987) by illustrating the uncertain environment in which they will have to find their way. The video contains precise facts and statistics on information growth, which address A-quadrant thinking preferences. It also provides the big picture of why students should acquire information literacy skills (D-quadrant) and reveals the importance of knowing how to find information (B-quadrant). C-quadrant preferences are mainly addressed through the music that is used in the video.

An interactive search exercise followed the video. The five-minute group exercise requires students to search for an article ('Angola: peoples and cultures' by J.C. Miller) that was purposefully selected as it is very difficult to find without the necessary information literacy skills (Figures 5.2, 5.3 and 5.4). The students are free to choose the search engine or database they want to use for the search (Figure 5.5). However, the article cannot be obtained through an Internet search engine such as Google or even by using a library database without rigidly applying information-seeking skills. After the five minutes, the lecturer shows the students why they could not retrieve the information and how it should be done (Figures 5.6 and 5.7). Students can also access a simulation on how to perform the search on the learning management system (Figure 5.8). The strategy followed in this learning task uses surprise and offers a challenging question or problem, two categories indicated by Keller (1987) as sure to get students' attention. In the course of the learning task the Whole Brain® Thinking quadrants are addressed as follows:

- *A-quadrant*: This task provides a challenging problem for the students to solve through analytical thinking. Students who rely strongly on the A-quadrant struggle with the vagueness and lack of logic locked up in the task.
- *B-quadrant*: The concrete example, and the procedure given at the end of the learning task, plays into the preference of B-quadrant thinkers, but they struggle with the 'risk' they have to take in finding information without clear guidelines on how to do so.
- *C-quadrant*: Students with C-quadrant preferences enjoy the group interaction to find solutions, and the hands-on search that is part of the task.
- *D-quadrant*: The element of discovery locked up in the task, and the freedom to choose the search tool, satisfies the expectations of students with a strong D-quadrant preference. Students with C- and D-quadrant preferences struggle with the short time allocated for the task as the C-quadrant thinkers want to obtain buy-in from the group, while the D-quadrant thinkers require more time to think.

Figures 5.2 to 5.7 show screen captures from the interactive search exercise.

The next learning task requires students to work in groups to generate ideas on the characteristics, skills or abilities required of a successful person in the information society. They are allowed to use the textbook and have to write a blog posting in the learning management system. The lecturer then facilitates a discussion on group blogs with the whole class. During this task, the Whole Brain® Thinking quadrants are addressed as follows:

- A- and B-quadrant preferences are addressed by reading and reviewing the textbook to find and organise the facts into a posting that makes sense.
- Students with C-quadrant preferences enjoy the small group discussions.
- D-quadrant thinkers enjoy synthesising the textbook information into a concise blog posting.

Figure 5.2   Navigating Information Literacy Slide 1: Title screen

Chapter 1 : Interactive exercise

Search for the article 'Angola: Peoples and cultures' by Joseph C Miller from the *Encyclopedia of Africa South of the Sahara.*

It is important to search in the correct place for this article.

This is a group exercise. Divide yourselves into small groups
(3–5 students).

You have 5 minutes for this activity.

Tip: Think **History!**

Figure 5.3   Navigating Information Literacy Slide 2: Introduction to the search exercise

Choose any of the links below for your search

Search engines
- Google: http://www.google.com
- AltaVista: http://www.altavista.com/
- Exalead: http://exalead.com/search/
- Gigablast: http://www.gigablast.com/
- MSN Search: http://za.msn.com/
- Bing: http://www.bing.com/
- Yahoo: http://www.yahoo.com/
- Ask: http://www.ask.com/

Meta search engines
- Clusty: http://clusty.com/
- DogPile: http://www.dogpile.com/
- Metacrawler: http://www.metacrawler.com/
- Mamma: http://www.mamma.com/
- Ixquick: http://ixquick.com/
- MetaGopher: http://www.metagopher.com/

Databases
- Databases available from UP's Library website:
  http://www.library.up.ac.za/eresources/eresourcesaz.htm

Figure 5.4	Navigating Information Literacy Slide 3: Suggested search engines and databases to use for the exercise

Why you couldn't find the answer

You needed to determine the category the article belongs to, which in this case is **History.**

You were not able to find the correct answer from searching a search engine or meta search engine, because the original article was retrieved from a Database entitled History Resource Center: World.

You need to search in this specific database from the Library's webpage to retrieve the article. The steps you needed to take are given on the next slide.

Figure 5.5	Navigating Information Literacy Slide 4: Explaining why the article could not be found

Steps to find the correct answer

- Go to the Library's web page
- On the the the 'e-Resources' tab, click on 'Databases A–Z'
- Click on the letter 'h' and click on the database
  History Resource Center: World
- Click on 'Proceed'
- Enter your login details to access the e-Resources page of UP's Library
- Click on 'Proceed' on the Cengage Learning page
- You should see a list of Gale databases
- Scroll down and click on the database: History Resource Center: World
- Type in your search query in the search box:
  'Angola: Peoples and Cultures'
- Click on the title to view the full text article

Figure 5.6 Navigating Information Literacy Slide 5: Steps to find the correct answer

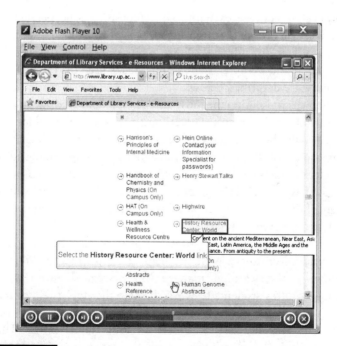

Figure 5.7 Simulation of the search process

Feedback obtained via a questionnaire (n=940) completed after the first class session showed that students agreed that it was beneficial to be an information literate person (93.7 per cent). They also agreed that information literacy was necessary to survive in an information and knowledge society (93.2 per cent), and to be successful at university (93.3 per cent) and at their future workplace (93.9 per cent). This was a much higher positive response than the one received in the initial analysis, where respondents admitted that the module was worth their time (75 per cent), and agreed that it would help them with their other subjects (79 per cent). The fact that such a large proportion of students now saw the value of the subject matter (93.7 per cent) implies that they would also think it was worth their time, and would be motivated to attend class, much more so than their predecessors (75 per cent). The students identified the search exercise as the task that contributed most to their learning (68 per cent).

After gaining students' attention during the first learning opportunity, it was necessary to sustain their motivation throughout the module. This was done by using Whole Brain® learning tasks in each of the subsequent classes.

Another chapter in the textbook, which focuses on concept identification and the construction of a search query, was also problematic. Lecturers stated that it was difficult to facilitate, while students said it was difficult to understand and execute. Two learning tasks used during this learning opportunity are described below.

The first was presenting the most important and most difficult concepts with the aid of Microsoft PowerPoint. Whereas the slides initially contained only bulleted lists of facts, pictures and animations that illustrate some of the concepts were added to additional slides. The bulleted lists of facts speak to the requirements of the A- and B-quadrants (Figure 5.8), while slides that contain pictures and animations illustrating the use of Boolean operators address the needs of students with D-quadrant preferences (Figure 5.9).

The second was requiring students to work together in groups to construct a search query with the help of an interactive Adobe Flash animation in the learning management system (Figure 5.10). The animation requires students to work through the steps that are required to construct a search query. It provides feedback to the students on their choices. This learning task addresses all four Whole Brain® Thinking quadrants. Critical evaluation of words that need to be included in the search string, and the logic in which these words need to be combined, is strongly dependent on A-quadrant thinking. Working through the steps

Formal Boolean Logic: AND

The function of the AND operator is to combine search terms in such a way that **all of the terms** combined by AND in the query must appear in the document for it to be retrieved. For example, if you want information on a cell phone having both a camera and bluetooth, the query will be 'camera AND bluetooth'.

If you look at Figure 6.4, which phones would qualify?

- The following cell phone models have cameras: A, B, D, E, G and H
- The following cell phones have bluetooth: A, E, G, H and J
- The only cell phones that have both a camera and bluetooth (camera AND bluetooth) are: A, E, G and H

6

Figure 5.8 Microsoft PowerPoint slide addressing A- and B-quadrant preferences

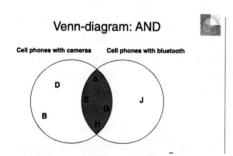

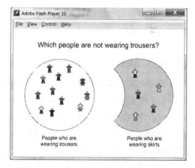

Figure 5.9 Microsoft PowerPoint slides addressing D-quadrant preferences

of constructing a query, with the opportunity to repeat the task, addresses the expectations of students with B-quadrant preferences. The interaction between members of a group who work together and share their personal reactions on the results of the learning task, and the hands-on approach of the task, supports C-quadrant thinking preferences. The expectations of students with D-quadrant preferences are met by allowing them the freedom to make choices in the animation.

During the initial analysis of the module students stated that they struggled with the applicable terminology. Keller (1987) indicates that

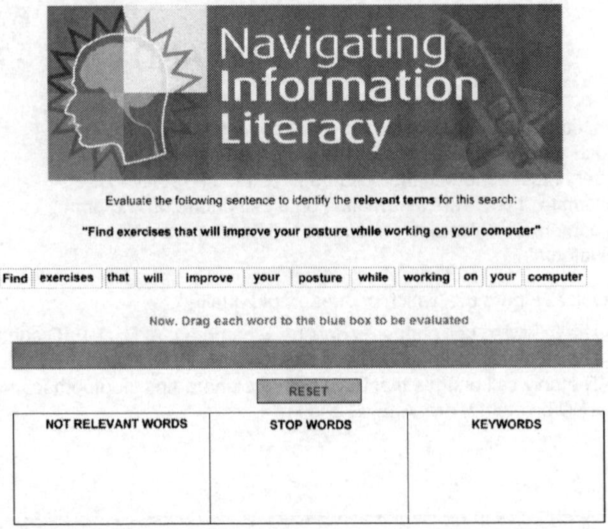

Evaluate the following sentence to identify the relevant terms for this search:

"Find exercises that will improve your posture while working on your computer"

| Find | exercises | that | will | improve | your | posture | while | working | on | your | computer |

Now, Drag each word to the blue box to be evaluated

RESET

| NOT RELEVANT WORDS | STOP WORDS | KEYWORDS |

Figure 5.10 Screen from the Flash animation to practise the skill of searching words to include in a search string

confidence and satisfaction are important requirements to ensure that students are intrinsically motivated. Confidence can be established if students have a method for estimating their probability of success. They obtain satisfaction through a sense of achievement, through receiving praise or through entertainment. In order for students to learn the terminology in such a way that they become confident and know the work, and enjoy mastering the terminology, games were developed to allow them to master the terminology in each chapter of the textbook. These games include crossword puzzles (Figure 5.11), flash cards, hangman, pick a letter (Figure 5.12), fill in the blank (Figure 5.13) and matching a word to a description (Figure 5.14). The games provide immediate feedback to students on the correctness of their answers and are available in the learning management system for students to use whenever they want. Although games are typically tasks that fall within the preferences of students who are strong in the D-quadrant, these tasks may also support learning of the three other quadrants as they contain facts (A-quadrant), opportunity for review and repetition (B-quadrant), and if the game is played with another student address the expectations of students who prefer C-quadrant tasks.

During the focus group interviews it became clear that students did not always understand the logic and relevance of specific work that formed part of the module. According to Keller (1987) such perceived lack of relevance demotivates students. In order to illustrate the relevance of the

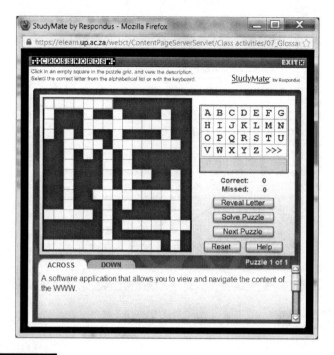

Figure 5.11 An interactive crossword puzzle

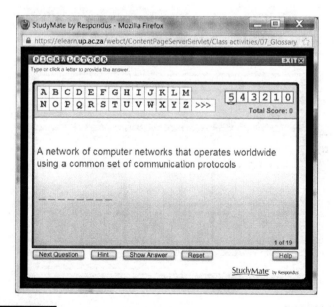

Figure 5.12 Interactive pick a letter

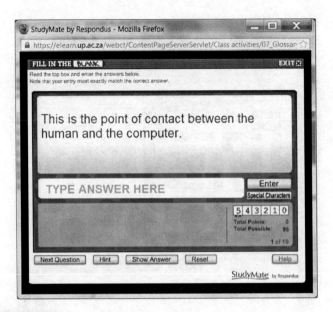

Figure 5.13 Interactive fill in the blank

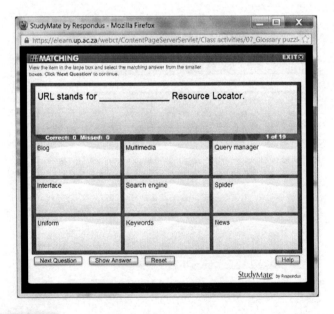

Figure 5.14 Interactive matching a word to a description

different topics of the chapters, a cartoon with three characters was developed to incorporate into each chapter (Figure 5.15). The storylines of the cartoons demonstrate how the topics tie in with real-life experiences, e.g. assignments students have to undertake or planning a vacation. Some cartoons also provide the steps a student has to take to perform particular tasks, e.g. searching information on the Internet or in databases. This task is aimed at providing case studies (A-quadrant), practical concrete examples (B-quadrant), human interest stories (C-quadrant) and visual illustrations (D-quadrant).

A fourth character was created, called 'ILLI' (Figure 5.16). This name was selected to illustrate the link the character has with information literacy. He was developed to serve as a friendly guide to relate the information literacy concepts to the reality of the students' life. The ILLI character has a Facebook profile and a Twitter account, which students are invited to join in order to address an outcome of the module; thus it requires students to know and use the latest social computing trends and

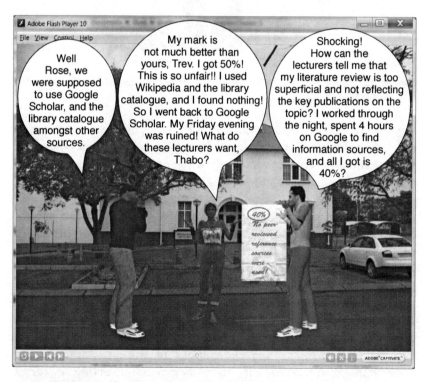

Figure 5.15 Cartoon stories demonstrating how topics of the module on information literacy relate to real-life experiences

Figure 5.16 The ILLI character, which serves as a friendly guide to students

services. The lecturers posted photos of the class, and interesting quotes and links to worthwhile websites that contain messages relevant to the subject on this Facebook profile and Twitter account. The ILLI character also showed up in the cartoons to apply the story in each cartoon to relevant information literacy concepts (Figure 5.17).

The learning material included examples of how to use specific databases. These examples contain the steps for each of the major databases to be searched for every field of specialisation. The verbal steps are enhanced with pictures of the screens that students will encounter (Figure 5.18). An online treasure hunt was developed to help students practise their web search strategies, either individually or in groups. The hunt consists of a series of questions that have to be answered. Each answer provides a clue for the next question. The game speaks to the exploration and discovering expectations of students with a strong D-quadrant preference, while it satisfies the expectation of the C-quadrant thinkers to carry out hands-on tasks. Students with a B-quadrant preference enjoy the skills practice, while the challenge to solve problems within the hunt motivates those students with A-quadrant preferences.

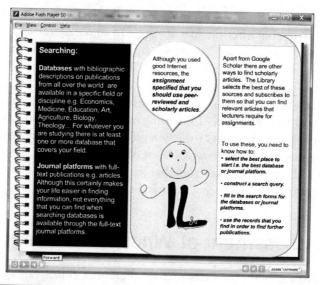

Figure 5.17   The ILLI character providing advice in a story

Searching for information about Facebook using databases & platforms

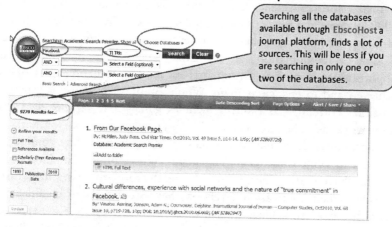

Figure 5.18   Verbal steps in searching for information enhanced with pictures of the screens

The success of the 'learning material toolkit' was illustrated through surveys carried out after the first semester of implementation. Students' motivation increased, as illustrated by the higher class attendance. Altogether 45 per cent of students indicated that they frequently experienced variety and change in the classroom, while 29 per cent indicated that they almost always had variety and change in the classroom as lecturers had moved away from using only lectures featuring Microsoft PowerPoint slides and started to include different tasks that accommodated the divergent thinking preferences of the students. The majority of lecturers (72.7 per cent) indicated that the learning opportunity plan had helped them to organise their classes and enriched their teaching practice.

5.6 Assessment of Whole Brain® learning

In accordance with the constructive alignment principle, assessment practice must illustrate that students achieved the set learning outcomes of a specific module. It is obvious that if Whole Brain® learning tasks form part of the assessment practice, assessment should also be carried out in a Whole Brain® Thinking manner. Assessment strategies for the information literacy module that was discussed earlier in this chapter are highlighted to indicate how this may be achieved.

The module on information literacy referred to above provides a challenge for assessment, as the module is presented to approximately 8000 students at a time. To overcome the marking load involved, the use of computer-based assessment is essential. In the information literacy module a combination of formative and summative assessment opportunities is used to ensure that all learning outcomes have been achieved and to engage as many Whole Brain® Thinking quadrants as possible. Formative assessment includes games and various class and homework tasks. Selected class tasks count towards a 'pool' of marks to be accumulated during the semester. This allows for continuous assessment while students are engaged in Whole Brain® Thinking tasks. The feedback that students receive during the formative assessment tasks enhances their motivation levels as they become more confident in knowing they can achieve the learning outcomes. The specific types of formative assessment also contribute to the different Whole Brain® Thinking quadrants in the following ways: A-quadrant thinkers master terminology and facts, and use concrete information and challenging problems; B-quadrant thinkers appreciate the repetition and review opportunities; C-quadrant thinkers enjoy the fact that these assessment opportunities may be undertaken as part of a group and as hands-on tasks, while students with a preference for the D-quadrant enjoy the discovery tasks and playing the games associated with these tasks.

The treasure hunt is an example of a class task that counts towards the pool of marks. The hunt comprises a set of questions within the quiz tool as part of the learning management system. As soon as the correct answer is submitted, the mark is automatically included in the grade book in the learning management system.

Summative assessment includes a compulsory assignment, semester tests on theory and practical application, as well as theoretical and practical examinations. The compulsory assignment students have to complete is linked to concept identification. This assignment consists of a number of scenarios where students have to choose the concepts that should be included in search terms. The task relies heavily on A-quadrant skills such as analytical thinking and critical evaluation. It also involves B-quadrant requirements to use practical, concrete examples.

The theoretical semester test and examination assess students' knowledge of the subject through multiple-choice, multiple-response and fill-in-the-blank question types. The practical tests and examinations require students to follow the steps facilitated during the semester and to perform searches for information. For instance, students would be asked to provide the year of publication of a specific article. Only the title of the article is provided and they have to search for the particular reference and, from the reference, retrieve the date of publication. These tests and examinations address mainly A- and B-quadrant thinking preferences as students have to apply facts and use information literacy skills. However, the simulation of the search for a specific reference during practical tests and examinations talks to the thinking preferences of the D-quadrant, while intra-reflection on how to do the search falls in the C-quadrant.

5.7 Conclusions

The use of Whole Brain® learning material and tasks improves student learning by addressing their diverse thinking preferences. The Whole Brain® Model for Learning and Facilitating of Learning (see Chapter 6) provides a rich source from which to analyse existing learning material and tasks so as to determine which Whole Brain® Thinking quadrants are addressed and which are omitted. The material currently used by the lecturer may already address the thinking preferences represented by the different quadrants and it may only be necessary to develop a few extra learning tasks or a little material to ensure that all the thinking preferences are covered within a module. The model can also be used with great success to create a variety of learning tasks and material that will enhance student learning. While one can choose separate tasks to address each of the quadrants, it is also possible to create a single task that addresses all four quadrants (as illustrated in the description of the information literacy learning material and tasks).

The Whole Brain® Model for Learning and Facilitating of Learning not only supports students' learning preferences, but may also be implemented with great success to increase and maintain their level of motivation. The instrument provides strategies that may enhance students' level of interest in and the relevance of the learning material presented, while also boosting their confidence and satisfaction (as illustrated in the information literacy module).

The development of Whole Brain® learning material and tasks is not a one-off exercise. It requires continued evaluation after implementation to ensure that the intended results are achieved and that the specific learning tasks are introduced at the correct stage of the module. Students may favour specific learning material and tasks more during the initial introduction of new concepts and prefer other learning material later in the module when they have to study for a test or examination. For example, during the information literacy module, students identified Venn diagrams and the Flash animation on constructing a search query as the material that contributed most to their learning directly after the class on creating search queries. However, after the semester test they chose the Microsoft PowerPoint slides and the graphics within the Microsoft PowerPoint as the learning material that enhanced the way they learned and that most contributed to their understanding.

It is advisable to involve lecturers or instructional designers with different thinking preferences when new learning material or tasks are created, because some individuals find it very difficult to create tasks that they personally would not prefer. One may be forced to choose team members with whom you do not necessarily collaborate easily, and the fact that you all have different thinking preferences may cause conflict.

The way forward

Abstract: In chapter 6 we propose a comprehensive flexible Whole Brain® Model for learning and facilitating learning as a tool for lecturers to accommodate students' diverse thinking preferences, as well as develop areas of lesser preferred modes of learning, thus contributing to the development of students' potential.

Keywords: Whole Brain® Model for learning, Whole Brain® Model for facilitating learning.

6.1 Introduction

In this last chapter we design a comprehensive Whole Brain® Model for Learning and Facilitating Learning that lecturers can use to accommodate the diversity of thinking preferences in their classrooms.

It is important to realise that a preference for a particular thinking style and an avoidance of another are of equal importance to an individual (Herrmann, 1996). Herrmann uses the term 'turn-on' work for work that is interesting, stimulating, pleasurable and satisfying, and gives a sense of fulfilment, and if individuals are given a choice, that is exactly what they select to do. He even purports that 'turn-on' work does not require constant external reward because doing the work is rewarding in itself. A preference will often lead to 'turn-on' work. This in itself is highly motivational and often results in a state of self-satisfaction (Herrmann, 1996). Dominance leads to the development of preference, which in turn establishes interests. Interest has a motivational impact on developing competencies and it influences career choices and ultimately the work we do (Herrmann, 1996). On the other hand, a lack of preference or actual avoidance results in 'turn-off' work, and this is highly demotivational.

Herrmann (1996) points out that if people are 'turned off', they drop out of the game, because they become selectively blind and deaf to the discussions and tasks that take place in their areas of avoidance.

As lecturers gain more experience with the Whole Brain® Model they tend to try to adapt their teaching practice. The more comfortable they become with the Whole Brain® Model, the more willing they are to change and implement strategies of facilitating learning to accommodate the diverse learning styles of their students.

6.2 Comprehensive Whole Brain® Model for Learning and Facilitating Learning

Based on Herrmann's expanded Whole Brain® Teaching and Learning Model (Figure 1.8) and lecturers' applied Whole Brain® facilitating of learning over the past 15 years, an adapted comprehensive flexible learning style model was designed to provide lecturers with a tool to understand the diversity of thinking preferences and learning preferences within each classroom. The model can be used by lecturers to enhance their teaching practice and specifically their facilitating of learning, while taking into consideration both learning preferences and avoidances of students. Our model is based on the Whole Brain® Model of Herrmann (1995, 1996) and consists of circles within circles and clusters within clusters. It has, at the core, different aspects, which motivate and activate students to learn (Figure 6.1).

The first cluster around the inner circle highlights individual preferences. It gives a brief description of the different mental preferences that individuals favour when processing information according to Herrmann's Whole Brain® Model. For the A-quadrant the preferences are analysing, theorising, logic processing and quantifying. For the B-quadrant, preferences include organising, sequencing and practising, to name a few. Sharing, internalising, moving and feeling involved are the preferences

Figure 6.1 The inner circle of Herrmann's Whole Brain® Teaching and Learning Model

for the C-quadrant, while D-quadrant preferences are exploring, discovering, conceptualising and synthesising (cf. Chapter 1) (Figure 6.2).

The ways in which people perceive and process information affect how they learn. Looking back on one's own learning experience, one recognises that one liked some subjects more than others, some methods of facilitating learning were more enjoyable than others, and we retained some material more accurately and for a longer period than other material that had been delivered typical of the old paradigm in a different way.

The next circle with clusters represents aspects within the four quadrant model that students typically struggle with if they have a least preferred or even an avoidance thinking style for that specific quadrant. These 'shirked' quadrants need to be developed and the model provides a tool

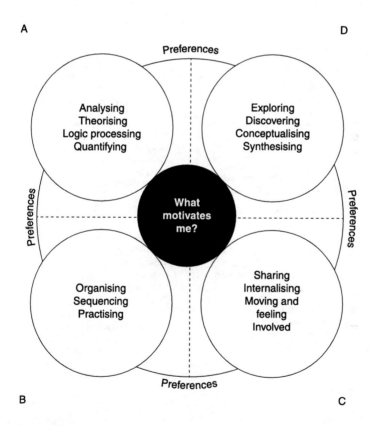

Figure 6.2 Individual preferences of students in each of the four quadrants

to assist lecturers to help students develop these skills. A student with a strong preference for the A-quadrant must be helped to express emotions and deal with vagueness, imprecise concepts or ideas, and lack of logic. Students with a strong preference for the B-quadrant need to start taking risks, and must be encouraged to overcome their aversion to unclear concepts and instructions, and ambiguity. Students with a strong preference for the C-quadrant have a problem dealing with too much data and analysis, and struggle when they lack an opportunity for interaction, sharing and building relationships. The student with a strong preference for the D-quadrant has a problem with autocratic and excessive strictness, strict time management, lack of flexibility, and too much detail (Figure 6.3). All of these antipathies and dislikes need to be

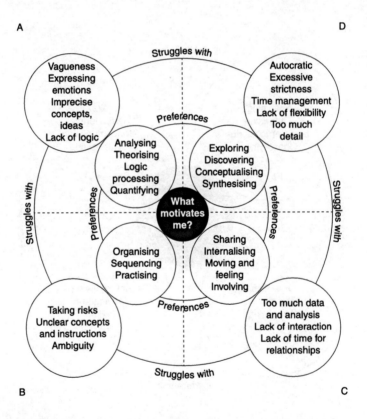

Figure 6.3 Emotions and tasks that students struggle with in each of the four quadrants

overcome to some extent to make the student an individual who situationally uses a Whole Brain® Thinking approach.

The next circle and clusters highlight the expectations of students within each of the four quadrants of the Whole Brain® Model.

For the individual with a strong preference for the A-quadrant, purpose, terminology, spreadsheets, challenging problems to solve, concrete information, presentations based on logic, expert resources and citations, and clear objectives are necessary. These individuals also appreciate the opportunity to ask challenging questions and participate in debates.

Someone with a strong B-quadrant preference enjoys the opportunity to practise newly acquired competencies and to participate in well-structured, well-organised tasks. These individuals prefer detailed agendas with clear outlines and welcome clear instructions. They appreciate a practical concrete example that is unfolded in a step-by-step process and appreciate repetition and review regularly.

Those with a strong preference for the C-quadrant enjoy group discussions and being involved in team projects, hands-on tasks, and small group discussions. They create time for human interest stories and narratives, and sharing of personal reactions and experiences. They also enjoy physical tasks.

Individuals with a strong D-quadrant preference appreciate mental imagery and discovering and exploring new possibilities. They rely on intuition, synthesise content and prefer to brainstorm concepts by using metaphors and visual illustration in the communication of concepts (Figure 6.4).

Just as in any design, approaches to facilitating at any learning, critical learning points across all four quadrants and modes of thinking should be kept in mind. Different design and delivery approaches improve learning in each of the four specialised quadrants. The quote from Felder remains essential:

> If professors teach exclusively in a manner that favors their students' less preferred learning style modes, the students' discomfort level may be great enough to interfere with their learning. On the other hand, if professors teach exclusively in their students' preferred modes, the students may not develop the mental dexterity they need to reach their potential of achievement in school (1996, 18).

Research from Houghton Mifflin College (n.d.) suggests that students learn best when they have moments in class where they are working in their preferred learning styles because it gives them the opportunity to

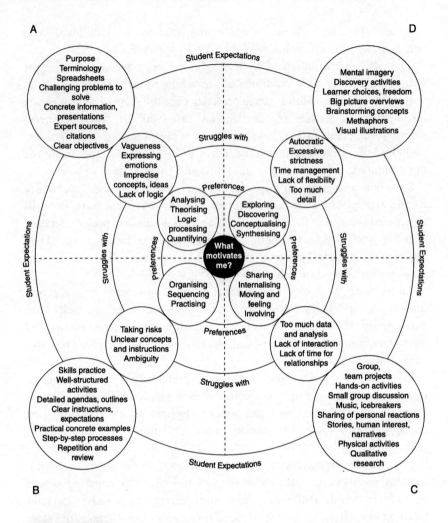

Figure 6.4 **What students expect in each of the four quadrants**

feel comfortable and to connect with the learning material. However, their research suggests that it is equally important for students to experience other styles, so they can expand their repertoire and be prepared for the world of work.

Incorporating all four preferences and avoidances will not only benefit students' preferred learning styles through facilitating learning in their preferred style of learning, but also assist students to develop their lesser preferred modes of thinking and help them become more competent in their least preferred Thinking Styles™.

The fourth circle and clusters highlight ways by means of which to facilitate effective learning and address four questions: what (A-quadrant), how (B-quadrant), who (C-quadrant) and why (D-quadrant).

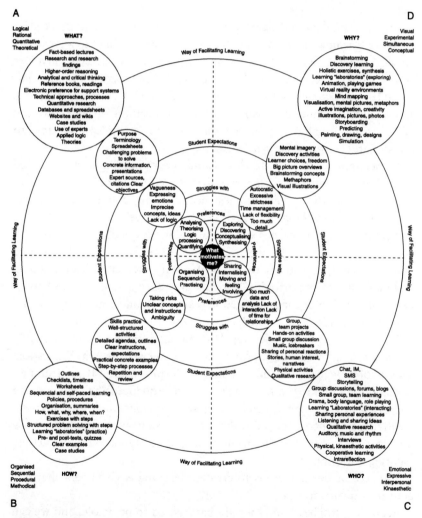

| **Figure 6.5** | Comprehensive Flexible Whole Brain® Model for Learning and Facilitating Learning |

To accommodate and develop A-quadrant thinking lecturers need to answer the 'what?' question. Their focus will primarily be on learning opportunities that highlight purpose, logic, theories and facts, all based on research, research findings and textbook references. Throughout the learning opportunities, attention should be given to stimulating higher-order reasoning and critical and analytical thinking, while incorporating modern technology and making use of simulations to supplement the lectures or case studies.

To accommodate and develop B-quadrant thinking lecturers need to facilitate learning in such a way that students are enabled to answer the 'how?', 'what?', 'why?', 'where?' and 'when?' questions. This involves clear outlines, checklists, timelines and worksheets, sequential and self-paced learning, which unfolds step-by-step through well-structured tasks and detailed learning material with clear instructions on where to find information. Emphasis is placed on concrete examples and time to practise and review what was learned.

To accommodate and develop C-quadrant thinking lecturers need to facilitate learning in such a way that students will be able to answer the 'who?' question. This implies incorporating and participating in group discussions, blogs and team learning, as well as creating forums and participating in forums in the classroom. C-quadrant thinking and acting can be enhanced when personal experiences are shared and individuals learn to listen to the ideas of others, interact with one another, and make use of opportunities for role-play. Groups of students should be encouraged to become engaged in team work and team projects, and to perform hands-on tasks such as writing a personal journal.

To accommodate and develop D-quadrant thinking lecturers should create learning opportunities for students to answer the 'why?' question. This involves field trips mainly for discovering purposes and opportunities. D-quadrant thinking and acting can be enhanced by encouraging creativity in assignments, embracing specific opportunities to express creativity, and incorporating tasks such as visualising metaphors, using imagination and performing mental imaging, storyboarding, predicting, painting and simulations.

The role of the lecturer is to create a learning environment that will activate students to learn.

According to Herrmann, 'we are hard wired to be whole, and we can become more so by taking more complete charge of our own development' (1996, 37). Therefore, to empower students to situationally use a Whole Brain® Thinking approach means that they continue to have the advantage of a dominant preference with a leading response to everyday situations, but they are no longer limited by that dominance. Developing their areas of lesser preference will equip them with a much broader spectrum of mental options that can be accessed, because they have been alerted to the existence of these modes and given the opportunity to practise them (Herrmann, 1996).

Our model in Figure 6.5 culminates from the work of Herrmann and our involvement over many years in facilitating learning using a Whole Brain® Thinking approach to researching, supervising students on the topic and offering workshops on applied Whole Brain® facilitating of learning in higher education. We are convinced that the model can assist lecturers to design learning material and create learning opportunities for students that will encourage them to embrace Whole Brain® learning.

Modern technology has added an array of possibilities for facilitating quality learning and creating tasks to assess students in all four quadrants. A-quadrant students ensure access to e-mail and to current research information on the Web, and B-quadrant students appreciate the practical application of computer software and simulation process opportunities. C-quadrant students are able to communicate with classmates and lecturers through e-mail, Skype and chat rooms, while D-quadrant students are able to create their own learning with software presentations and tools like Microsoft PowerPoint (Herrmann-Nehdi, 2012).

6.3 Conclusion

The value of the comprehensive, flexible Whole Brain® Model for Learning and Facilitating Learning will assist lecturers and instructional designers to design better learning interventions and meet the unique requirements of their students. Teaching tasks and activities should ideally be designed to move back and forth dynamically for each key learning point and be equally distributed across all four quadrants in a balanced way (Herrmann, 1996).

Developing thinking skills in least preferred thinking modes can be practised, and these newly acquired thinking skills can help individuals to establish competencies in their least preferred thinking preferences. By using the comprehensive, flexible Whole Brain® Model for Learning and Facilitating Learning, the lecturer can experiment with diverse strategies for facilitating learning, which can assist in building learning experiences that are meaningful for all involved.

The effort does not demand a radical change. We suggest that you start the journey by redirecting a small part of your course work towards using Whole Brain® Thinking in the facilitating of learning. Evaluate the outcome and then incorporate more tasks and activities, and so on. Focus on the two to five approaches that will best serve your design and the diverse group of students. Put together a check list for yourself: evaluate what you want to do, and ask 'does this make sense?' If it does, you will gradually start to develop all of these skills, and over time enable your students to develop competencies in all four thinking modes. These ideas can be monitored by executing the principles of action research.

List of references

Ammons-Stephens, S., Cole, H.J., Jenkins-Gibbs, K., Riehle, D.F. and Weare, W.H. (2009) 'Developing core leadership competencies for the library profession', *Journal for Library Leadership and Management*, 23(2), 63–74.

Ash, S.L. and Clayton, P.H. (2004) Service learning: Integrating inquiry and engagement. In V.S. Lee (ed.), *Teaching and Learning Through Inquiry: A Guidebook for Institutions and Instructors* (Sterling, VA: Stylus), 229–44.

Bedwell, W.L., Wildman, J.L., Granados, D.D., Salazar, M., Kramer W.S. and Salas, E. (2012) 'Collaboration at work: an integrative multilevel conceptualization', *Human Resource Management Review*, 22, 128–45.

Benade, S. (2006) Engineers: Left-brain oriented only? The myth dispelled. GSM@UP news. Alumni newsletter Graduate School of Management.

Bender, C.J.G. and Du Toit, P.H. (2007) 'Innovative scholarship development in curriculum-based service-learning'. Paper presented at HELTASA Conference: *Learning and Teaching Innovation in Higher Education: Expanding the Frontiers*, 27–29 November, St George Hotel, Pretoria.

Berliner, D.C. and Gage, N.L. (1998) *Educational Psychology* (Boston, MA: Houghton Mifflin Company).

Biggs, J. (1996) 'Enhancing teaching through constructive alignment', *Higher Education*, 32(3), 347–64.

Biggs, J.B. (1985) 'The role of metalearning in study processes', *British Journal of Educational Psychology*, 55, 185–212.

Biggs, J.B. (1999) *Teaching for Quality Learning at University* (Buckingham: SRHE and Open University Press).

Biggs, J.B. and Telfer, R. (1987) *The Process of Learning*, 2nd edn (Sydney: Prentice Hall of Australia).

Bleed, R. (2006) 'The IT leader as alchemist: finding the true gold', *EDUCAUSE Review*, 41(1), 32–43, available at: *http://www.educause.edu/ero/article/it-leader-alchemist-finding-true-gold*

Bothma, T.J.D., Cosijn, E., Fourie, I. and Penzhorn, C. (2011) *Navigating Information Literacy: Your Information Society Survival Toolkit*, 3rd edn (Cape Town: Pearson Education South Africa).

Boud, D. (2006) 'Aren't we all learner-centred? The bittersweet flavour of success'. In P. Ashwin (ed.), *Changing Higher Education: The Development of Learning and Teaching* (London: Routledge), 33–46.

Brandes, D. and Ginnis, P. (1996) *A Guide to Student-Centred Learning* (Cheltenham: Stanley Thornes Publishers Ltd).

Burton, D. and Bartlett, S. (2005) *Practitioner Research for Teachers* (London: Paul Chapman).

Buscaglia, L. (n.d.) BrainyQuote.com, available at: *http://www.brainyquote.com/quotes/authors/l/leo_buscaglia.html*

Carr, W. and Kemmis, S. (1986) *Becoming Critical: Education, Knowledge and Action Research* (Geelong: Deakin University Press).

Center for Creative Leadership (2012) Campbell Leadership Descriptor, available at: *http://www.ccl.org/leadership/pdf/assessments/CLD.pdf*

Charan R., Drotter S. and Noel J. (2001) *The Leadership Pipeline: How to Build the Leadership-Powered Company* (San Francisco: John Wiley & Sons).

Chew, E. and Jones, N. (2010) 'Driver or drifter? Two case studies of the blended learning practices in higher education'. In F.L. Wang, J. Fong and R. Kwan (eds), *Handbook of Research on Hybrid Learning Models: Advanced Tools, Technologies, and Applications* (Hershey, PA: Information Science Reference), 71–93.

Clayton, P. and Kimbrell, J. (2007) 'Thinking preferences as diagnostic and learning tools for managerial styles and predictors of auditor success', *Managerial Finance*, 33(12), 921–34.

Clement, M. and Frenay, M. (2010) 'Faculty development in Belgian universities'. In A. Saroyan and C. Amundsen (eds), *Rethinking Teaching in Higher Education: From a Course Design Workshop to a Faculty Development Framework* (Sterling, VA: Stylus Publishing), 82–103.

Coffield, F., Moseley, D., Hall, E. and Ecclestone, K. (2004) *Learning Styles and Pedagogy in Post-16 Learning: A Systematic and Critical Review* (London: Learning and Skills Research Centre).

Cohen, S.A. (1987) 'Instructional alignment: Searching for a magic bullet', *Educational Researcher*, 16(8), 16–20.

Cranton, P. (2010) 'Adult learning and instruction: Transformative learning perspective'. In P. Peterson, E. Baker and B. McGaw (eds), *International Encyclopaedia of Education*, 3rd edn, Vol. I (London: Academic Press).

Dale, E. (1969) *Audiovisual Methods in Teaching*, 3rd edn (New York: Dryden Press; Holt, Rinehart and Winston).

Dalsgaard, C. and Godsk, M. (2007) 'Transforming traditional lectures into problem-based blended learning: Challenges and experiences', *Open Learning*, 22(1), 29–42.

Darwin, A. and Palmer, E. (2009) 'Mentoring circles in higher education', *Higher Education Research and Development*, 28(2), 125–36.

De Beer, M. (2009) 'Memory-based expression of self: Demonstration/expression of identity through the art of making'. In K. Pithouse, C. Mitchell and R. Moletsane (eds), *Making Connections: Self-study and Social Action* (New York: Peter Lang Publishing, Inc.) 43–58.

De Boer, A. and Steyn, T.M. (1999) 'Thinking style preferences of underprepared first-year students in the Natural Sciences', *South African Journal of Ethnology*, 22(3), 97–102.

De Boer, A., Bothma, T.J.D. and Du Toit, P.H. (2011) 'Enhancing information literacy through the application of whole brain strategies', *Libri*, 61 (March), 67–75.

De Boer, A., Bothma, T.J.D. and Olwagen, J. (2012) 'Library leadership: Innovative options for designing training programmes to build leadership competencies in the digital age', *South African Journal for Libraries and Information Science*, 78(1), 79–92.

De Boer, A., Coetzee, H.S. and Coetzee, H. (2001) 'Teaching cataloguing and classification at the University of Pretoria: Thinking preferences of second-year students', *Libri*, 51(2), 114–23.

De Boer, A., Steyn, T. and Du Toit, P.H. (2001) 'A whole brain approach to teaching and learning in higher education', *South African Journal of Higher Education*, 15(3), 185–93.

De Boer, A., Du Toit, P.H., Bothma, T.J.D. and Scheepers, D. (2012a) 'Constructing a comprehensive learning style flexibility model for the innovation of an Information Literacy Module', *Libri*, 62 (June), 185–96.

De Boer, A., Du Toit, P.H., Bothma, T.J.D. and Scheepers, D. (2012b) 'Whole brain teaching for whole brain learners', paper presented at the Lily Conference on College and University Teaching: Brain-Based Learning and Teaching, Washington DC, available at: *http://lillyconferences.com/dc/schedule.shtml*

De Jager, T. (2011) Beginner-Teacher Professional Development: An Action Research Approach to Mentoring, unpublished master's dissertation, University of Pretoria.

De Vries, M. and Du Toit, P.H. (2007) 'Collaborative learning and the use of action learning: my zoo experience', paper presented at HELTASA Conference: Learning and Teaching Innovation in Higher Education: Expanding the Frontiers, 27–29 November, Pretoria.

Donald, J. (2004) 'Clarifying learning'. In A. Saroyan and C. Amundsen (eds), *Rethinking Teaching in Higher Education: From a Course Design Workshop to a Faculty Development Framework* (Sterling, VA: Stylus Publishing).

Donche, V. (2005) *Leren, Onderwijzen en Leren Onderwijzen* (Ghent: Academia Press).

Driscoll, M.P. (2000) *Psychology of Learning for Instruction*, 2nd edn (Boston: Allyn & Bacon).

Drotter, S. (2003) *The Leadership Pipeline: The Right Leader in the Right Job*, Management Forum Series, Salem, OR.

Drucker, P. (1997) 'I got my degree through e-mail', *Forbes*, available at: *http://www.forbes.com/forbes/1997/0616/5912084a.html*

Duderstadt, J.J. (2008) *Engineering for a Changing World: A Roadmap to the Future of Engineering Practice, Research, and Education* (Ann Arbor, MI: University of Michigan).

Du Toit, P.H. (1995) 'Diagnostic assessment of learning: Reflection technique for the evaluation and development of a learning process-driven curriculum', paper presented at 21st Annual IAEA Conference: New Horizons in Learning Assessment, 13–17 June, Montreal.

Du Toit, P.H. (2009) *An Action Research Approach to Monitoring One's Professional Development as Manager* (Pretoria: Foundation for Professional Development).

Du Toit, P.H. (2012) 'Using action research as process for sustaining knowledge production: A case study of a higher education qualification for academics', *South African Journal of Higher Education*, 26(6), 1216–64.

Du Toit, P.H., Bothma, T.J.D., De Boer, A-L., Fourie, I. and Scheepers, D. (2011) 'From creativity to innovation to transformation in information literacy for university students: learning material that makes a difference', paper presented at the Librarians' Information Literacy Annual Conference, London, available at: *http://lilacconference.com/WP/programme/abstracts-mon/*

Du Toit, P.H., De Boer, A-L., Bothma, T.J.D. and Scheepers, D. (2012) 'Multidissiplinêre samewerking:' n Noodsaaklikheid vir onderwysinnovering', *Suid-Afrikaanse Akademie vir Wetenskap en Kuns*, 52(2), 236–251.

Entwistle, N., McCune, V. and Walker, P. (2001) 'Conceptions, Styles, and Approaches Within Higher Education: Analytic Abstractions and Everyday Experience', In R.J. Sternberg, and L. Zang (eds), *Perspectives on Thinking, Learning, and Cognitive Styles* (London: Lawrence Erlbaum Associates).

Felder, R. (1996) 'Matters of style', *ASEE Prism*, 6(4), 18–23.

Fringe, J. dos S. F. (2012) Promoting Critical Reflection for Academic Professional Development in Higher Education, unpublished doctoral dissertation, University of Pretoria.

Gardner, H. (1993) *Multiple Intelligences: The Theory in Practice* (New York: Basic Books).

Garrick, J. (2000) 'Flexible learning, work and the management of intellectual capital'. In V. Jakupec and J. Garrick (eds), *Flexible Learning, Human Resource and Organizational Development* (London: Routledge), 239–56.

Garrison, D.R. and Kanuka, H. (2004) 'Blended learning: uncovering its transformative potential in higher education', *The Internet and Higher Education*, 7(2), 95–105.

Gazzaniga, M.S. (1998) 'The split brain revisited', *Scientific American*, 279(1), 35–9.

Goode, H. and Du Toit, P.H. (2010) 'How can I improve strategies of facilitating learning from a whole brain theory perspective?', paper presented at conference Action Research: Exploring its Transformative Potential, 19–20 August, Nelson Mandela Metropolitan University.

Gravett, S. (2005) *Adult Learning: Designing and Implementing Learning Events – A Dialogical Approach*, 2nd edn, (Pretoria: Van Schaik).

Greyling, W.J. and Du Toit, P.H. (2008) 'Pursuing a constructivist approach to mentoring in the higher education sector', *South African Journal of Higher Education*, 22(5), 957–80.

Haigh, N. (2006) *Everyday conversation as a context for professional learning and development*, available at: *http://www.tandfonline.com/loi/rijazo*

Harris, R. (2004) 'The challenge to unlearn traditional language'. In A. Saroyan and C. Amundsen (eds), *Rethinking Teaching in Higher Education: From a Course Design Workshop to a Faculty Development Framework* (Sterling, VA: Stylus Publishing), 169–86.

Harrison J., Dymoke, S. and Pell, T. (2006) 'Mentoring beginning teachers in secondary schools: An analysis of practice', *Teaching and Teacher Education*, 22, 1055–67.

Henneman, E.A., Lee, J.L. and Cohen, J.I. (1995) 'Collaboration: A concept analysis', *Journal of Advanced Nursing*, 21(1), 103–9.

Herrmann, N. (ed.) (1995) *The Creative Brain*, 2nd edn, (USA: Quebecor Printing Book Group).

Herrmann, N. (1996) *The Whole Brain Business Book: Unblocking the Power of Whole Brain Thinking in Organizations and Individuals* (New York: McGraw-Hill).

Herrmann International (2009) Understanding the Herrmann Whole Brain® Model, HBDI® Profile Package.

Herrmann-Nehdi, A. (2012) 'The best of both worlds: Making blended learning really work by engaging the Whole Brain', available at: *http://www.hbdi. co.za/documents/Blending%20learning.pdf*

Heunis, C. (1997) Avontuurgerigte spanbou in 'n eietydse samelewing: 'n Menslike bewegingskunde perspektief, unpublished doctoral thesis, University of Pretoria.

Hills, T. and Van Oordt, M. (2012) 'Two teachers are better than one', paper given at the Johannesburg Regional Conference of the Southern African Accounting Association, University of the Witwatersrand, 7 September 2012.

Hopper, R. (2005) 'Emotional intelligence in academic library leadership', Library Staff Publication 1, available at: *http://scholarsarchive.jwu.edu/staff_pub/1*

Horak, E. and Du Toit, J.W. (2002) 'A study of the thinking styles and academic performance of civil engineering students', *Journal of the South African Institute of Civil Engineering*, 44(3), 18–24.

Horak, E., Steyn, T.M. and De Boer, A. (2001) 'A four quadrant whole brain approach in innovation and engineering problem solving to facilitate teaching and learning of engineering students', *South African Journal of Higher Education*, 15(3), 202–9.

Houghton Mifflin College (n.d.) 'Thinking Styles and Learning Styles', available at: *http://www.facultytraining.com*.

Huber, M.T. (2004) *Balancing Acts: The Scholarship of Teaching and Learning in Academic Careers* (Sterling, VA: Stylus).

Huber, M.T. and Morreale, S.P. (eds) (2002) *Disciplinary Styles in the Scholarship of Teaching and Learning: Exploring Common Ground* (Washington, DC: American Association for Higher Education and Carnegie Foundation for the Advancement of Teaching).

Hughes, G. (2007) 'Using blended learning to increase learner support and improve retention', *Teaching in Higher Education*, 12(3), 349–63.

Kachelhoffer, P.M., Malan, S.P.T. and Knoetze, J.G. (1990) 'Riglyne vir kurrikulumontwikkeling'. In S.P.T. Malan and P.H. du Toit. (eds), *Suksesvolle Onderrig: Riglyne vir Dosente, Onderwysers en Opleiers* (Pretoria: Academica), 7–28.

Keller, J.M. (1987) 'Development and use of the ARCS Model of Motivational Design', *Journal of Instructional Development*, 10(3), 2–10.

Keller, J.M. (2006) ARCS website, available at: *http://www.arcsmodel.com/home.htm*

Kember, D. (2000) *Action Learning and Action Research: Improving the Quality of Teaching and Learning* (London: Kogan Page).

Kimeldorf, M. (1996) *Creating Portfolios for Success in School, Work and Life* (Minneapolis, MN: Free Spirit Publishing).

Klasen, N. and Clutterbuck, D. (2002) *Implementing Mentoring Schemes* (Oxford: Butterworth-Heinemann).

Knobbs, C. (2011) 'Employing small groups to promote independent learning and to develop social skills', *Innovate*, 6, 44–5.

Knowles, M. (1990) *The Adult Learner – A neglected Species*, 4th edn, (USA: Gulf Publishing Company).

Kolb, D.A. (1984) *Experiential Learning: Experience as the Source of Learning and Development* (Englewood Cliffs, NJ: Prentice Hall).

Korthagen, F.A.J. (1993) 'Two modes of reflection', *Teacher and Teacher Education*, 9(3): 317–26.

Korthagen, F.A.J. (2001) *Linking Practice to Theory: The Pedagogy of Realistic Teacher Education* (Mahwah, NJ: Lawrence Erlbaum Associates).

Le Cornu, R. (2005) 'Peer mentoring: engaging pre-service teachers in mentoring one another', *Mentoring and Tutoring*, 13(3), 255–366.

Lee, V.S. (ed.) (2004) *Teaching and Learning Through Inquiry: A Guidebook for Institutions and Instructors* (Sterling, VA: Stylus).

Lee, V.S., Greene, D.B., Odom, J., Schechter, E. and Slatta, R.W. (2004) 'What is inquiry-guided learning?' In V.S. Lee (ed.), *Teaching and Learning through Inquiry: A Guidebook for Institutions and Instructors* (Sterling, VA: Stylus), 3–16.

Liebenberg, L. and Mathews, E.H. (2012) 'Integrating innovation skills in an introductory engineering design-build course', *International Journal of Technology and Design Education*, 22, 93–113.

Lotriet, M., Jorissen, W. and Nagel, L. (2008) 'A diamond metaphor to promote a flexible blended teaching and learning model'. In J. Luca and E. Weippl (eds), *Proceedings of World Conference on Educational Multimedia, Hypermedia and Telecommunications* (Chesapeake, VA: AACE), 3472–8, available at: *http://www.editlib.org/p/28866*

Lovat, T., Toomey, R., Clement, N., Croty, R. and Nielsen, T. (2009) *Values Education, Quality Teaching and Service Learning: A Troika for Effective Teaching and Teacher Education* (Sydney: David Barlow).

Lumsdaine, E. and Binks, M. (2003) *Keep on Moving! Entrepreneurial Creativity and Effective Problem Solving* (Hightstown, NJ: McGraw-Hill Higher Education).

Lumsdaine, M. and Lumsdaine, E. (1995) 'Thinking preferences of engineering students: Implications for curriculum restructuring', *Journal of Engineering Education*, 84(2), 193–204.

Lumsdaine, E., Lumsdaine, M. and Shelnutt, J.W. (1999) *Creative Problem Solving and Engineering Design* (New York: College Custom Publication Group; McGraw-Hill Higher Education).

Mandela, N.R. (2012) Lighting Your Way to a Better Future, speech, available at: *http://db.nelsonmandela.org/speeches/pub_view.asp?pg=item&ItemID=NMS909&txtstr=education%20is%20the%20most%20powerful*

Marquardt, M.J. (2002) *Building the Learning Organisation: Mastering the 5 Elements of Corporate Learning* (Palo Alto, CA: Davies-Black).

Masebe, J. (2007) Meta-evaluation for Programme Reviewing at a University of Technology, unpublished master's dissertation, University of Pretoria.

McGill, I. and Beaty, L. (1992) *Action Learning: A Guide for Professional, Management and Educational Development* (London: Kogan Page).

McNiff, J. (2002) 'Action research for professional development: Concise advice for new action researchers', available at: *http://www.jeanmcniff.com/booklet1.html#12*

McNiff, J. and Whitehead, J. (2006) *All you need to know about action research*. (London: Sage).

Molenda, M. (2003) 'In search of the elusive ADDIE model', *Performance Improvement*, 42(5), 34–6, available at: *http://www.comp.dit.ie/dgordon/Courses/ILT/ILT0004/InSearchofElusiveADDIE.pdf*

Morris, R.J. (2006) Left Brain, Right Brain, Whole Brain? An examination into the theory of brain lateralization, learning styles and the implications for education, PGCE thesis, Cornwall College, St Austell, available at: *http://singsurf.org/brain/rightbrain.html*

Mouton, J. (2001) *How to Succeed in Your Master's and Doctoral Studies: A South African Guide and Resource Book* (Pretoria: Van Schaik).

Mullen, C.A. (2000) 'Constructing Co-mentoring Partnership: Walkways we must travel', *Theory Into Practice*, 39(1), 4–11.

Multidisciplinary Oxford Dictionary (2012) 3rd edn, available at: *http://oxforddictionaries.com/definition/english/multidisciplinary?q=Multidisciplinary*

Neave, G. (2008) 'On Scholarly Communities, *Lieder* and Systems: Ulrich Teichler and their Structural Dynamics', in B.M. Kehm (ed.), *Hochschule im Wandel: Die Universität als Forschungsgegenstand* (Frankfurt am Main: Campus Verlag), 267–80.

Nicholas, D., Rowlands, I., Wthey, R. and Debrowolski, T. (2008) 'The Digital Consumer: An Introduction and Philosophy', in D. Nicholas and I. Rowlands (eds), *Digital Consumers: Reshaping the Information Professions* (London: Facet), 1–13.

O'Connor, K.B. (2009) 'Finding my story and place in researching indigenous education: the formation of a narrative identity'. In K. Pithouse, C. Mitchell and R. Moletsane (eds), *Making Connections: Self-study and Social Action* (New York: Peter Lang), 43–58.

Olivier, C. du T. (1998) *How to Educate and Train Outcomes Based* (Pretoria: Van Schaik).

Oosthuizen, M. (2001) An Investigation into Facilitating Learning via The Whole Brain Model in the Study Unit Tooth Morphology, unpublished master's dissertation, University of Pretoria.

Orlikowski, W.J. (2002) 'Knowing in practice: Enacting a collective capability in distributed organizing', *Organisation Science*, 13(3), 249–73.

Ornstein, R. (1997) *The Right Mind: Making Sense of the Hemispheres* (New York: Harcourt Brace & Company).

Østerlund, C. and Carlile, P. (2005) 'Relations in practice: Sorting through practice theories on knowledge sharing in complex organisations', *The Information Society*, 21(2), 91–107.

Petri, L. (2010) 'Concept analysis of interdisciplinary collaboration', *Nursing Forum*, 45(2), 73–82.

Phuthi, N. (2012) Enhancing Quality Academic Practice Through Integrated Industry-Based Learning, unpublished doctoral dissertation, University of Pretoria.

Picciano, A.G. (2006) 'Blended learning: Implications for growth and access', *Journal of Asynchronous Learning Networks*, 10(3), 95–102, available at: *http://www.sloan-c.org/publications/jaln/v10n3/pdf/v10n3_8picciano.pdf*

Pillay, V., Wolvaardt, G. and Du Toit, P.H. (2010) 'Introducing action research as process for higher learning in an advanced course for health managers offered by a private higher education institution', paper given at the conference Action Research: Exploring its Transformative Potential, 19–20 August, Nelson Mandela Metropolitan University.

Pithouse, K., Mitchell, C. and Moletsane, R. (2009a) 'Going public with scholarly collaboration: Reflections on a collaborative self-study book process'. In K. Pithouse, C. Mitchell and R. Moletsane (eds), *Making Connections: Self-study and Social Action* (New York: Peter Lang), 25–39.

Pithouse, K., Mitchell, C. and Moletsane, R. (eds) (2009b) *Making Connections: Self-study and Social Action* (New York: Peter Lang).

Pretorius, J.P., Scheepers, D. and De Boer, A. (2011) 'Using the Whole Brain® Model to innovate teaching and learning for information literacy learners', paper presented at the Higher Education Learning and Teaching Association of Southern Africa, Port Elizabeth, South Africa, available at: *http://www0.sun.ac.za/heltasa/file.php/1/Conferences/Conf_2011/HELTASA_2011_Abstracts.pdf*

Pulko, S.H. and Parikh, S. (2003) 'Teaching "soft" skills to engineers', *International Journal of Electrical Engineering Education*, 40(4), 243–54.

Ramsden, P. (1999) *Learning to Teach in Higher Education* (London: Routledge).

Reiser, R.A. (2001) 'A History of Instructional Design and Technology: Part L: A History of Instructional Media', *Educational Technology Research and Development*, 49(1), 53–64, available at: *http://www.springerlink.com/content/8284v653u064 1h87/*

Republic of South Africa (2000) 'Norms and standards for educators' *Government Gazette*, 415(20844).

Rooke, D. and Torbert, W.R. (2005) 'Seven transformations of leadership', *Harvard Business Review*, April, available at: *http://hbr.org/2005/04/seven-transformations-of-leadership/ar/1*

Scheepers, M.D., De Boer, A-L., Bothma, T.J.D. and Du Toit, P.H. (2010a) 'A mental model for successful interdisciplinary collaboration in curriculum innovation for information literacy', paper presented at the IFLA-ALISE-EUCLID satellite meeting of the IFLA conference, Boras, Sweden, available at: *http://repository.up.ac.za/bitstream/handle/2263/17259/Scheepers_Mental(2011)pdf?sequence=1*

Scheepers, M.D., De Boer, A-L., Bothma, T.J.D. and Du Toit, P.H. (2010b) 'Towards excellence in a mega class: collaborative design and development of learning materials to facilitate Whole Brain learning in an information literacy course', poster presented at the IFLA-ALISE-EUCLID satellite meeting of IFLA conference, Boras, Sweden, available at *http://tinyurl.com/d4675s8*

Scheepers, D., De Boer, A., Bothma, T.J.D. and Du Toit, P.H. (2011) 'A mental model for successful interdisciplinary collaboration in curriculum innovation for information literacy', *South African Journal for Libraries and Information Science*, 77(1), 75–84.

Scherman, V. and Du Toit, P.H. (2007) 'Cooperative learning in postgraduate lectures: Possibilities and challenges', paper presented at the HELTASA Conference: Learning and Teaching Innovation in Higher Education: Expanding the Frontiers, 27–29 November, St George Hotel, Pretoria.

Schön, D.A. (1987) *Educating the Reflective Professional: Toward a New Design for Teaching and Learning in Professions* (San Francisco: Jossey-Bass).

Singh, H. (2003) 'Building effective blended learning programmes', *Educational Technology*, 43(6), 51–54.

Singh, H. and Reed, R. (2001) *Achieving Success with Blended Learning: A White Paper*, ASTD State of the Industry report, American Society of Training and Development, available at: *http://chriscollieassociates.com/BlendedLearning.pdf*

Slabbert, J.A., De Kock, D.M. and Hattingh, A. (2009) *The Brave "New" World of Education: Creating a New Professionalism* (Lansdowne: Juta).

Steyn, T.M. (1998) Graphical Exploration as an Aid to Mastering Fundamental Mathematical Concepts: An Instructional Model for Mathematics Practicals, unpublished master's dissertation, University of Pretoria.

Straka, G.A. (1997) *European Views of Self-directed Learning: Historical, Conceptual, Empirical, Practical, Vocational* (Münster, New York, München and Berlin: Waxmann).

Strong-Wilson, T. (2009) 'Seeing what I mean: The student teacher portfolios object of self-study/formation'. In K. Pithouse, C. Mitchell and R. Moletsane (eds), *Making Connections: Self-study and Social Action* (New York: Peter Lang Publishing Inc.), 153–68.

Taylor, K.L. and Colet, N.R. (2010) 'Making the shift from faculty development to educational development'. In A. Saroyan and M. Frenay (eds), *Building Teaching Capacities in Higher Education: A Comprehensive International Model* (Sterling, VA: Stylus), 139–67.

Teare, R. and Prestoungrange, G. (2004) *Revans University – the University of Action Learning: Accrediting Managers at Work in the 21st Century* ([Prestonpans]: Prestoungrange University Press).

Troha, F.J. (2002) 'Bulletproof instructional design: A model for blended learning', *USDLA Journal*, 16(5), available at: *http://www.usdla.org/html/journal/MAY02_Issue/article03.html*

US Department of Education. (2009) *Evaluation of Evidence-based Practices in Online Learning: A Meta-analysis and Review of Online Learning Studies*, Washington, DC, available at: *http://www.ed.gov/about/offices/list/opepd/ppss/reports.html*

Van der Horst, H. and McDonald, R. (1997) *Outcomes-based Education* (Pretoria: Kagiso).

Van Knippenberg, D. and Schippers, M.C. (2007) 'Work group diversity', *Annual Review of Psychology*, 58, 515–41.

Vermunt, J.D. (1995) 'Process-oriented Instruction in Learning and Thinking Strategies', *European Journal of Psychology Education*, 10, 325–39.

Von Glasersfeld, E. (2001) 'Radical constructivism and teaching', *Prospects*, 31(2), 161–73.

Wilkie, K. (2004) 'Becoming facilitative: Shifts in learners' approaches to facilitating problem-based learning'. In M.S. Baden, and K. Wilie (eds), *Challenging Research in Problem-based Learning* (Maidenhead: Open University Press), 81–92.

Wolvaardt, G. and Du Toit, P.H. (2011) 'Action research-driven professional development: Developing transformational health care managers and creating learning organisations', *South African Journal of Higher Education*, 26(6), 1249–63.

Wysocki, R.K. (2002) *Building Effective Project Teams* (New York: John Wiley & Sons).

Young, J.R. (2002) '"Hybrid" teaching seeks to end the divide between traditional and online instruction', *Chronicle of Higher Education*, 48(28), A33–A34.

Zuber-Skerritt, O. (1992) *Action Research in Higher Education: Examples and Reflections* (London: Kogan Page).

Zuber-Skerritt, O. (2000) *Action Learning, Action Research and Process Management: Theory, Practice, Praxis* (Brisbane: Action Research Unit, Faculty of Education, Griffith University).

Index